THE
COUGAR
DOESN'T
LIVE
HERE
ANY
MORE

THE
COUGAR
DOESN'T
LIVE
HERE
ANY
MORE

LORUS J. MILNE and MARGERY MILNE

Line drawings by Stanley Wyatt

Prentice-Hall, Inc., *Englewood Cliffs, N.J.*

The Cougar Doesn't Live Here Any More by Lorus J. Milne and Margery Milne

ISBN 0–13–181149–5

Library of Congress Catalog Card Number: 76–131870

Printed in the United States of America   T

Prentice-Hall International, Inc., London
Prentice-Hall of Australia, Pty, Ltd., Sydney
Prentice-Hall of Canada, Ltd., Toronto
Prentice-Hall of India Private Ltd., New Delhi
Prentice-Hall of Japan, Inc., Tokyo

Unless otherwise credited, photos by Lorus and Margery Milne.

Acknowledgment is gratefully made to *Audubon Magazine* for
permission to include some paragraphs, with modification, from
our article "The cahow—10 years to doom?" in vol. 70, no. 6,
pp. 46–51, the issue for November/December 1968.

For helping round out our illustrations of major wildlife, we particularly
appreciate the assistance of Luther C. Goldman and Beatrice Boone of the
Bureau of Sport Fisheries and Wildlife, and Bob Williams, Bureau of
Commercial Fisheries, all in the U.S. Department of the Interior.
Special thanks go to Carol Cartaino, editor at Prentice-Hall, for her
enthusiastic efficiency in working on the text and pictures.

Second Printing........June, 1972

For Herb and Jessie Nichols,
explorer friends who travel each year
to cougar country

Books by Lorus J. Milne and Margery Milne

The Cougar Doesn't Live Here Any More
When the Tide Goes Far Out
*The Nature of Life: Earth, Plants, Animals, Man, and
    Their Effect on Each Other*
North American Birds
The Nature of Animals
The Phoenix Forest
*The Ages of Life: A New Look at the Effects of Time
    on Mankind and Other Living Things*
Patterns of Survival
Living Plants of the World
Gift from the Sky
Biological Frontiers
The Crab That Crawled Out of the Past
Water and Life
Growth and Age
Because of a Tree
The Valley: Meadow, Grove and Stream
The Senses of Animals and Men
The Mountains [with the Editors of LIFE]
The Balance of Nature
*The Lower Animals: Living Invertebrates of the World
    [with Ralph and Mildred Buchsbaum]*
Plant Life
Animal Life
Paths Across the Earth
The World of Night
The Mating Instinct
The Biotic World and Man
Famous Naturalists
A Multitude of Living Things

FOREWORD

HENRY THOREAU once complained that, even in his day, many of "the noblest animals" had disappeared from New England, leaving him "but a tamed, and as it were, an emasculated nature." More than half a century later Theodore Roosevelt was exclaiming that the loss of animal species was like "the loss of a gallery of masterpieces."

But it is doubtful if even these early spokesmen for what we call "conservation" realized as compellingly as we do the broadest implications of the phenomenon they were observing or would have guessed just how soon a nostalgic regret was to be succeeded by something like terror. Both were regretting the loss of an aesthetic, quasi-mystical experience which many—perhaps most—Americans had never shared. They could be dismissed as men riding a hobby. What real difference did it make that the passenger pigeon was extinct and Thoreau's "noblest animals" banished from the rapidly spreading areas of dense population?

No doubt many feel the same today. But what we are now beginning to realize is that the disappearance of wildlife over most of the earth is not an isolated misfortune. It is simply one aspect of a process which threatens the very existence of every member of the human race, be he a "nature lover" or not. Its underlying cause is the same as that which created the population explosion, air and water pollution, the epidemic of pesticide poisonings, the specter of hunger, and the threat that our earth is becoming one huge junk pile. All are the result of the great miscalculation, of the assumption that the earth can be treated as belonging to man alone and that he can pursue his immediate aims without regard to the fact that he, no less than the humblest animal, is part of an interrelated complex to which he must adjust himself. The determination to "conquer nature" will lead ultimately to death; to cooperate with nature can lead to a more abundant life.

The present book considers, in the broadest possible perspective, everything related to the rise and extinction of animal species. Evolution is, of course, as much the history of extinctions as it is of the new appearance of animal and plant species. But what has created the new crisis is the simple fact that man is the most successful animal that ever lived and the only one that has, one might say, been capable of outsmarting himself. In that fact lies his great danger. He can, as no previous species ever could, destroy the system of which he is a part and upon which his survival must, in the long run, depend. The idea of the earth for man alone is simply unrealizable.

Like all the many books written by the Milnes, this one exhibits virtues not often found together. It is thoroughly researched and at the same time not merely a collection of facts. For all their familiarity with the literature of the subject, the authors are much more than armchair naturalists. They have traveled widely both "in Concord" and in faraway places. They are always ready with a personal observation to illustrate and enliven a fact. They have the competence of the professional plus the enthusiasm of the amateur. And there is no better combination for the production of a readable as well as a valuable contribution to natural history.

Joseph Wood Krutch

CONTENTS

THE
COUGAR
DOESN'T
LIVE
HERE
ANY
MORE

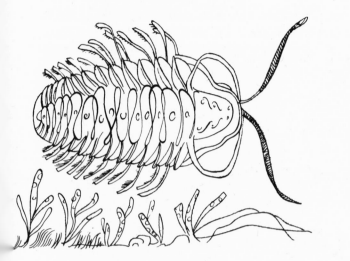

INTRODUCTION: THE VANISHING ACT

WHEN A WHITE rabbit or a cooing dove appears suddenly out of a black hat, or vanishes as abruptly and completely, we know that a magician has had a hand in the trick. Usually his act is reversible, and it reminds us of the way we lose our laps when we stand up or our fists when we open our hands. Wild creatures and familiar scenes have a way of disappearing too, with various degrees of permanency.

Sometimes the vanishing act involves only a predictable transformation, as when a tadpole vanishes while the frog appears. The individual insect is still there after it sheds its caterpillar skin to become a pupa, and later its pupal armor to emerge as a moth.

Thousands of ponds and lakes have filled with silt and organic matter and have transformed into grass-clad prairies or dense forests, according to the climate. These changes occur naturally. Man may speed them up, but the earth's long history has been a constant replacing of one scene and one community of life with another. Chicago was once a swamp, inhabited by muskrats and many other animals. The muskrats and the plants they fed on vanished from where pavement and tall buildings now stand. But they still live within the city limits, as do others of their kind in New York and Boston. They continue to thrive in patches of marsh and waterways from Alaska to Newfoundland, throughout most of the United States and Canada.

However, when the last passenger pigeon died of old age on September 1, 1914, in the Cincinnati Zoological Garden, no sleight of hand could produce another live one. A species had died forever. In its *Bulletin* for July, 1968, the International Union for the Conservation of Nature and Natural Resources listed 161 other kinds of birds that have vanished since the year 1600. By comparison, between the beginning of the Christian Era and 1600 A.D. less than 10 species of birds became extinct—at a rate of one in each 177 years. The IUCN list includes 12 species lost in the 1600's, 21 in the 1700's, 75 in the 1800's, and 54 already in the 1900's. Another 334 are presently in the endangered category. This rapid increase in the rate of disappearance is matched in the records for mammals. Cold-blooded animals and plants have fared little better, but information about them is less explicit.

Probably the last heath hen graced some hunter's table, although laws were passed to protect these birds after they vanished from the American mainland in 1835. Their last outpost was on the island of Martha's Vineyard, off Cape Cod, where no more were seen after 1932. At that time there was less cause for alarm over the loss of the heath hen than there is today. Until a few years ago, the alarmists could be quieted by pointing to two more races of the same species of bird—the greater prairie chicken and Attwater's prairie chicken—and a closely related species—the lesser prairie chicken—still living along the eastern flank of the Rocky Mountains from Canada to Colorado and among more arid foothills of western states. Now all of these splendid birds are on the official danger list. East of the Mississippi River and west of the Rocky Mountains, wild prairie chickens of all kinds are extinct, except for a small population in Illinois. Although the survivors have changed their habits, to stay in woodland wherever they can find cover, the last of them seems likely to vanish in this century unless they are left suitable places to live and receive more effective protection. Their loss would not only add to the tally of extinct species but deprive the world of a whole genus of birds that developed special habits and body features in relation to the North American scene.

We make no claim that any species, including our own, is indispensable or unthreatened. We know well how great has been the turnover in species during the past, while life as a whole has continued and increased its hold upon the planet. During more than a billion years, millions of kinds of creatures have vanished, after having their life spans to spend energy from the sun.

Ultimately, we realize, the finite amount of solar energy the earth can intercept each year will set a limit on the total quantity of life. Green plants in water and on land capture and put to use less than a tenth of one percent of the available energy. The rest goes unutilized because no plant operates at maximum efficiency. Yet the only food available to members

Each spring, progressively fewer prairie chickens arrive on their traditional courting grounds, the males to inflate the display sacs on each side of the neck, raise their neck feathers and tail, strut and boom out their calls, while females approach and choose a suitor. (MALE, LEFT, BY LUTHER C. GOLDMAN, BUREAU OF SPORT FISHERIES AND WILDLIFE; FEMALE, BY ALFRED M. BAILEY FROM NATIONAL AUDUBON SOCIETY.)

of the animal kingdom comes from the net annual productivity of the green plants—the amount that can be spared after they have used the energy they need for their own processes. The net productivity has been estimated for the world to be 500,000,000,000,000,000 Calories, perhaps half of it in lignin, cellulose, and other organic compounds for which no vegetarian animal has the proper digestive agents.

Greater utilization of both energy and space has always awaited an increase in the diversity among living things. Right now, more kinds of animals can inhabit the earth than ever before because so many species have evolved special ways to make useful to them the resources that formerly were wasted. Until less than 500 million years ago, no plant or animal possessed suitable adaptations to live on land; all of the surface of the continents was useless space, and the sun's energy received there produced only heat. Until about 100 million years ago the prairies and steppes were equally inhospitable to life. Changes in the living things themselves made the difference.

Given a chance, the evolution of adaptations by plants and animals can be expected to continue toward the day when there is no useless space, not even deserts, ice caps, and pools of petroleum. Already a few pioneers are testing their tolerances against these adverse environments. Slowly, too, the better adapted forms of life displace the less suited. Old ones become extinct as new species take their place. Progress is served, but only at a gradual pace.

The explosive rate of extinction today continues only because one species—our own—has become overwhelmingly successful so quickly. Except where we spread into the inhospitable deserts and ice caps, we and the living things we raise for food take space in the sun and other resources from wild animals and plants that are our contemporaries. If we multiply the 2,200 Calories of useful food that each person is supposed to consume per day by the 3.5 billion people estimated by the Statistical Office of the United Nations to be alive, we see a total food requirement amounting to 2,810,000,000,000,000 Calories annually. This is about 1¼ percent of the total useful productivity of the world's green plants. For one species among the more than a million species in the animal kingdom to lay claim to more than one percent of the food resources of the planet is surely a measure of our dominance and our ecological impact on the world.

Almost always our efforts simplify the environment and decrease the total efficiency of life. To raise crops that capture carbon through photosynthesis and show a net productivity of 154 (potatoes) to 306 (sugar beets) units per acre annually, we clear forests with a net gain of from 625 (deciduous) to 1,272 (coniferous) units. We replace humid grasslands, whose annual gain averages 179 units, with grain that nets only 149. Despite all of our efforts, crop plants today account for only 2.6 percent of the world's net productivity, as compared to 3.0 percent from wetlands, 3.6 from grasslands, 37.2 from the open sea, and 53.6 from forests. The forests produce mostly wood, for which we lack the necessary digestive agents. The seas contribute little, for their appearance of great productivity is an illusion arising from their vast area—nearly three-quarters of the surface of the world. Per acre the oceans produce less than a quarter as much as the land. To gain an equal amount of nourishment from them would require harvesting food from nearly four times the area, were it not for the fact that the productivity is concentrated near the coasts; beyond is almost the equivalent of a desert.

No one can question the need of people for suitable food to keep them alive and healthy. The need for so large a human population, let alone a larger one in the immediate future, is harder to justify when it is seen to be at the expense of all other forms of life. Yet some of the straits in which nonhuman animals and plants are now and have been in the past stem from the activities of people who lay claim to the instincts of a house cat which, although well fed, must sneak after birds and mammals it can kill. When we learn that well-fed hunters have decimated the few remaining members of another species tottering on the brink of extinction, we think of the quotation in the *Political Precepts* of the venerable Greek biographer Plutarch: "It was the saying of Bion [a Greek pastoral poet of the second century B.C.] that though the boys throw stones at frogs in sport, yet the frogs do not die in sport but in earnest."

Each species of animal consists of living individuals. Every individual moves about, just as we do, seeking to satisfy its needs for food, shelter, and the companionship of its own kind. In doing so it competes with others of the same species and with individuals of unrelated kinds. Success for the individual depends upon what resources it can reach and use. For the species, success rests upon the ability of individuals in each new generation to compete at least as vigorously as their parents did. For a modern animal to compete successfully with modern man takes special adaptations. The conspicuous winners in the contest are those that can benefit from man's existence even if, by doing so, they become pests.

As we think about the animals whose fortunes are evidently waning, we can best understand why each creature is endangered by considering what space it has, what it eats, and what eats it, all in the context of its own surroundings. Seen in its habitat, the animal often reveals that it is susceptible to a hazard met by other imperiled animals elsewhere under similar circumstances. From recognizing this pattern we may hope to help a number of different species to survive in the same world with man, rather than to seek a separate remedy to perpetuate each kind.

For an increasing number of people in the technologically advanced countries, the ecological effects of human success in subduing the earth are becoming obvious. As some unknown philosopher commented, these effects are not rewards or punishments—merely consequences. But, fortunately, mankind is attaining the state of mind in which thought can be given to the dangerous simplification in the world consequent to human presence. With thought and consideration, the devastating changes in the environment can be slowed or corrected for the benefit of the potential losers in the contest, before they vanish without issue.

CHAPTER 1

ANIMALS
IN
SUCCESSION
THROUGH
THE
GARDEN
OF
EDEN

EVERYBODY LOVES A lavish parade, one with imaginative variety and rich detail in the individual displays. If we arrive long after the beginning, we wonder what we have missed and how it will end. Many people experience the same sensations when they become aware of the succession of animals that have populated the earth. Today, as never before, the end of the parade may be approaching while we are finding out what features it showed before we arrived on the scene.

Many of the traffic rules for the natural parade apply firmly to animals and, with some special dispensations, to mankind as well. Discovery of these rules was a major achievement made by scientists of the last few generations and some who are still active. Indeed, the first recognition that an ever-changing parade of animals flows along the streets of time was a feat of human understanding we can credit to men of the nineteenth century. Detecting organic evolution and offering explanations for it rank near the top among scientific achievements of any age. The first of these ideas were those of Jean Baptiste de Lamarck, expressed initially in 1801. Later and far more comprehensive ideas by Charles Darwin and Alfred Russel Wallace reached printable form in 1858, but gained broad support through the work of contemporary men.

Georges Cuvier, at the Paris Museum, opened up the pages of the fossil record, hoping to find scientifically acceptable support for the conflicting idea of Special Creation. Instead, as his successors realized, the fossil evidence demonstrated beyond cavil that living things have evolved progressively for half a billion years. Gregor Johann Mendel secluded in his monastery garden, discovered the genetic basis that neither Darwin nor Wallace could imagine to explain the variability upon which natural selection works. Louis Pasteur, while establishing the germ theory of disease, vanquished the old notion of Spontaneous Generation. He showed that, even among the microbes, life comes only from preexisting life. We need these facts, which seemed so unrelated when first they were discovered, to build upon in thinking back to the beginning of the animal parade.

In this century we have gained a marvelous amount of knowledge about how the world was before the parade began. Evidence offered by biologists, geologists, and biochemists shows that, following an immense period of time during which no life of any kind we know could have lived on earth, conditions changed. Spontaneous Generation became possible—perhaps inevitable. But no active multicellular animals could participate in those beginnings because the planet's atmosphere contained no oxygen for them to breathe.

In reaching these conclusions, scientists make one assumption and then test its consequences. They assume that the physical and chemical laws and geological forces operating today, all of which depend upon discoverable features of the chemical elements that compose the universe, have operated in the same ways for an indefinite time in the past. From measurements of the rate at which water vapor has been discharged from volcanoes during the last century, and evidence that this rate has been about the same for at least 140 million years (since Jurassic times), they are willing to credit that all of the water on earth had this origin and that it has accumulated from none to the present volume of the oceans and lakes and rivers within 3,000 million years. Until water was available, life could not begin.

The force of gravity on earth, which depends upon the planet's constitution and dimensions, suffices to hold some gases to provide an atmosphere. But hydrogen and helium are too light; no matter how much of them the earth's gas covering may have contained to begin with, they would escape progressively—just as they still do today. Geologists believe that 3,000 million years ago the concentration of hydrogen in the atmosphere was still high enough to favor the many possible combinations with other elements, such as with carbon to form methane (CH_4), nitrogen to form ammonia (NH_3), and sulphur to form hydrogen sulfide (H_2S), as well as with oxygen to form water (H_2O). Any other oxygen present would probably have been combined in carbon monoxide (CO) and various nitrates ($-NO_3$), sulfates ($-SO_4$) and phosphates ($-PO_4$), which dissolve in water. Seemingly the atmosphere contained no free oxygen and little nitrogen as such.

But as the hydrogen gas was lost to outer space, escaping from the earth's gravitational field, the ammonia and nitrates might slowly decompose under the action of ultraviolet light and other radiations. Although the atmosphere now is four-fifths nitrogen, all of the gas could be accounted for from these sources.

Scientists at the University of Chicago, Columbia University, and other research centers have experimented with an artificial atmosphere containing these gases, which continually emanate from volcanoes. When heat is used to cause water vapor to circulate through the gases and past an electric spark or other source of energy, the elements recombine and form organic compounds. Most, if not all, of the building blocks for living things appear under these conditions, in milligram amounts. Without oxygen, they do not decompose. Over an immense period, chemical evolution might produce a living organism, one able to absorb these compounds from its environment, combine them into more of its own constitution, and reproduce itself. It could get energy by fermentation, as yeasts do in the absence of oxygen, and release carbon dioxide (CO_2) as waste. When carbon dioxide became available, the process of photosynthesis and the evolution of green plants could take place.

No one doubts that green plants had to be present, at least along the sunlit shallows of earth's warm seas, before there could be any Garden of Eden. The photosynthesis of green plants is a necessary step toward modern times, if only because green plants liberate oxygen whenever the sun shines on them, and because they make food in abundance—enough to sustain their own growth and that of all the animals too. Only under such conditions could the many representatives of the animal kingdom appear.

Oxygen is an extremely active element. It not only clings to hydrogen tightly in water, but joins readily with many other substances. Once present in the earth's atmosphere, it would oxidize both inorganic and organic materials. It would destroy the organic compounds in solution that are essential for Spontaneous Generation. Never, so far as can be learned, since animals appeared on earth has any form of life arisen spontaneously.

Not one of the earliest kinds of animals possessed the combination of features that is needed for life in the present day. Every one had to adjust to changes as the price of surviving. Even the lowly amebas in modern ponds, which lack a distinctive shape and seem simplest of all animals alive, show that they have become specialists. Everything that lives is a product of variation away from the original style, with astonishing adaptations to its present situation.

Some of the variants in the past were better equipped than others to meet the challenges of competition for limited resources. These kinds perpetuated themselves and gained time to vary further. The ones less well fitted lost out and disappeared. Both the losers and the winners left marks of their existence in the fossil record; but none of these marks made by very early animals match in detail any creature that is alive today.

To examine the remains of early animals in the parade—ones we can recognize easily—we need only visit a big museum where fossils are on display. Doing so is like getting a ticket aboard an imaginary time machine. We go first to the exhibits from Cambrian times, for this is the earliest period in which the sedimentary rocks in many parts of the world preserved large numbers of obvious animals in good condition. Some museums have earlier animals from the Precambrian rocks of Australia, but they are more than 600 million years old and challenge our imagination even more.

The phyla of animals represented among these Cambrian fossils include most of those in a tide pool along a modern coast. Even some soft-bodied medusae (jellyfishes) and segmented worms settled gently in death on soft oozy mud and were preserved. There are sponges, and corals, and mollusks and lamp shells (brachiopods), and moss animals (bryozoans), and echinoderms. The invertebrate animals with jointed legs (arthropods) include crustaceans and trilobites. Not a single modern species or genus is among them. Most of the families and many of the classes have disappeared in the intervening years. Yet one feature unites them with the present: every one of the Cambrian fossils is of an aquatic animal living in shallow marine environments.

Like many people, we are attracted particularly by the trilobites, some of them less than half an inch long, others more than 6 inches. They remind us of certain present-day crustaceans that appear like magic in shallow salt lakes formed by rare rains on deserts in the American Southwest. Trilobites were not crustaceans, for they lacked jaws and must have sucked in tiny plants as food. Yet we find it easy to imagine them in all sizes, creeping and swimming along the shores of Cambrian seas. They were animals we could have caught in cupped hands, or grasped firmly. So far as we know, all trilobites became extinct at the end of the Paleozoic era, about 250 million years before mankind appeared.

After we have had a few encounters with fossil trilobites, the different kinds become recognizable and the names that have been given them roll trippingly from the tongue. The Cambrian kinds always lie horizontal, outstretched in the sedimentary rocks, for they had not yet evolved the ability shown by later trilobites in the parade—to curl up like a pillbug. *Olenellus,* with its broad head shield and spiny tail, suggests a horseshoe crab, whereas *Paradoxides* has long backward extensions from its head shield and no tail spine at all. Some of these fossils are as perfect as a bas-

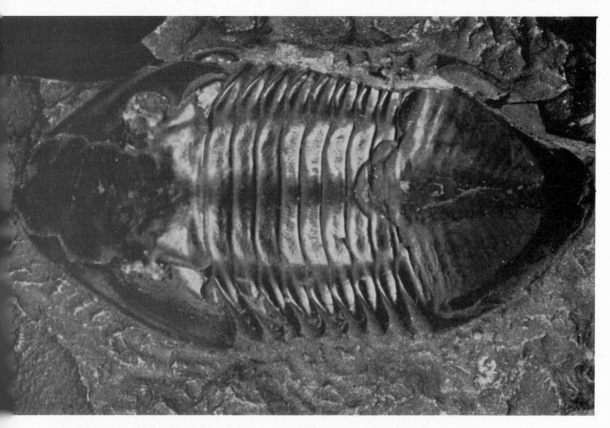

Trilobites of many sizes and kinds were fossilized among the sediments of the Paleozoic era, but their numbers decreased rapidly when fishes with jaws and the predatory nautiloid mollusks appeared.

relief, while others are mere fragments—bits of shells that were shed in the normal process of growth.

From the succeeding geological periods, the Ordovician and Silurian, we meet the trilobites *Calymene* and *Phacops,* the latter named because its eyes are the size and shape of lentil seeds. Both kinds grew two-inch bodies, one inch wide, which often formed solid little fossils the shape of a whole walnut, as though made to be carried in a small boy's pocket, to be taken out and petted from time to time. It seems a shame they did not survive long enough for anyone to be able to admire them as living individuals. Each of these trilobites could turn its broad flat tail underneath and bring it up against its head, concealing and protecting its many feet and gills.

No great stretch of the imagination is needed to comprehend why trilobites grew scarce by Devonian times, which began about 405 million years ago, or why the last of them disappeared during the next 160 million years. Predatory animals began appearing in great numbers, their abundance almost certainly made possible by the availability of trilobites to eat. The

Devonian did have a few large kinds of trilobites, such as 27-inch *Teratas-pis*. But these creatures, which had abounded in the shallow seas of the Cambrian and Ordovician periods, were replaced by newer kinds of life, by animals of which few fossils are found among the Cambrian contin-gents.

Predatory mollusks suddenly diversified during the Ordovician period. One type that might attract our eyes produced long tapering shells divided internally by cross partitions. The animal lived in the largest chamber which, for *Endoceras,* was as much as a foot across in a shell 15 feet long. Limestone blocks in which these giant shells are exposed now line the halls of the National Research Council of Canada building in Ottawa, On-tario. We can walk slowly along these corridors, marveling at the fossils, and unwinding in our minds the similar but spiral shells of the chambered nautiluses which are the direct descendants of these ancient mollusks.

Scientists suspect that the soft body of the Ordovician nautiloids was very similar to that of the modern survivor. Presumably the creature con-trolled the buoyancy of its long, straight, chambered shell, and could hover above the ocean floor while grappling for trilobites with its many tentacles.

The nautiloids were still there, as formidable predators, in Devonian times. But they no longer produced straight conical shells. Instead, they curved their external armor into a flat spiral, like a coil of rope upon a ship's deck or an expanding spiral like a cornucopia. This may have given the buoyant chambers greater strength with less weight of inert lime. Perhaps the change made the nautiloids more efficient in capturing trilo-bites.

Certainly the trilobites dwindled in numbers and in variety as the nauti-loids flourished. But the nautiloids soon had competitors, which seem to have hurried virtually all of them to extinction. So far as the fossil record shows, there have been none of these predatory mollusks alive during the last 100 million years except the four species of chambered nautiluses that now remain as "living fossils" at modest depths in the seas off Malaya and Indonesia.

The new predators in the seas were hungry fishes with strong jaws, in-vading the ancient seas from fresh water where their jaws had evolved. Scientists have no doubt that the fishes gobbled up the trilobites, gulping down with special ease those that curled into the shape of a big pill. If any trilobites still hide somewhere in the deep sea, no scientific expedition has yet uncovered even a fragment to suggest their whereabouts.

The Devonian became the Age of Fishes. Although differing consider-ably from those of today, the fishes almost certainly showed the same combination of three-dimensional mobility, keen sense organs, and basic intelligence that have served them well in all succeeding years. Probably

An eight-inch bony fish preserved in fine-grained limestone of Permian age about 250 million years ago.

the seas teemed with fishes—carnivorous ones, herbivorous ones, and omnivorous scavengers. The time was ripe for the world to expand, for a few plants to begin growing upright on the muddy shores of estuaries and tidal rivers, braving the burning sun, the cold nights under the stars, the desiccating and sometimes violent winds.

Almost at once, certain kinds of animals began utilizing the food produced by the new land plants. These animals, which included the ancestors of insects and spiders, turned their backs forever on the salty oceans. They soon forsook the fresh waters too, at least during their adult lives. Their own adaptations let them survive exposed to air while feeding on the terrestrial vegetation.

As the land plants evolved their stems, roots, leaves, and reproductive parts, the fungi evolved too as both parasites and partners. The insects, in particular developed matching adaptations that let them gain nourishment and a place to live in myriad ways. These relationships seem so familiar to us that, as we move along to the displays of the Carboniferous age, we feel on slightly firmer ground. Although this period began 345 million years ago, the fossils are of impressive plants and animals in freshwater swamps. It was there that cockroaches in all sizes became recognizable. The giants

among ancestral dragonflies attained a wingspan as great as 27 inches—
more than three times as great as any dragonfly alive today.

Insects burgeoned and diversified, chiefly as specialists feeding on and
in definite kinds of land plants or scavenging on plant remains. They provided food for dragonflies and for many other animals of the shallow fresh
waters, the land, and the air. We think of insects as rewarding the versatile
among contemporary kinds of life, being food for the earliest amphibians,
the first reptiles, the mammals, and probably the birds as well when the ini-
tial kinds appeared. In this sense, there had to be a generous supply of insects in the parade of animals before reptiles could diversify. They
nourished the trend that led to the great dinosaurs and the impressive Age
of Reptiles.

During the Mesozoic era, when reptiles attained their all-time dominance, the emphasis among land plants changed radically. The old-style
seed ferns of the Carboniferous evolved into more modern styles of vegetation, or they became extinct. The newcomers replaced the giant club
mosses and horsetail trees. Forests grew upon progressively drier land.
And gradually the shift in style left less space to cycads and other early
gymnosperm trees, more to the later conifers and to the new flowering
plants (angiosperms) of all sizes.

According to Dr. Verne Grant, who directs the Boyce Thompson
Southwestern Arboretum in Arizona, these changes in early seed plants
probably were required to match a new development in the insect hordes:
beetles with strong jaws and a taste for the reproductive parts of seed
plants. One adaptive modification led to the conifers, which developed res-
inous cones, shutting out the insects while continuing to rely on the wind
for distribution of pollen from one tree to the next. Other seed ferns
changed the pattern of growth in the leaves close to their seed parts. They
enclosed the seeds with a fruit wall, displayed colorful leaves as petals,
took the insects into partnership as carriers of pollen, and became flowering plants.

The consequences altered the world drastically for animals on land.
The fact that insects would use their sense organs and wings to hunt out
showy flowers at any level in the forest let many flowering plants become
herbs instead of woody trees, and become annual or biennial instead of
perennial. The possibilities expanded again when mammals and birds appeared and began transporting edible fruits or hoarding seeds in the soil,
distributing these reproductive parts far more efficiently than the wind had
ever done. Yet few of these changes are evident among the displays representing the Age of Reptiles.

When we walk through the hall of reptilian giants in the museum, and
feel dwarfed by the reconstructed skeletons of *Brontosaurus* and *Tyranno-*

saurus, we marvel that such mighty creatures could have existed and then vanished so completely. Until recently, when aerial surveys of the last unexplored parts of the continents filled in blank spaces on the map, there still was hope of finding live dinosaurs in some isolated "lost world." Now we feel confident that every one of these reptiles yielded its territory to more familiar, less fearsome forms of life.

The Cretaceous period—when dinosaurs and their relatives were the most conspicuous life on land, in the air, and in the seas—lasted 70 million years. It ended about 63 million years ago with an incredible series of mass extinctions that closed the Age of Reptiles. Surely so great a catastrophe should have left clear evidence in the rocks and allowed a convincing explanation.

Actually, in the most recent sedimentary deposits of the Cretaceous, the fossil record simply dwindles to include other kinds of life. None of the early interpretations drawn from the change had broad appeal. Few scientists could credit a selective crippling of inheritance, due to some sudden burst of radiation from the sun. Eggs in the soil and creatures more than a few feet down in water would have been completely protected.

It does not seem reasonable that the weather from the poles to the Equator grew cold, letting warm-blooded birds and mammals roam widely, destroying every egg and juvenile reptile of the particular kinds that became extinct. The adult dinosaurs could scarcely respond to cold weather by fatal inanition while crocodiles, turtles, and the ancestors of snakes and lizards continued to evolve. Terrestrial insects and spiders, like the green plants that provided their nourishment directly or indirectly, did not dwindle noticeably. Yet something eliminated the big and little dinosaurs, the birdlike ornithosaurs, the flying pterosaurs, and the sea-going plesiosaurs and ichthyosaurs. At the same time, the carnivorous ammonites and belemnites among the marine mollusks vanished in a similar fashion, leaving no descendants of any kind.

A geologist from Scripps Institution of Oceanography, Dr. M. N. Bramlette, offered in 1965 a more convincing interpretation of the debacle that ended dinosaurs. He pointed out that during the entire 167 million years of the Mesozoic era, virtually no mountain building took place. Slowly the quiet earth eroded. Its mountains crumbled. Its rivers slowed, and meandered. They spread no fertilizing silt upon their former flood plains and carried little in solution to the sea. Terrestrial vegetation must have suffered from mineral malnutrition and must have been able to support no large mass of animal life—particularly no massive animals. Living things in waters over the continental shelves must have been in comparable difficulties. Only the small, versatile, the undemanding, the preadapted could survive in numbers. They inherited the earth after the convulsive activities at the era's end raised the Rocky Mountains, the Andes, the Sierra Nevada, the Alps, the Himalayas. All of these mountains gathered rain from the winds and sent rivers again rushing with dissolved nourishment to the seas.

Although we like to think of the Cenozoic era, which followed Cretaceous times, as the Age of Mammals and Birds, it is even more an Age of Insects and of Flowering Plants. Of all the different kinds of animals passing in the modern parade, more than 750,000 kinds are insects, as compared to 4,500 of mammals and 8,600 of birds. In the plant kingdom today some 295,000 out of 415,000 kinds are flowering plants. If variety is the true measure of success on earth, the insects and flowering plants are supreme. In becoming adapted to all of the ecological nooks and crannies in fresh waters and on the land, these living things have shown greater versatility than any that ever inhabited the seas. They have spread the world of life into the polar regions, up the mountain slopes, across the plains into the deserts. Animals have never before had so much living space to colonize, so many opportunities to diversify.

Animals of most kinds now live on land, close to the world's most available oxygen, in a gaseous medium that impedes their movements far less than a liquid one, and where green plants and fungus plants show the greatest variety. All of these kinds of life evolved as additions to the total, as colonists from the seas, and their descendants. In the seas, where all life began, new kinds of animals and plants have replaced the old, but not in such a spectacular way.

The pace of replacement in the seas can be appreciated from the fossil record. Late in 1966 the retiring president of the American Society of Paleontologists, Dr. J. Wyatt Durham, made some "educated guesses" on this topic from his specialized knowledge. He noted that about 100 kinds of marine invertebrate animals with hard parts, suitable for fossilization, were known from Early Cambrian times some 600 million years ago. Focusing on this type of animal throughout those millions of years, he gave his reasons for believing that about one in every hundred had now been identified. This would indicate that Early Cambrian seas probably had 10,000 species of invertebrates with hard parts, as compared to about 150,000 species in modern seas. The 15-fold increase in diversity during 600 million years would be a measure of increased specialization and efficiency. It seems plausible, and extremely modest as contrasted with the explosive rate of evolution that followed colonization of the land.

These estimates by Dr. Durham are consistent with some approximations offered in 1952 by the distinguished paleontologist Dr. George G. Simpson, indicating 500 million as a probable total number of species for all living things since the beginning on earth. Of these 500 million, perhaps 5 million species are alive today as the total genetic stock among which biologists continue to discover unnamed kinds of animals, plants, and microbes. The other 495 million would then be organisms of the past that have become extinct, their places taken by newer forms of life. This suggests a loss by replacement of one species in each 500 years on the average as a normal pattern throughout the immense past.

When we think of an event that occurs naturally once in 500 years, we realize the challenge in identifying the factors that combine to produce the event so infrequently. Many of them, moreover, may be as subtle as the continuous cycling of nutritional substances between sea and land. Today, many areas of the ocean (such as the Sargasso Sea) are too remote from coasts, too isolated by eddying currents, to receive this fertilizer from the shores and rivers. They are virtual watery deserts, their clear depths supporting few plants and fewer animals. Organic nutrients, including the vitamin B_{12} made by soil microbes, are probably needed. The nitrates and phosphates are among the most significantly missing. Only a slight reduction in the amounts of these materials in the biogeochemical cycles would cause major changes in the communities of animals, whether terrestrial, freshwater, or marine.

The spectacular events may actually have less effect on life than we might anticipate. It is tempting to look for major changes in more modern times. Late in the Cenozoic era, which began less than 65 million years ago, was the Ice Age. Immense glaciers a mile or more thick overlay much of North America and Europe, and lesser parts of Asia. They weighted the continents, deformed the crust of the earth, and contained so much frozen water that the oceans were depleted. While the ice exterminated life on northern parts of the continents, land closer to the Equator expanded because the continental shelves were exposed to the sun. The change in weather must have caused virtually all of the animals and plants to shift southward, adjusting rapidly to the spreading cold and ice. Many must have been too slow, too intolerant, or cut off by barriers such as open water.

Yet the fossil records show few clear-cut instances of extinction due to the ice, and none that can be distinguished with certainty from the slow waxing and waning of animal groups due to their competition for limited resources. Although this evidence is fairly fresh—all within the last two million years—the paleontologists find little to show that the gigantic glaciers had selective action. The deep cold obliterated all life from large areas, and then let the descendants of most of the same species return.

All through the Cenozoic era the animals and plants represented in the fossil record are much like those of today. Examining their remains, we gain confidence that the climatic conditions they survived were comparable to those we can still experience between the Equator and the poles. Yet the distribution of the many types of life has changed markedly as the continents and islands on which they lived evolved into the land we know. The fossil history consistently shows the readiness of living things to spread into new territories as fast as opportunities appear. Land animals and plants traveled according to the rise and fall of solid bridges between the continents. Correspondingly, the sea routes for marine life were blocked while terrestrial organisms found an open avenue. Then the straits reappeared, while the shorelines separated and a water barrier—often with a strong current through it—stopped the further movement of animals that could not swim well at sea.

While the Ice Age was still far in the future, the rumbling earth raised a dry highway between North and South America. Along it, into the previously isolated tropics of the New World, went many pouched mammals (marsupials) and also the ancestors of modern anteaters, armadillos, and sloths. Then the bridge sank beneath the waves and these mammals diversified, with their own descendants as their principal competitors. On the southern continent they became specialized as herbivores and as carnivores of many kinds. Yet they did not develop the features needed for later coexistence with the new types of placental mammals that were evolving in the Northern Hemisphere.

Briefly, during Miocene times, a land bridge between Siberia and Alaska allowed animals such as deer, parrots, and carp to spread from the Old World into the New. The deer took a firm place among the horses and camels that had evolved in North America from less distinctive mammals. Perhaps the competition that the deer added proved too much for the rhinoceroses. After being widespread in the world, these immense animals disappeared from the North American scene. It seems unlikely that they were exterminated by the cats that had evolved, including the famous saber-toothed "tigers" whose oversized upper canine teeth appear well fitted for stabbing downward through armored hide.

When, late in the subsequent Pliocene period, a new land bridge developed between North and South America, there were no rhinos left to cross it. But the deer and cats spread southward. So did some camels, just as they had to Asia earlier, in the period when Siberia and Alaska were linked again by land—letting bears, elephants, crows, and giant salamanders reach the New World from the Old. In South America, the carnivorous and herbivorous marsupials vanished, unable to compete with the newcomers. Only the omnivorous opossums remained, and a few of these came northward across the same land bridge into Central America.

Warping of the continents during the Ice Age allowed more terrestrial mammals to travel beyond their former boundaries. Crows followed the new land connection southward, all the way to Tierra del Fuego. Porcu-pines came north into Canada, and peccaries into the American South-west. From Alaska into Asia, the horses crossed a bridge that led them on into Africa. Musk-oxen came eastward into North America and braved the cold weather along the fringes of the ice fields, probably in company with wooly mammoths. Bison from the Old World reached the New, and found grazing land farther south. There their principal competitors were native grasshoppers, horses, camels, pronghorns, and colonial ground squirrels called prairie dogs. Following all of this edible flesh came an omnivorous animal of the Old World with a craving for meat: a two-legged primate of African origin, with stone tools and a knowledge of how to start a fire.

CHAPTER 2

THE
RISE
OF
CULTURE
AND
THE
FALL
OF
WILDLIFE

HAND TOOLS AND charcoal often seem the marks of emerging man, distinguishing him from the prehuman ancestors who accepted the world without attempting to change it.

Man is not alone in using tools. The woodpecker finch on the Galápagos Islands is a tool user. After cutting a hole with its blunt beak into a plant and exposing an insect grub to view, the bird chooses a cactus spine with which to extricate the edible insect. In equatorial Africa the chimpanzee selects a suitably slender stick to push into the doorway of a termite nest, giving soldier termites something to grasp in their hard jaws. The chimp pulls out the loaded stick and eats off the termites. Even an African vulture can pick out a stone and use it as a tool to batter through the hard shell of an ostrich egg and reach the nourishing contents. More than the ability to use a tool is needed to start a culture and to change the world.

We give more credit to the unknown savages in many parts of the world who learned to throw a stone or a straight stick—a spear—and kill animals at a distance. The men who invented the spear and the bow, the catapult and the blowgun, advanced our heritage much further. They extended man's power far beyond the reach of his arm. To tip the spear with obsidian or flint, making it penetrate and stick, or to coat with poison the points of arrow and dart, the quicker to subdue a victim, also increased man's power. Long before metal and explosives entered the armament of our species, these tools that worked at a distance made our ancestors immensely influential in the community of life.

21

By the patient and rapid rotating of a stick pressed into a slight depression in a piece of wood, a minute fire can be started with frictional heat. The fire becomes bigger when blown gently and fed with the right dry fuels. No animal except man has learned this trick, let alone used it to build a warming, flickering, impassable fence across the mouth of a sleeping cave. With practice, any apprentice can learn how to do it; knowledge of fire is a cultural heritage. Yet the first animals dispossessed by this wonderful discovery may have been bats and bears that would not return to a smoky cave. The fire dispelled the chill of night, cast restless shadows on the cave walls, and warded off the hungry predators beyond the cave. None of these effects changed the world immediately.

The use of fire to make inedible foods edible proved almost as important a cultural advance, for it added to man's diet a whole array of hard cereal grains and starchy vegetables. These could be harvested and stored, solving the problem of what to eat during a winter snow storm. Later, when men became more skilled at planning ahead and changing their environment to suit their tastes, this chain of discovery progressed to deliberate cultivation of plant crops, preempting major areas of the earth's fertile lands so far as possible for the good of our own species and no others.

As we look about, we see few animals of other kinds that approach us in the variety of foods they will accept. In one place or another, people subsist on cooked roots and stems and starchy seeds, on cooked and raw leaves and berries, nuts and tree fruits, sea foods, and almost every kind of meat. Raw hamburger and cooked flesh, raw fish or boiled or broiled or baked or fried, raw oysters or cooked shellfish, bêches-de-mer (sea cucumbers) and sea urchin eggs, live ants or cooked caterpillars, the list is almost endless.

We have a friend who has taught his horse to eat raw fish, but the horse would prefer a handful of oats or an apple any day. Most animals are quite particular. In fact, our closest competitors as far as versatility in food seem an undistinguished lot: pigs and bears, domestic fowl, rats and mice, ants and cockroaches, vultures and gulls, and to a distinctly lesser extent dogs, goats, and skunks. North Africans assure us that a camel will eat anything it can find. Few of these versatile animals have much chance to demonstrate their full catholicity of taste unless they gain access to foods man has prepared or discarded. The bear, the rat, and the gull at the garbage dump are beneficiaries of human culture.

In some parts of Africa today tribal custom decrees that, as boys reach the age at which they should be initiated into manhood, they spend a lunar month in groups of two or three, living off the land and in small thatched shelters they build far from the village. Hunger sharpens the skill of these boys in surviving, eating whatever small birds, lizards, insects, or other animals they can kill, together with parts of wild plants that can be made edible with the simplest procedures. The accuracy with which they can throw a stone or a crude spear verges on the incredible. The scarcity of animal life smaller and slower than an antelope is a consequence.

Another custom on this great continent is even more widespread south of the Sahara and other deserts. People set fire to the dry grasslands several times a year. They claim that the practice reduces the number of ticks, improves the food supply for edible animals, and puts a human hunter on a more even relationship with local predators (such as lions) in competing for antelopes and other prey. We wonder whether the custom began through a vague recognition that any bird or mammal, reptile or insect overtaken and killed by the flames is already half-cooked and an easy meal, or through some conscious plan to drive terrified antelopes toward waiting hunters. Whatever the original reason, the custom dates from long ago and changes the world for most kinds of living things in the area.

Whether set by man or started by a bolt of lightning, the grass fire spreads rapidly. Where the grasslands meet the forest, it burns under the nearest trees. It scorches the bark and dries the leaves to death on many live trees, turns dead ones into torches, and transforms organic matter on the forest soil into gases and mineral ash. Thereafter the sun and any rain reach the ground, where previously the foliage of the forest intercepted both. Forest animals find nothing to eat, but grass eaters have additional territory as grass spreads among the dead trees. Only an occasonal fire is needed to maintain the new grassland, even where the climate would otherwise support a dense forest.

The fossil record shows that, two million years ago, forests extended across Africa from the Atlantic Ocean to the east coast, where now the continent has grasslands and vast savannas, whose trees are of kinds tolerant to fire. So far, no way has been found to learn whether the changing climate during the Ice Age caused grasses to replace the forest, or whether this alteration in the landscape was the first large-scale effect of emerging man. The place is right. The time is right. But did mankind spread northward from the forest fringes into natural grasslands because they were rich with big, meaty, herbivorous animals, or use fire to progressively expand this extraordinary hunting area? Some day soon, a scientist may discover a way to decide whether Africa's big game country is man-made.

Ecologists know that natural fires start chiefly during electrical storms, usually in the wettest part of the year, and do little damage to either the food for grazing animals or the wild grazing mammals. The fires men start, by contrast, are most frequent during the dry season, when the dead tops of dormant grasses contribute to a raging wall of flame that sweeps across the land. Afterward, the sun parches the bared soil, readying it to

Kirtland's warbler, which nests only among the jack pine stands of northern Michigan and winters in the Bahamas, has been called the "bird worth a forest fire." (ROGER TORY PETERSON FROM NATIONAL AUDUBON SOCIETY.)

blow away in any steady wind. Today the deliberate use of fire to extend grasslands is well known. But experiments designed to test the effects of fire at different seasons on the range for grazing animals give results that are inconsistent—sometimes good and often bad.

The Plains Indians in America set fire to the prairie grasses so frequently during the millennia before Europeans arrived, that no one can be sure to-day how far the grassy plains extended eastward and to the north as a normal expression of the natural climate. The Indians recognized the advantages in more territory for edible bison and less for inedible trees. Probably they were responsible for the existence of tall-grass prairies toward the eastern forests, where trees would grow if protected. Instead, the fire-tolerant grasses sometimes attained a height so great that a mounted man could ride through them without disclosing his whereabouts.

On lands with greater rainfall, where a forest of hardwood trees would normally grow and shelter a modest array of animals, a program of regular burning often maintains a completely different forest of coniferous soft-woods or a grassy savanna studded with fire-resistant trees. In the American Southeast, man's cultural pattern favors the longleaf pine and other eastern yellow pines, generally with an understory of dogwood and a sparse ground cover of wiry shrubs. Live oak and other slow-growing trees would replace the pines and make a habitat for a far greater assortment of animal life if, for a few decades, no flames cleared the forest floor of pine needles, fallen branches, and oak seedlings. Even in the areas of Central America where the annual rainfall would support a dense rain forest full of amazing tropical animals, savannas of pine and tropical grasses are common. They are the product of changes that begin with cutting the valuable timber, such as magnificent tall mahogany trees, then clearing the rest of the forest for agriculture, finally abandoning the unproductive fields to the few plants and animals that can survive with frequent fires. The whole character of the landscape changes in just a few years. If the affected area is large, it may never recover.

Prevention of fire is a cultural tradition too, best developed by people who have combustible property they wish to protect. Their success affects the welfare of many kinds of wildlife. One example became famous in the early 1960's, when American biologists began seeking a reason for the dwindling numbers of a particularly rare warbler. This bird, Kirtland's warbler, spends the winter in the Bahamas and nests only in the northern part of Michigan among young stands of jack pine. Suitable stands were vanishing because of fire prevention or prompt control. Jack pines, which are native also in adjacent Canada, hold their cones unopened, on the branches, each cone a prison within which the dormant seeds normally die of eventual starvation. Scorched by a forest fire that bares the ground and destroys many of the mature trees, the cones pop open, showering winged seeds unharmed into the breeze. On the soil the seeds germinate and start a new pine grove in competition with fire-resistant grasses, blueberry bushes, and other low vegetation—plants a jack pine can shade out as it grows. Now Kirtland's warbler has become "the bird worth a forest fire," and the basis for an experimental program of deliberate burning under the most careful supervision of the Michigan Department of Conservation and the United States Forest Service.

The plight of California's famous condors seems to be a consequence of a policy of fire prevention, which expanded over North America at the same rate as the colonists. Formerly these birds were not "California" condors, but were widespread. They visited the Atlantic shoreline, the Gulf states, and across the central plains into Canada. Soaring magnificently on wings spread wider than those of any other North American bird, they peer sharp-eyed at the ground for carrion, such as a dead rabbit. Today the condors find little to eat, and their numbers have shrunk to fewer than 100 birds, all nesting in a moderately inaccessible part of the California coast.

Many areas of former condor territory are now planted with crops or used as pastures, both too well managed to have animal bodies lying about. No cougars or wolves now make a kill and leave the remains in view. In the West, where neither use of land is encouraged by the climate, shrubby sagebrush and other woody plants now form a dense screen a few feet above the ground. Without frequent fires spreading unchecked, this growth decreases the opportunities for grasses and herbs, for rabbits and other animals that would feed on the low soft plants; it also shields the few dead bodies from aerial reconnaissance. It is far easier to protect the nesting areas for the California condors, and to keep people away so that the birds will have privacy for their slow reproduction, than to restore their habitat by fire, increasing visibility and their food supply at the same time.

Only recently have scientists begun to measure the benefits and detriments of fire, and the impact of other ways in which man alters the natural history of the world. Until the twentieth century, neither travel nor communication were easy enough to let anyone grasp the real limitations of our planet. Almost half of that century passed before progress in technology let archeologists learn, from the radiocarbon content of charcoal and fossil bones and other organic matter, reasonably accurate dates within the past two million years for human artifacts and objects associated with expanding culture.

Human hunters, armed with crude weapons and a knowledge of fire, have been far more influential than had been credited previously. As primitive people spread out of Africa into Asia and Europe, into North Amer-

The North American condor, now represented by only a few birds near the California coast, was once widespread over the continent. (CARL B. KOFORD, BUREAU OF SPORT FISHERIES AND WILDLIFE.)

ica and then South, and across the East Indies to Australia and Pacific Islands, the edible animals diminished in numbers. Many disappeared forever.

In North America, the elephants, camels, and native horses perished completely. The saber-toothed cats became extinct, no doubt in part because so much of their natural food had been exterminated. Although technically in prehistoric times, these disappearances cannot have been long ago. The tusks and teeth of elephants get tangled in the trawl nets of fishermen off the shore of the eastern continental shelf from Virginia to Maine, where these animals died less than 15,000 years ago. Probably the Indians hunted them there while the continent was still warped, exposing its shelves, after the Ice Age. Perhaps we should be surprised that so many other meaty animals survived until Europeans arrived. The pronghorns may have been too fleet, the deer too secretive, the bison herds too formidable, the prairie dogs too quick and fertile, to meet the same fate.

In the Old World, the presence of mankind and of favored domestic animals has had the same effect. Eurasian caribou vanished, except for the herds of captive animals that Laplanders and other nomadic people learned to maintain and to call reindeer. Early hunters in southern France and Spain were familiar with these and other vanished mammals, for they drew good pictures of them on caves in which they took shelter.

The giant roc or elephant bird (*Aepyornis*) of Madagascar, which is the largest relative of the ostrich for which evidence has been found, disappeared so recently that men were still using its huge eggshells as storage jars for drinking water when explorers from Europe arrived. Similarly in New Zealand, when Captain James Cook visited during the southern summer of 1770–1771, the Polynesian settlers (Maoris) had handsome ceremonial cloaks made from the plumes of extinct moas. Prehistory hides the details of the fate that befell many an animal that could not survive close to man.

If the human species is a special type of animal, and not merely the most versatile competitor for resources the world has ever known, then extinction due to human activities is a special way in which animals are vanishing from the earth. It is a phenomenon of the past two million years, and matches the novel evolution of a cultural heritage in place of the usual inheritable changes with time in body build and function. The question is whether the parade of animals will continue, merely swerved by this new feature of the environment, or will end with mankind and two categories of companions: those man calls "vermin," which he cannot quite exterminate, and those he can no longer get along without—his pampered livestock of various kinds.

CHAPTER 3

NONHUMAN PARTNERS OF MAN'S CHOOSING

NOT LONG AGO a young man of 11 years who had just been introduced at school to animals in a drop of pond water went to a university professor of biology as the nearest oracle. "Sir," he asked, "have there always been amebas?"

His question has no certain answer, for amebas leave no fossil evidence of their existence. Amebas may be the most ancient style of life on earth, or the degenerate descendants of something different. But some of the animals the 11-year-old knows best are equally enigmatic. No single wild ancestor is known for most of the domesticated kinds of animals: dogs, cats, horses, cattle, sheep, goats, pigs, honeybees, or silkworms. The only wild members of these domesticated species known today are the off-spring of individuals that have escaped and reproduced in sheltered places, and hence are feral.

We are sure that all these animals had wild ancestors, but we don't know how many. Did early man, some six to ten thousand years ago, sympathize with rare creatures that were almost extinct, take them into his household, and upgrade their qualities until each beast, bird, or insect could serve him? Or, having learned to breed these animals in captivity, did he exterminate all that remained then in the wild? Certainly to protect his herds, flocks, and hives, he managed to erase a great many species, at least locally. Perhaps there is some magic about these animals that limits them to so few kinds.

No indication that domesticated species are peculiar is in the classic books by the Swedish physician-naturalist who signed himself in Latin as

Carolus Linnaeus. As he groped for uniformity and found it in naming all the living things he knew on earth, his concept of a "kind" was embodied in the species he grouped in genera. Any breed or age or sex of dog was included in *Canis familiaris,* of beef animal in *Bos taurus,* of horse in *Equus caballus,* and of domestic pig in *Sus scrofa.* His names for them are still in use.

Charles Darwin discussed these and other familiar kinds of life in his 1868 book *Variation of Animals and Plants under Domestication.* He believed that the diversity evident in the many true-breeding types had evolved as a consequence of human selection (instead of natural selection) from among the offspring of single species. Not until the present century and from a better understanding of the mechanism of inheritance did biologists begin to question whether the word "species" holds the same meaning when applied to domesticated animals as it does among creatures in the wild.

Scientists regard each species as a population of individuals so similar as to be capable of interbreeding with full fertility. When crossed with individuals of a different species from the same part of the world, they are expected to produce no offspring, or young with reduced fertility, such as a sterile mule. Rarely does the scientist who classifies living things take time to test fertility. Yet the tests that have been tried show that judgments based on features such as body build are reasonably reliable. Under wild conditions, at least, hybrids are rare and usually sterile. The rarity is an outcome of inherited adaptations that tend to isolate each species in reproduction.

Penned together in a zoo, a captive lion from Africa may mate with a tigress from Asia, or a lioness with a tiger. The outcome is a "liger," which is often fertile when test-crossed with either parental type. Under normal circumstances, geographical separation keeps these hybrids from arising and maintains the genetic purity of both the African *Panthera leo* and the Asiatic *Panthera tigris.* The leopard (*Panthera pardus*) ranges close to the territories of both lion and tiger, but generally keeps to the forest instead of savannas or swamplands. Neither its scent nor mating calls attract the other species, and the leopard shows no interest in theirs.

By contrast, the domestic dog is willing to interbreed freely with many wild species, such as coyotes and wolves, that do not normally cross. Students of human history are challenged to explain how early man managed to maintain so sociable and variable a beast under domestication, while exterminating all wild members of *Canis familiaris.* But if the dog is a multiple hybrid, fortuitously· fertile, we have no need to look for it as a species that vanished in the wild. Its multiple ancestors could include the circumboreal gray wolf (*Canis lupus*) that lived around the fringes of human communities. This modern view is reinforced by the regularity with which Eskimos cross their husky breed of sled dogs with gray wolves to benefit from hybrid vigor. Recently, mammalogists have begun to regard as something new the fertile "coy-dogs" that have commenced to maintain themselves under wild conditions in eastern North America, from crosses between domestic dogs and coyotes (*Canis latrans*). Coy-dogs show an obvious blend of features.

If the ancestors of many domesticated animals were multiple, so probably were the characteristics that early man noticed and put to use. Edibility may have ranked high. The pups from a den of wolves, of jackals, or other doglike animals could be taken home and raised in pens on table scraps until each grew big enough to eat. In a number of nations today dogs are eaten routinely with no more qualms than we have in cooking a fish we have caught, or a chicken, or a yearling lamb.

Dogs can dig, and a pen is a nuisance. Dogs that began as pups may have escaped, stayed around the community, bred with their wild neighbors, scavenged at every opportunity, and often ended in the stew pot. Outdoor dogs, half wild and half starved, are common in the streets and environs of many small communities in Asia and Africa. Strongly territorial and brave in packs, they set up a great commotion when a stranger appears—and they may attack. Otherwise they are less watchdogs than street cleaners, showing a behavior that is rarely seen in countries where babies are diapered and adults use privies or plumbing facilities. Where dogs are commoner than diapers, and sanitary engineering has yet to be introduced, these animals show an extraordinary eagerness to eat human feces. This service to mankind cannot have been overlooked by primitive people.

Today the principal working dogs are the collies and similar breeds that are trained to obey commands at a distance. They herd sheep and cattle where neither a horse nor a motorized vehicle can carry a man fast enough. Without dogs, New Zealanders could scarcely raise sheep in such numbers on their roadless, rounded mountain tops, isolated from adjacent country by steep slopes clad in dense underbrush. On foot, the climbing man commands the dog, and the dog controls the sheep.

In many countries the history of the horse as a partner of mankind has followed a similar course. Rarely now are horses raised primarily as meat animals. Possibly we have eaten horse at restaurants more often than we know. Only at the Faculty Club of Harvard University did the authors see it offered on the menu, order a horse steak, and enjoy it for what it was. As draft animals their value is small. No longer would a mechanical en-

gineer think of rating his machines in horsepower—a unit devised by
James Watt in relation to extraordinarily strong dray horses.

A few years ago a conversation with specialists in animal husbandry
made us realize more fully the changing relationships between mankind
and horses. It began when we asked about horse nutrition, based on a
sudden awareness that without having a four-part stomach and chewing a
cud as cattle do, horses get most of their winter nourishment from hay,
which is largely cellulose. The cattle, we knew, have rumen bacteria as intestinal partners that are able to split cellulose molecules into digestible
substances. How does a horse manage? It has some suitable bacteria in its
large intestine. Yet until recently there seemed no point in spending time
and money on research toward improving the diet of horses. So rapidly
were they being replaced by tractors and motor vehicles that their virtual
disappearance was foreseen. The U. S. Department of Agriculture ceased
to include them in its annual inventory of farm animals. Now horses have
returned to favor and recovered their numbers, but in a new guise. The nutrition of the animal is important today because so many people find horse-
riding a delightful hobby and horseracing a gambler's sport.

Western stories and motion pictures never reveal how much the jeep
with its four-wheel drive replaced the horse as a mount for cattle ranchers.
The machine goes farther in a day, longer without maintenance, gets its
energy from compact gasoline instead of bulky hay, and often lets a cow-
hand be home at night by traveling along the highway at a pace half
again as fast as the best race horse on the home stretch. Slowly the famous
gauchos of the South American pampas are disappearing, along with their
mounts. They are becoming part of history, like the chariot racers of Roman days, the mounted Vandals who vanquished Rome, and the terrible
warriors of Genghis Khan riding their Mongol ponies. We may see the
day when the cattlemen of Botswana give up their life in the saddle, and
the Arabs their handsome horses. The long partnership between man and
horse as a matter of actual utility seems doomed.

It is ironic that the mustangs or broncos of the western United States
had to be rescued by sentimental people a few years ago when these feral
animals, which may be descended from the war horses of the days of the
Spanish conquest, were threatened with extermination. The cattle and
sheep ranchers cared little when hunters for pet-food companies began
with jeeps and low-flying aircraft to flush from each mountain canyon
the horses that sheltered and bred there. Every feral horse fewer meant
more grazing and water for domestic stock, and added profit. But ad-
mirers of the mustang rallied to its defense and got laws passed prohibiting
use of aircraft in this way. Now they may have to do their lobbying again

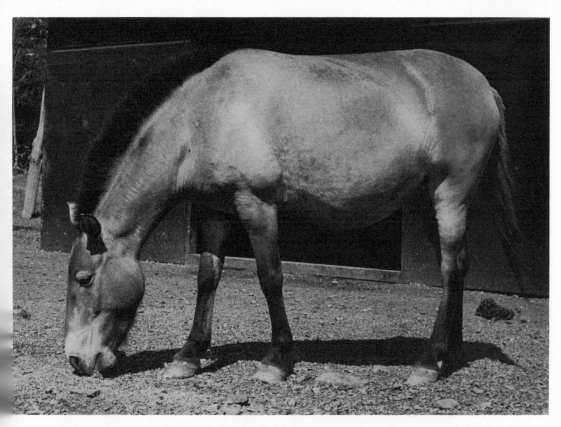

Once numerous on the grasslands west of Mongolia, Przewalski's horse is losing its distinctive identity through loss of its isolation, for it interbreeds with domestic horses that have been introduced. (COURTESY OF DR. HEINZ HECK, CATSKILL GAME FARM.)

to prevent the rounding up and killing of the mustangs from the newer snowmobiles. It seems hard to keep a breeding stock of horses on the continent where fleet grazing animals of the genus *Equus* originally evolved.

Long ago, ancestral horses of several now extinct species migrated across the land bridge to Siberia and diversified as they spread out in Asia. There during prehistoric times, man managed to tame and then breed horses of some kind. But whether their stock was primarily that of the then-widespread, now-extinct tarpan, which lived in southern Europe too, remains to be learned. The only wild relative in this part of the Old World today is the Mongolian wild horse (*E. przewalskii*). A stocky, short-legged and thick-headed animal, it is now on the vanishing list. To some extent it is endangered by the ease with which it hybridizes with Mongol ponies—a breed of the domestic horse. This may merely indicate a shared ancestry, which thousands of years of geographical separation did not shape into a genetically isolated species.

Probably the dog, the horse, and cattle all entered human culture toward the end of the Stone Age or the beginning of the Bronze Age, which in eastern Europe and Asia Minor seems to have come around 3500 B.C.

The Ankole cattle herded in equatorial Africa bear heavy diverging horns like those depicted on monuments of ancient Egypt (photographed in southwestern Uganda).

The cattle too are beasts of mystery, widely treasured under domestication, but nowhere wild except as feral animals, and on a broad range from which native predators have been largely eliminated.

The partnership between *Bos taurus* and man may have begun centuries before the founding of the first civilization in the valleys of the Tigris and Euphrates. Remains of domestic cattle of medium size, with rather ordinary horns, are among the oldest artifacts of man excavated in this area. Cattle with extraordinarily long and sturdy horns are depicted on monuments of early Egypt. They are almost identical, in fact, with the head armament of the Ankole cattle herded today by tall Watusis in equatorial Africa. We have gaped at these beasts passing in single file along a road, each wearing slightly curved horns that taper smoothly from a thick base. The angle of divergence makes plausible the story told us in this region: that the letter **A** was invented from looking at the head of such an animal turned upside down.

Some archeologists believe that cattle were caught and penned from river valleys in Asia Minor and perhaps the lower Nile, and confined until used as impressive sacrifices to placate the powerful gods. Animals that accepted captivity enough to breed could reduce the effort required for hunters to go out and capture wild, unruly beasts. A different species of cattle (the humped zebus or Brahmans, *Bos indicus*) somehow got isolated on the Indian peninsula and adjacent land. Only recently has this species been interbred with the domestic cattle of Europe, Africa, and more northern Asia, chiefly to spread a tolerance for hot weather among cattle to be raised in warm countries. In Europe, at least, cattle were similarly modified millennia ago by crosses with a now-vanished European species called the auroch ("original ox," *Bos primigenius*). The auroch, an enormous animal as much as six feet high at the shoulder with spreading, forward-curving horns as described by Julius Caesar and many other writers, had more the character of a Texas longhorn. The last known example died in 1647. Attempts to reconstruct the aurochs by "reverse breeding" from hybrids have been only partly successful. The Texas longhorns, which were descended from cattle the Spanish introduced, have largely vanished too, being replaced by newer breeds that grow faster to marketable size.

Other cattle have been domesticated in Southeast Asia, but seldom crossed successfully with the familiar *B. taurus* or *B. indicus*. The yak or grunting ox (*B. grunniens*) is well adapted to life at high elevations in the Himalayan foothills and plateau country, but does not tolerate conditions at lower altitudes. Tibetans tamed and bred some of these animals centuries ago and developed a smaller, more docile creature than the wild yak, used for riding, as a beast of burden, and as a source of milk, meat, leather, bone, fat, soap, glue, and fertilizer. Less familiar is the gayal (*B. frontalis*) which is a medium-sized animal with heavy, short, diverging horns, unknown in the wild but raised in northern Burma, Assam, and the Chittagong Hills of India.

Perhaps because the word "cattle" is so closely related to "chattel," as a human possession, it is used to include also the distinctive water buffalo that serves man from Egypt to the Philippines. Animals of this kind run wild in marshy parts of Assam, Bengal, and Nepal. But whether they are feral, like those released and now numerous in northern Australia, is yet to be proved. Probably they are descended from domestic stock, making the water buffalo, too, of uncertain origin with all truly wild relatives extinct. It is well named, for its health depends upon a daily bath and frequent access to drinking water. To people that it recognizes by sight, it is usually docile; to strangers it is generally belligerent. A water buffalo pulling a plow through a rice paddy in the Philippines, seeing us pause for a photograph from the narrow dike between one field and the next, snorted and wheeled toward us so suddenly that one of us (LJM) fell into the mud

—one leg knee deep on one side of the dike and the other on the opposite! By contrast, water buffaloes with blindfolds were oblivious to our presence in Egypt while they walked in circles, goaded occasionally by a child, to turn water wheels dipping into canals from the Nile and serving irrigation. Water buffalo milk is rich and palatable; the hides make superior leather; but the meat offers little to recommend it.

Cattle require more space and more food in proportion to the milk they yield than the domestic goat, whose partnership with man dates back at least eight and possibly nine thousand years. It originated near mountains of Southwest Asia, probably from a combination of several related species. Often the bezoar goat (or pasang) is mentioned as the principal ancestor, but these wild natives of old Persia show many differences from the modern goats that are raised for milk, wool, leather (particularly soft kidskin from young animals), and meat.

The goat is a browser, needing shrubby vegetation that grows slowly, and hence it affects its world quite differently from a cow, which feeds on grass and herbs that regenerate quickly. To reach its food, a goat will climb trees with low branches or precipices that challenge a man to follow. So catholic is the animal's taste that it eats and digests many objects made of paper. When goats ate off the identifying paper labels from the first tinned steel cans to be marketed, no actual demonstration was needed to start the rumor that these animals would eat the metal cans as well. With the help of sheep, they have destroyed much of the native vegetation across North Africa and southern Europe, as well as in parts of Asia to which their wild ancestors were surely native.

As we think back through two-thirds of the time since the last glacial period, when men of the Old Stone Age were looking about them for ways to make their lives easier, we suspect that medicines and magic held greater attraction than any investment in captive animals for next year's feast. How could a man fail to benefit from maintaining a small flock of bezoar goats, in whose stomach he might find bezoars? Each of these stonelike objects grows like a brown organic pearl with concentric layers of secretion over some pebble or wad of hair that the goat has been unable to pass through its digestive tract. Bezoars are still prized—bought and sold—in many countries as trusted antidotes for poisons, and as amulets affording protection against the unknown. A pregnant she-goat would hold additional benefits: two or three kids that could become offerings to the gods, and a supply of pure white milk whose fat droplets are so fine they fail to rise to the top, making the liquid naturally homogenized. Tended carefully, a superior milch goat may continue producing milk for a whole year after giving birth. The record is more than 16 pounds of it (more than a gallon) daily, containing half a pound of butterfat. To treasure such an animal is most logical.

Left on a deserted island, with no large four-footed carnivores to trouble them, goats can fend off attacks from predatory birds and reproduce until they starve to death from destroying all of the vegetation. These activities have hurried quite a number of the world's rare local animals into extinction.

The domestic breeds of sheep seem more vulnerable, unable to protect their young from birds of prey. This so unfits them for feral existence that free-ranging herds gradually die out from failure in reproduction. Unlike goats, sheep have a good sense of smell, which they use in following narrow trails upon which others of their kind have stepped. Every print of their sharp, two-toed feet contains a small daub of an odorous secretion from a special gland. Where many have trod, the odor may be strong enough to alert other sheep downwind, inducing them to join the herd and follow the leader.

For a reason we do not comprehend, lambs have held a place of special esteem as sacrificial animals in religious ceremonials from ancient times until the present. Their importance may have induced some men of the Stone Age to evolve a new occupation: the herding of the sacred sheep. Like goats, these animals originated somewhere in mountainous southwestern Asia, but a little later—about seven thousand years ago. The earliest known remains are bones of domestic sheep found near altars of temples dating from the New Stone Age. Since no wild sheep of this species have been discovered anywhere, it seems likely that the familiar animal that Linnaeus named *Ovis aries* was derived from either a species long extinct or some combination of wild sheep. The nearest living kin, whose ancestors may have made the principal contribution toward *Ovis aries*, are the urials of northern India. Often called red sheep or Asiatic mouflons, they range from Cyprus through the southern U.S.S.R. to Kashmir and Pakistan, chiefly as mountain dwellers in rough and precipitous country. European mouflons from Corsica and Sardinia have been interbred with domestic sheep on many occasions in recent years, and possibly long ago as well. Even the larger argali or Marco Polo sheep, which are native to the eastern U.S.S.R. and western China, may have contributed to the pool of inheritance from which sheep breeders have selected more than 200 special varieties with distinctive features and names.

Equally tailored into many different styles to match local needs is the domestic pig. Linnaeus lumped it with the Eurasian wild hog under the same name, and for centuries no one has been able to prove that they were distinct back in the Old Stone Age. Certainly the domestic animal will

A striped coat distinguishes the young of the wild pig in Europe and northern Asia, but the domesticated animals derived from wild ancestors have lost this feature. (P. BERGER FROM NATIONAL AUDUBON SOCIETY.)

cross with the wild hog, but so it will also with small pigs of several other species native to southern Asia. The wild hog may have been introduced into the British Isles, but it seems native to the area from the Atlantic coast of Europe proper across North Africa, through southern Asia (including some of the East Indian islands), and possibly to Japan. Yet in all of its many geographic subspecies, the wild hog bears young with lengthwise white stripes, following a pattern among the swine of the world that has only two exceptions: the peculiar babirusa of the East Indies, which is on the vanishing list, and the domestic pig. In all of its 300 different breeds, the domestic animal is like the babirusa in producing unstriped young. Chance would be against such uniform loss of striping unless, in the ancestry of the domestic pig, an unknown and totally vanished species had an important share. Another consistent difference is that the domestic pig farrows from eight to twelve piglets at a birth, compared to the wild boar's four to six. Perhaps the pig's chief ancestor was more fertile and docile than the wild hog to the extent that men of the Stone Age chose it to become a human partner, thereby saving it from total extinction.

In ancient Egypt the pig was sacred to Osiris; in classical Greece, it was similarly dedicated to Demeter. In New Guinea and islands of the South Pacific the distinction between sacred and special is often unclear. Each family may own a pig or two and keep it penned beneath the house as an animated garbage grinder and feces disposal system combined. But suckling pig—usually one big enough to be weaned—is the central dish of a small feast for a special occasion, and a whole one roasted over hot stones in a pit is the major attraction in a big celebration. This is very different from buying a roasting loin or a few pork chops or a pound of bacon at the butcher shop. The pig is killed ceremoniously, as befits an animal of real importance.

Recent discoveries by archeologists and geneticists combine impressively as we think about the world's principal domesticated animals. Pig, sheep, horse, dog, and all of the widespread kinds of cattle were taken into partnership with mankind in southwestern Asia during the Stone Age. They now combine a heritage of contributions from species of other areas; but in almost every instance they represent the sole survivors incorporating genes from species that now have vanished.

Today we can appreciate better than ever before why the environs of ancient Babylon, near the junction of the Tigris and Euphrates Rivers, cradled so many civilizations in sequence. Nowhere else on earth may have afforded so many different kinds of animals suitable to be taken into partnership with mankind. Subdued, their welfare looked after while their surplus numbers were cropped, they outlived the wars and man-made devastation. They made some men herders and farmers, while freeing others to try their hands at new enterprises in growing communities. As the domesticated forms of life came to depend upon man for perpetuation, they also generated culture. From their modern esteem comes their recognition as a special category of life, each referred to today as a cultigen.

In a sense, our own species and some nonhuman life have taken analogous courses in overcoming the limitations imposed by the environment. Our ancestors went into partnership with useful plants and animals, improving them and becoming dependent upon them as a resource for more people. These alliances were basic to the spread of our species over almost all of the lands in the world. Wild animals and plants have found partners too, and become able to colonize areas that previously were closed to them.

It is tempting to credit much of the difference between the cultures of the West and of the East to the combination of domesticated animals upon which each depended. Western men possessed sheep and goats, which devastated the land and forced the men to move. Empires with these cultigens spread northwest into Europe and metastasized into distant continents: the Americas, Africa, Australia, and New Zealand. Simultaneously a counterpart culture evolved in the Far East in relative isolation, without sheep or goats. It had no need to shift to other lands, remained introspective, but acquired some of the other animal resources common to the Eurasian continental area. The China pig became an equivalent of the European one. The Peking duck was derived from circumboreal mallards, just as were the domestic ducks of Europe. But swan geese, which winter in northern China, contributed a domestic goose in the Orient that is completely distinct from the Western barnyard goose, which came from greylags—perhaps birds that migrated from northern Europe to winter in the Persian marshes.

Long before Europeans arrived in America, people of mongoloid stock had spread widely in the New World, with only the dog to represent cultigens from Asia. They had, however, domesticated a few kinds of American plants as culture-generators, with no widespread meat animal to go along. Maize, for which no wild ancestor is known, and various kinds of beans were staples. Locally, the Andean people maintained the guinea pig as a prolific, harmless creature that could reproduce indoors and run about the house, to be cooked whenever the housewife had no more exciting ingredients for a meal. Today it is a vanishing animal in the wild.

The Peruvians transformed a breeding stock of captured guanacos into the New World's only beast of burden (the llama) and a somewhat smaller, hairier version (the alpaca), both of which are known only as domesticated animals—a status they have held for at least a thousand years. In the high country to which these South American camels are well adapted, almost everything they produce is used: wool from both alpaca and llama, woven into fabrics or braided into rope; fine hairs to be felted into thick textiles and hats; hides for crude sandals; jerked meat to be chewed strenuously; hard fat (tallow) for making candles; and dry droppings as the best fuel above the altitudes at which trees and shrubs grow. Some scientists regard the guanaco, llama, and alpaca as separate species, and assume an independent ancestry antedating domestication. They must then regard the llama and alpaca lines as extinct in the wild, vanished like the forerunners of so many of man's cultigens.

In Mexico the Spanish met one more domesticated animal: the Mexican race of the American turkey. They took some of these magnificent birds as trophies to Europe, and gradually shared them through the barnyards of the continent. The Pilgrims brought the bird to New England, unaware that this largest and most edible of American birds was native in the forests paralleling the Atlantic coast. Benjamin Franklin voted for the American turkey, rather than the bald eagle, to become the country's emblem. But wild turkeys faded away through slaughter and destruction of their habitat.

So thoroughly were the native wild turkeys of eastern North America hunted by European settlers that restocking seemed important—with the descendents of Mexican turkeys brought from Europe. (WILLIAM J. JAHODA.)

The turkeys of eastern North America, which have a brown-tipped tail instead of the white tail tips and tail coverts of the Mexican race, are almost gone. Generally the introduced Mexican breed is chosen for restocking forests where protection can be given. We have encountered a few in open woodlands from New York State and Virginia to Arizona, and continue to regard them as feral rather than wild. The principal wild turkey in the New World now is the separate species called the ocellated turkey, native to Guatemala, where its future can no longer be regarded with confidence.

It seems incredible that the explorations of new territory by Alexander the Great, Marco Polo, Columbus, Magellan, da Gama, Cook, and the other great men in history should have had their greatest effect in promoting the spread of horses, cattle, goats, sheep, pigs, and poultry. Far less significant to other living things have been the achievements of which cultured man is justly proud: accurate maps, quick communication, a detailed familiarity with the living world, and now space travel. Surely here on earth, with so much perspective from modern knowledge, it should be possible to survey our planet for wild species that, even if few, could be domesticated, perhaps combined, to benefit mankind while furthering the survival of more kinds of life, instead of fewer.

We sense an urgent need to expand our mutually beneficial relationships with the animals and plants of each naturally different part of the world. By doing so, we would stave off the cultural homogenization that now threatens to engulf us. Neither human dress nor food need be the same in Nome, Nassau, and Nairobi. Nor is there just cause today for people, who can so clearly choose their own destiny, to hurry toward oblivion their own or any other kind of life.

CHAPTER 4

OUTDOOR HARVESTS AND AN ETHIC FOR THE LAND

THERE MAY STILL be people in the mountains of New Guinea and other remote places who believe unswervingly that a spirit, benevolent or malevolent, inhabits each river, stone, tree, and animal. Surely the number is shrinking and fewer pray devoutly, fearfully, for forgiveness from the spirits of living things they must kill to eat. Yet when a pagan sets aside his polytheism and accepts any one of the great modern religions in its place, he cuts himself off from any reverence for nonhuman life. No longer need his conscience restrict his outdoor harvests, or his behavior follow any ethic for the land.

We speak of the savages in New Guinea as "Stone Age people," and sympathize with their bewilderment in discovering how differently the citizens behave and live in other lands, where cultigens and technological progress have been incorporated into culture for many centuries. Rarely does it occur to us that the religious patterns that unify large areas of the civilized world arose after all of the major cultigens had been gained. The Mosaic laws of the Hebrews were codified around 1300 B.C.; Confucius and Buddha were contemporaries around 500 B.C.; Mohammed followed Jesus of Nazareth by about six centuries. All of these religions served primarily to help people get along with people. They focused attention on perfection and an indefinite future, rather than on present needs. As Walter Shepherd wrote in his *New Survey of Science,* they made man "a disinterested wisdom-lover." He became concerned with the welfare of an immortal soul, and not with the mortal world.

These religious frameworks for social action appealed to men who had found empiric techniques more useful than polytheism in wresting a livelihood. They were already specialists and custodians of wealth. The wealth of the agriculturalist was a herd of domesticated animals or a field of grain, endangered by flood, drought, and other vagaries of weather, by diseases and assorted pests, by hungry wild animals, and by lawless men. To guard these possessions, the husbandryman had to stay close, using his ingenuity and physical strength wherever he could. Merely to profit from the natural increase, to reap a crop, he became a partial prisoner of his productivity. So long as his products reached urban dwellers, they could concentrate on expanding their realm of interests with ever more nonliving possessions. The city people could ignore the problems confronting the rural citizens, who alone contended with outdoor harvests.

The custodians of cultigens were practical men, who had to change their plans to match the weather and the welfare of their particular crops. The nomadic Laplander must keep his reindeer moving to fresh lichen ranges. The nomadic Bedouin follows the green in the desert with his flocks of sheep and goats, pampering his horses, looking after the welfare of his camels and donkeys; together these animals take most of his time, while providing him with beasts of burden, sources of milk and fuel (dry dung), of meat in emergency, and of commodities for sale and barter. Farther south in Africa, the black herd boys routinely move their cattle and goats into a thorn-scrub corral each night, out of reach of lions and leopards. Men of Eurasian ancestry prefer to let their animals roam freely, and to make the land hospitable to this method by eliminating every predator for miles around. These facets of culture gradually change the land, and the animal life that inhabits it.

During the last four centuries the transfer of cultigens and hangers-on around the world has been faster than in all previous history. In each new land it has been a substitution, rather than an addition, and disruptive because of the speed with which the change occurred. Each increase in the numbers of people and of domesticated life has brought about a matching decrease in the numbers and variety among wild plants and animals. Great cattle ranches and wheat fields in the American West now utilize the energy from the sun that formerly supported buffalo grass, other native plants, bison, pronghorns, prairie dogs, prairie chickens, and the spectacular predators of the plains, such as wolves and grizzly bears.

The fossil record shows that similar successions in the past have affected far more kinds of life, but over a much longer time. Rarely has one type of plant or animal diversified and spread over a major area without others losing their access to energy and shrinking toward extinction. Increase and decrease are generally simultaneous and equal. The total variety of life may remain almost unchanged while this slow changing of the guard—a permanent change—occurs. But the quick changes caused by man have a totally different quality, for they replace the many species by a few: the human pioneers, the cultigens that act like pioneers so long as they receive protection, and the pests.

Initially, the total variety among living things in any community is increased when cultigens are introduced from distant lands. So long as a pioneer tends a farm in isolation, raising almost everything he needs for himself and his family, his investment is small and his effect on the environment unimportant. It is when too many subsistence farms are operated side by side or when they are combined into a larger and more efficient operation that the native life is replaced and the soil itself endangered. Primitive hunting and food gathering have no such effects.

Often the impact of the cultigens is oblique, yet increasingly disastrous. In equatorial Africa, for example, the world's most spectacular array of wild hoofed animals can find plenty to eat on the grassy highlands where scattered trees provide some shade. Domestic cattle there are scrawny, famished for lack of acceptable foods. They are ill-adapted for getting enough moisture from the plants they choose, and cannot go more than about a day's walking distance from a water hole in search of more to eat before they must be herded back for another drink. In these restricted areas they trample more vegetation than they devour, much of it of types that the native wild animals would eat but that tame cattle ignore completely.

During prolonged droughts the herdsmen drive away from the shrinking water holes all but their domesticated livestock. No matter how thirsty the antelopes and zebras become, they can have no water if sharing the limited resource will deprive the cattle. This seems harsher than it actually is, for the wild animals are wary even where they are little hunted and where the natural predators, such as lions, have been driven off. If the way is open to them, the antelopes will migrate over the dusty savannas for hundreds of miles, away from dry areas into greener ones. Rarely can men with herds contemplate comparable journeys, if only because doing so would take them into the territories of unfriendly tribes. But with more people, more small communities, more artificially constructed water holes, more cattle, and less unclaimed land between, the old migration routes are being blocked. The wild hoofed animals lose out. Even without raising a hand against wildlife, mankind decreases the space and resources available to native animals and plants.

Whether following the Judeo-Christian tradition as directed in the chapters of Genesis, or attempting to subdue and dominate the earth merely for commercial gain, man tends to classify the living resources around him as usable and hence good, or harmful to his enterprises and hence to be eliminated, or neutral and hence replaceable and expendable for any slight gain or convenience. Most animals and plants are in the neutral category. Often their disappearance is barely noticed.

The second-largest land animal in the world, the Indian elephant, is appreciated when trained and tractable, whether as a work animal and prestige mount in Southeast Asia or in circuses and zoos. Yet little effort is made to breed this elephant in captivity, because adult males are generally dangerous and unpredictable. Consequently the supply is maintained by capturing young elephants in the wild and taming them. But both wild animals and wilderness are fast disappearing, which leaves these elephants a dim future. Particularly in Ceylon, as the forested hills are cleared to make room for plantations of tea and other crops, the big beasts have nowhere to go. So long as they keep their distance, no hand is raised against them. Their numbers diminished to about 5,000 at the beginning of the present century, and to less than 1,000 by the latest census. Proposals to set aside land for elephant reserves find scant support where an exploding human population sees neither space nor food for its own immediate future.

From our customary frame of reference in temperate lands, we can appreciate the difficulty in leaving space and food for animals the size of elephants. We are less likely to realize how disastrous can be the selective elimination of a single species of smaller animal or of a green plant, even as big as a tropical tree. Yet that one tree may be the essential source of nectar or soft fruits in season for dozens of species of bats. Our own experience does not prepare us to think of this, because all of these flying mammals that we meet are insectivorous. We hear of the blood-feeding vampire bats of tropical America, and of the rabies they sometimes transfer. But in the tropics, nectar-sipping and fruit-eating bats constitute the majority. Actually the world has more kinds of bats, mostly tropical, than members of any other order of mammals except rodents. Generally lumped as "fruit bats," they depend upon a constant supply of flowers or suitable fruits, each in its season, with never a gap of more than a day in the continuity. A short period without food, due to elimination of some critical tree, leads to sharply diminished numbers of these nocturnal fliers. Without them, a great array of different plants lose their customary pollinators, fail to set seed (and to nourish animals that live on the surplus seeds), leading to progressive changes in otherwise untouched members of the wild community.

The limited tolerances in foods shown by domestic animals often upset man's plans. The sheep in Scotland close-crop the green grasses and keep them as low as though freshly cut by a lawnmower. They nibble on

A young red-shouldered hawk from a nest in a moist woodland close to cultivated fields helps control the number of rodents and insects that compete with man for crops.

The golden eagle, with its 78-inch wing span, has become a rare bird—a rodent-hunter of the tundras, remote mountains, deserts and grasslands. (KARL MASLOWSKI, BUREAU OF SPORT FISHERIES AND WILDLIFE.)

shrubby gorse and heather only as a last resort. The short grass, however, cannot smother the seedlings of gorse and heather, which grow to become invading weeds. Scotsmen complained to us that in their lifetimes they had seen this woody growth encroaching on the famous sheep pastures, from which comes the wool for all of the wonderful tweeds and tartans. Yet on the steep slopes, with so many rocky outcroppings, machines can scarcely be used to uproot the shrubs—even if the sheepmen could buy the machines.

Most animal husbandrymen are in this same predicament in some form. Ultimately their livelihood depends on grasses and herbs that grow best where periodic fires destroy all woody growth. The sheep raisers and cattle ranchers have good reason to fear fire, for wariness of flames (as well as of wolves and men) has been bred out of their domesticated animals toward increasing the yield of wool or meat.

In our trying to increase the efficiency of raising crops outdoors, it is easy to forget that the whole pattern of nature works against biasing an environment for production of one species. In trying to protect and favor domesticated animals and plants, man pulls at a complex web of interrelated wildlife, often with unexpected consequences. He sees a big hawk or a golden eagle tearing at the dead body of a newborn lamb or calf, concludes that the bird of prey has killed it, and condemns every hawk or eagle. He may refuse to believe a scientific report that shows how rarely the bird preys on anything larger than a mouse, and how ready it is to scavenge—cleaning up any small animal, wild or domestic, that it finds dead. These easy meals use victims of accident and disease, carcasses of no commercial value. They space out for the bird its chancier dining on live-caught rodents and grasshoppers. Unless the man is prepared to replace the bird as a governor on the populations of rodents and insects, he does himself a disfavor to take its life. Unopposed, the plant eaters multiply and diminish the supply of vegetation upon which domesticated livestock depend. Merely by removing the top predator, or an animal that combines predation with scavenging, he diminishes significantly his own chance to gain from the land.

We think of the hawks, eagles, owls, wolves, foxes, coyotes, and weasels that were killed for the benefit of people trying to raise sheep and poultry, now eliminated from land where no sheep or hen has lived for years. More than a decade has passed since last we saw a mink or otter within miles of our home, or since a bear with her cub made news by raiding a neighbor's beehives night after night. Yet restoration of the natural predators would neither be easy nor welcomed. The people who live near us now have pet dogs and cats to guard. They would not appreciate any increase in the numbers of birds or beasts of prey. Pleasure possessions, rather than animals raised for profit, stand in the way of modern action that would be meaningful ecologically, reversing the long-term decrease in the variety among native life.

Over most of the United States and adjacent Canada, we sadly admit that the cougar does not live here any more. To meet one of these long-tailed, sand-colored cats, we have to travel. Between 100 and 200 of them survive in the Florida Everglades, and perhaps 5,000 in the western mountains. Three centuries ago this was the most wide-ranging large predator in the New World. Known variously as mountain lion, puma, panther, painter, and léon, it was native from the Pacific to the Atlantic and Gulf coasts, from British Columbia to New Brunswick and south to Patagonia. Rarely did one attack a person, even a child, unless in the immediate vicinity of a den where helpless young cougars needed protection.

New Englanders called it a catamount ("cat-a-mountain") and expected each hill to have a solitary individual that would hunt over an area about nine miles across. This much territory normally offered enough herbivorous animals as prey that the cougar could make a kill every night or two, eat seven to eight pounds of meat, and cover the rest with leaves. Smaller carrion-eaters generally finished off each carcass.

A few years ago we examined carefully the mounted skin of the last known cougar from the state of New Hampshire. Its final resting place is among the natural history specimens in the Woodman Institute of the town of Dover. It was killed on Cartland Farm in Lee, during the autumn of 1853, and its skin stuffed by an unskilled taxidermist. No doubt the trophy stood in the home of the hunter, William Chapman of Newmarket, from then until 1919, when his son donated the specimen to the Institute for safekeeping. Still in good shape, the body is more than five feet long, the tail an extra two feet. Although we realize that the specimen is priceless historically, it was listed on an inventory for insurance purposes at $250. Surely this estimate is conservative, and the exhibit worth ten times the bounty still being paid for cougars killed in California.

A recent study made of cougars in a wilderness area of Idaho revealed that while mule deer and elk are their principal prey, these predators dine frequently on jack rabbit, snowshoe hares, wood rats, squirrels, mice, and occasionally on nothing but grasshoppers. Of the mule deer and elk killed, from 62 to 75 percent are less than 18 months or more than 9 years old; in each category, at least half are suffering from malnutrition—an affliction that strikes hardest at the young and aging, often causing their deaths by starvation in late winter. Commonly, when a cougar makes a kill, the rest of the herd (whether elk or deer) move away from the area quickly, giving the vegetation on which they have been feeding time to recover.

High in the western mountains, where snow lasts much longer than at lower elevations, the cougar clings to its old way of life. It bears its spotted kittens in rocky shelters, and trains them as efficient predators. (WILFORD L.MILLER, FROM NATIONAL AUDUBON SOCIETY.)

A young bull moose feeding from vegetation in a shallow pond at Moose, Wyoming, can seek sanctuary among the spruce thickets on the soggy mountain slopes beyond the aspen grove.

The reason given for eliminating cougars is that, particularly when old, they took a liking for unwary horses and sometimes cattle. But now, over much of the big cat's former range in North America, the horses have been replaced by tractors. Beef cattle are few except in the West—rarer than cougars near the California mountains, where the predators live mostly on mule deer and keep the population from exploding. Dairy cattle now spend the night indoors, eating an artificial diet that promotes lactation, while being close to the milking machine. Except as a hazard to free-running pets, we could use cougars again in New England to help control the deer and porcupines.

Deer are ordinarily thought of as the cougar's first choice in prey. This belief may be a quirk of American history, due to the changing numbers of its other two favorites: moose and elk. Today the continent has far more deer than when the Pilgrim Fathers landed, whereas moose and elk are less conspicuous. Deer habitat, and deer, increased rapidly as pioneering men opened up the forest, creating countless borders and edges where second growth from roots of surviving trees presented shrubby browse at deer height. The deer ate, hid, and reproduced there. They still do, in amazing abundance.

Moose have always been swamp dwellers. They continue to hold a place in the northern coniferous forest belt that lies across the New World like an evergreen sash from northern New England and eastern Canada to Alaska.

Apparently the colonists had heard of elk, but did not recognize the animal when they saw it among North America's wildlife. Forced by circumstances to choose between the largest hoofed animals in the North Temperate Zone, called *moos* by Indians of Algonquian dialects, and the second-largest (called *wapiti* by the same Indians), they assigned the word elk to the *wapiti* and adopted moose for the one called elk in northern Europe. Where *wapiti* have a counterpart in the Old World, they are known as red deer.

Elk (*wapiti*) could not hide so easily as moose. They need space in which to move from winter browsing to summer grazing ranges. At first they were shot to provide meat, hides, and bones. Then their carcasses were left to rot while just the two canine teeth from the lower jaw were saved as good-luck charms—an idea adopted from the Indians, who wasted nothing.

Among the souvenirs one of the authors (LJM) inherited is an elk "tusk" three-quarters of an inch long, mounted in 24-carat gold on a stick tiepin. Its history is lost. We compared it once and found it an almost perfect match for the teeth sculptured into the slightly gaping mouth of an

On the floor of the valley known as Jackson Hole in Wyoming, the Fish and Wildlife Service maintains a winter refuge for elk that migrate up into the adjacent mountains for other seasons. (E. P. HADDON, BUREAU OF SPORT FISHERIES AND WILDLIFE.)

elk statue in bronze, of the kind standing in front of meeting places in cities and towns all over the country. Once a logical symbol for a fraternal order to choose in America, this animal was common from the Pacific coast to the southern Appalachians, from the northern edge of the Great Basin to the southern extent of the coniferous forest in Canada.

Progressively the elk vanished. The last record in Pennsylvania is of one shot in 1869. By 1900 they were practically exterminated over about 90 percent of their former range. The principal herds remained in Yellowstone National Park, Wyoming, in Montana, and in parts of Canadian provinces from Manitoba westward. During the winter of 1915, 500 elk bodies were found in Yellowstone Park, left by the poachers who removed only the canine teeth. Subsequent improvements in policing this herd let it build up again until a need for culling developed. Excess animals are now being reintroduced into suitable reserves in states where elk formerly abounded.

An isolated local race of elk with shorter, heavier antlers on a darker body seems to be holding its own among the peaks of Olympic National Park and on Vancouver Island. Two small herds of a dwarf race, called the tule or California elk, seem in constant danger; the latest census showed 300 in Owens Valley and another 80 in the Cache Creek area, some of them competing with livestock grazing on national forest land; another 35 are semidomesticated on a Tule Elk Reserve, and 10 more are in American zoos.

Just south of Yellowstone Park, in the magnificent valley known as Jackson Hole, ranchers have complained to us about the refuge provided by the Federal government for elk that summer in the mountain forests. Why should good hay be cut, stored, and distributed to these animals in winter, when commercial cattle could be raised instead. Throughout the American West, in Australia and other countries, we have heard men who raise livestock for a living make similar comments and calculations. The range could support more domestic sheep and cattle if the native herbivores were eliminated. Three European rabbits in Australia eat as much as one sheep; kill 30 rabbits and raise 10 sheep in their place. One red kangaroo eats as much as two sheep; only 15 kangaroos need be killed to provide for 30 sheep. How many American prairie dogs eat as much as one cow?

Rarely does the rancher ask whether the plants the wild herbivore eats are the same kinds as those his domestic animals would choose among the vegetation, or what predators would be forced to change their ways to stay alive. If a rancher finds a way to get rid of jackrabbits, but not mice and grasshoppers, the coyotes that formerly lived on all three types of native animals are unlikely to survive on the remaining two. They may turn to attacking sheep, or move away altogether, letting the grasshoppers and mice multiply unchecked. In either case, the rancher loses more than he gains by killing jackrabbits. Neither their pelts nor meat has much value. And if he kills the coyote too, he finds little market for its skin. It is one of the least handsome of the beasts of prey. As J. Frank Dobie knew, its charm is in its versatility and its voice.

A great many predatory animals have been brought close to extinction by trappers and hunters for the fur trade. Much of the original exploration of North America and of the seas distant from Europe was done by intrepid men bent on satisfying the wealthy market for prime pelts. Initially they traded and competed with the Indians for beaver, while this fur was popular for millinery use. Previously they had almost exterminated Europe's beavers, which survived mostly by changing their habits. Now the animals burrow in stream banks and, unlike the American beavers, make neither lodges or dams of sticks and mud. When the beavers of the New World became equally scarce, the savage persecution turned to the carnivorous fur-bearers.

Today, when we think of furs, our minds turn first to seal, mink, ermine, otter, fox, perhaps fisher, marten, wolverine and imported leopard.

The alert, adaptable coyote has changed its geographic range and preferred foods, finding new dens in which to care for its pups, as raisers of livestock persecuted the animal in the West. (E. P. HADDON AND E. R. KALMBACK, BUREAU OF SPORT FISHERIES AND WILDLIFE.)

So long as a beaver can reach poplars or other trees close to running water, it can dam the flow and make a pond around its lodge. Photographed on the east coast of Kodiak Island, Alaska. (E. P. HADDON, BUREAU OF SPORT FISHERIES AND WILDLIFE.)

The ecological consequences from killing these predators was far greater than from harvesting the omnivorous raccoon or skunk or such herbivores as chinchilla, nutria, muskrat, squirrel, vicuña, and Persian lamb. The fur-bearing beasts of prey were also fewer and sooner liquidated. Sometimes we marvel that men were desperate enough to brave the wilderness in winter, when pelts were in best condition, or the high seas and little-known coasts where fur seals hauled out or sea otters lolled among the kelp. Yet they submitted to legislation and international agreements only after southern fur seals, northern fur seals, and sea otters had almost disappeared. With few more pelts to be had, it did not matter much that pelagic sealing was forbidden.

While the marine predators took the brunt of exploitation, the fresh-water mink and otter, the terrestrial ermine (a weasel in a winter coat) and fox, and the often arboreal marten and fisher had their day too. A reduction in mink and otter let fish and shellfish thrive. Removing the weasels and foxes helped small rodents and large insects to increase in numbers. When marten grew scarce, squirrels multiplied enormously. Bringing the fisher to low ebb released porcupines to slowly rise in population. By 1959, when the New Hampshire state legislature was called upon to consider the pros and cons of a proposed program to reduce forest damage by poisoning porcupines, fishers had almost been forgotten. While the law-makers argued about the hazards in leaving apples flavored with strychnine where porcupines might find the bait, fishers made an unexpected resurgence and attended to the superfluous quill-bearers without cost or human effort. Now the legislators have a new topic for study: should fishers be protected, or hunted legally for unfashionable pelts, or be subject to a bounty because they are predators?

Today the wild mink and fox have had a reprieve, being displaced on the fur market by mutant captives of unusual colors from fur farms. Leopards, cheetahs, ocelots, and other spotted cats are endangered by being fashionable temporarily. Despite the speed with which our culture changes, it bears heavily upon wild animals of many kinds. The survivors after years of persecution may need a century to readjust to relative scarcity and rebuild even part way their shattered populations.

So much has happened during the present century that, well before its three-quarter mark is reached, memories of the early decades have faded. We forget how ruthlessly the fruit growers in the southeastern United States exterminated North America's only member of the parrot family —the sociable, fruit-eating Carolina parakeet, last seen alive in 1920— before their orchard lands were turned to other purposes. Introduction of innerspring mattresses and nonallergic pillows of foam rubber has made the world safe for many birds. If the last great auks had not been killed to supply the feather trade, and mostly for featherbeds, these queer flightless creatures could nest in reasonable security today on rocky islets around the North Atlantic Ocean. The market for plumes can now be satisfied from captive domestic birds (including ostriches in South Africa) without a need to smuggle in exotic feathers obtained by killing wild birds. Sixty years ago an intensive trade in fancy plumes and whole stuffed birds was so profitable in America and Europe that anyone in the field who objected was liable to be shot.

Presently our sympathies and support go to park wardens who risk their lives in Africa to limit the number of poachers bent on slaughtering giraffes and brindled gnus for tails to sell as fly swatters, and elephants for just the tusks. We can become alarmed that the world's seven kinds of scaly anteaters (pangolins), which merit an order to themselves in the classification of mammals, are endangered because of a market for their scales in mainland China. A recent survey in Sarawak indicated that about 7,000 anteaters of one species were killed there annually, their scales smuggled mostly through Indonesian Borneo to Singapore and Hong Kong for re-shipment. In our culture, powdered anteater scales are not regarded as a sure cure for skin eruptions caused by venereal disease.

In our part of the world, a measure of the effect of culture on wildlife can be seen in the number of small and large birds that crash to their death on tall buildings, or from flying into wires strung across the landscape from poles and pylons. We approve the floodlighting of these obstacles in season, and all measures aimed at humanely dispersing birds or other animals from airports before they get sucked into the jet engines or collide with airplanes taking off and landing. We are disturbed over the millions of animals killed annually while attempting to cross busy highways, and doubly so when the collision is fatal to both motorist and animal as so often happens when the encounter is with a heavy moose or deer.

Farmers and foresters, we find, sometimes get grim satisfaction over the killing of deer in this or any other way. These animals do damage to their crops, and there is no compensation except through expensive legal claims based on indisputable proof. Yet until about two decades ago, both farmer and forester kept reasonably aloof from direct conflict with wildlife. They waged a never-ending war with rodents and insects, with fungus diseases and weeds, for which no one had many kind words. Drought and hurricanes took erratic tolls, and so did the occasional fire that got out of control. On the site, the damage was impressive. So were statistics in dollar value or in acres destroyed.

About 1946 these agriculturalists began taking advantage of a new tool offered by the culture of technology. The fresh approach was chemical: a series of organic compounds at attractive prices, guaranteed to kill insects, fungi, and weeds. Preliminary tests proved that in the concentrations required for 99 percent effectiveness, neither mankind nor domestic animals were affected. Eagerly the farmers and foresters adopted the techniques, unaware that their action would reach out to every species of animal on earth and influence its destiny. No one foresaw that the program, begun with such high hopes, would end by poisoning the planet from pole to pole.

Dichloro-Diphenyl-Trichloro-Ethane (DDT) was just the first of the synthetic compounds that seemed perfectly tailored to rid mankind of insect pests. Unlike any nonvolatile, noncorrosive substance, it penetrated readily the waterproof body covering of insects and, in minute concentrations, killed almost all that came in contact with it in any way. Its application could be modified to suit man's crops, whether wheat and potatoes or cotton and pulpwood. At last, man could hope to win in his war with insects.

Initially this chemical boon to mankind was dusted inside the clothing of civilians and soldiers during World War II. Seemingly it prevented the spread of body lice and fleas that carry typhus fever and bubonic plague. Sprayed on ponds and marshes, or inside dwellings where mosquitoes might rest and absorb lethal doses, the poison controlled malaria and spared millions of people from death or debilitating disease. Later, DDT spread from farm vehicles and slow-flying biplanes over fields and forests almost wiped out potato beetles, boll weevils, spruce budworm, and other pests. It doubled the yield of food and fiber and helped in producing pulpwood toward all the myriad uses of paper. Virtually everyone who knew about DDT approved when the Nobel Prize for physiology and medicine in 1948 was awarded to Swiss chemist Paul Müller, who discovered the insecticidal properties of this material.

No harm beyond the croplands was foreseen from applying the new cheap insect-killer once or twice a season. But the surviving pests reproduced and their offspring showed a tolerance for two or three times the dose that had killed 99 percent of previous generations. Chemists modified the formula and began producing and marketing a whole series of related compounds, each a chlorinated hydrocarbon. Ecologists came to know them as the "deadly seven," the others being marketed under the names aldrin, chlordane, dieldrin, endrin, heptachlor, and lindane, to distinguish them from DDT. Meagerly soluble in water but dissolving in fats, they resist the ordinary processes of organic decomposition. This property makes them ideal for "residual" poisons that can be spread on surfaces and left, ready to kill whatever insect walks or settles there at a later date. Ten or fifteen years after application they maintain 50 percent or more of their concentration. Some scientists estimate that of the 1.5 million tons of DDT alone that have been produced and used, fully two-thirds is still in its original form or in equally toxic products of partial disintegration, such as one called DDE.

Few people noticed that less than a third of these poisons reach their target. Two-thirds blow away in the wind as dust, or are carried off by water, eventually to reach the oceans. At first no one realized that the chlorinated hydrocarbons accumulate both inside and outside animal bodies through a failure to enter significantly into any of the usual avenues for excretion. Until recently, no quantitative tests had been devised for DDT and related substances. No one gave a thought to the phenomenon now known as "biological magnification" of toxic concentrations.

By 1962, when Rachel Carson's book *Silent Spring* put the makers and users of agricultural poisons on the defensive, a few people had noticed a cause-and-effect relationship between American elm trees sprayed with DDT to kill bark beetles that transfer Dutch elm disease, and the death of robins. Residual spray still clung to the elm leaves in autumn, when the foliage died naturally, fell to the ground, and began to decompose. Earthworms dragged the soggy leaves into their tunnels, speeded the process of decomposition, absorbed DDT from each sprayed leaf, and stored the poison in their fatty tissue. By spring when robins arrived and began catching earthworms, the DDT was still there. Experimenters saw no evidence that a worm with a large amount of poison was slower and more likely to be caught than one with less, but the indications were clear that the more poison-containing worms a robin ate, the sooner the bird went into a progressive pattern of twitching movements and convulsions that ended in death.

Improvements in assay methods let Dr. Charles F. Wurster, Jr., of the State University of New York at Stony Brook, Long Island, measure seemingly trivial amounts of DDT and related hydrocarbons (including DDE) in surface waters of Long Island Sound soon after the completion of a program of aerial spraying for mosquito control in marshes along the coast. Dilution lowered the amount to a mere .000003 parts per million. But microscopic plants, particularly diatoms which produce buoyant droplets of oil rich in vitamin D, absorbed the DDT and stored it. Tiny crustaceans, feeding on the plants, retained enough oil during their short lives to build up an average concentration of .04 ppm of DDT. Herring and other fishes that feed on these crustaceans transferred the DDT into their own fatty tissues until it measured .5 ppm. Cod and other fish-eating fishes of larger size—many of them of commercial value—showed the next stage in this biological magnification of poison, with an average of 2.0 ppm.

The top predators, whether sharks or fish-eating birds (such as ospreys, bald eagles, cormorants, albatrosses, shearwaters, and petrels), are most vulnerable to this new chemical hazard because they specialize in eating the unwary, the sick, the dying and dead from prey populations. Under ordinary circumstances, their role is to prune away the infected individuals and the least fit. Their principal risk is acquiring a few parasitic worms from this customary food. But when their victims contain poison, the predators are in real trouble. Each meal is likely to add to the concentration held in their own bodies. Even if they, as full-grown, mature, long-lived individuals, can tolerate the material, their eggs and young often cannot. Reproduction falters, if only from a failure to provide the usual amount of lime in the eggshell. Down sinks the predator population.

The thickness of empty eggshells of birds has now been measured from specimens long treasured in museums, each shell carefully labeled with its date and place of collection. Those of golden eagle, peregrine, and sparrow hawk vary little and at random until 1946; then comes progressive thinning of the shells. Some sea birds now fail to add a limy shell at all, and lay an egg that spreads out disastrously in the nest. Ospreys that lay eggs containing 3.0 ppm of chlorinated hydrocarbons raise no more than half as many young as ospreys did in the same locations during years prior to DDT. Ospreys and eagles are now threatened with extinction

A banded osprey returns to its nest along the Connecticut shore—one of the few remaining birds of this kind in eastern North America. (WILLIAM C. KRANTZ, BUREAU OF SPORT FISHERIES AND WILDLIFE.)

more by chemical residues than by any direct action taken against them as birds of prey.

Agricultural poisons have made the earth one world, just as have radioactive wastes from "dirty" nuclear explosions. No country can keep them out, for they ride the stratospheric winds and every ocean current. Tragically, they are reminiscent of the story of the Sorcerer's Apprentice, for scientists have found ways to produce these materials and not yet learned to make them harmless.

We take pride in our species for being unique in recognizing opportunities, making short-term plans, and changing the environment in ways that seem likely to benefit the planners. But as never before we are comprehending the broad consequences of human action and inaction, the array of detriments that have constituted an unanticipated corollary to the benefits. With space probes and moon explorers we have demonstrated both our potential and our limitations. We and other living things on earth occupy a hospitable island in an immense and essentially lifeless, uninhabitable universe.

With information compiled since 1950 by the offices of the United Nations, cultured man has become a classifier, critically examining the earth for the first time. Estimates of value and measures of resources generally relate to mankind and favored animals and plants, as though these alone merit consideration. Yet from these surveys comes a new appreciation for the actualities faced by every kind of life and for our own relationship to our world.

Of nearly 200 million square miles of the earth's surface, some 56.5 million are land. Of these, about a quarter (14 million) are too cold, too dry or jagged for any except the most highly adapted creatures. The 5.5 million square miles of Antarctica, for example, are home to emperor and Adélie penguins, some skua gulls, and almost nothing else with warm blood. A few lichens and mosses and one kind of grass constitute the complete flora.

Another quarter (15.2 million) is called forest land, although nearly half of it is too poor to yield trees at a rate that is commercially significant. Forest animals and those of the desert edge are likely to survive on this quarter of the land because man cannot seem to put it to a better use than producing well-adapted trees. This multiple use, which provides opportunities for recreation, produces the biggest crop (wood) and a place for some wild animals too.

A third quarter (14.3 million) is used, with little effort toward improving it, as range and pasture for meat animals. Most of it is relatively unproductive because of chronic cold or drought, or is unsuited to raising plants from which man might get food directly. Our ancestors cleared some of it of forests; the rest originally was grassland. It is a fine place for

The 57 million square miles of land on earth can be classified according to their uses. Until man began cutting the forests, they occupied about 23.4 million square miles—nearly 41 percent of the total. The asterisk indicates the 5.3 million square miles of Antarctica.

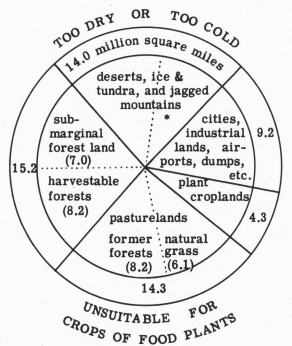

dung beetles and other scavengers, and for the decomposers that capture the energy they need while cycling the chemical substances out of non-living matter and into forms that plant roots can absorb.

The remaining quarter of the terrestrial world is divided unequally between some 9.2 million square miles from which almost no food comes, and 4.3 used for raising plant crops. The 9.2 million are increasing at the expense of the 4.3, for they are areas of urban development, industrial sites, airports, refuse dumps, and similar land. Of the 4.3, about 4.0 are for edible crops and the remainder for fibers such as cotton. This quarter of the total land is home to most of the world's people. Nearly all of the others live on the 14.3 million square miles of range and pastureland, and dream of the day when they can move to the nearest city. To increase productivity of food for mankind on the 4.0 plus 14.3 million square miles is easier than to reclaim the wilderness that is naturally too arid, too cold, or too steep, or to get significantly more from the broad oceans. Wild animals have their chance to survive or vanish according to whether they can maintain a place on the productive land, or scattered through the forests, the deserts, the mountains, and the open seas.

As we think about the cultural patterns that relate to human food, we realize that essentially no one feels concern over the live plants that die for us to eat, for our wooden buildings, for our newspapers and other paper products, for fuel, or to allow us a view and space. So far as we can learn, those people in India who wear a cloth over nose and mouth are more concerned about killing a fly they might inhale than saving microbes from being killed; they are glad to eat cheese that still contains living microbes —the ones that transformed the milk into a different food. Throughout cultured countries we hold that, since plants and perhaps some animals must die for us to live, at least the animals must be nonhuman. If people are to be killed, it can be only for the good of the society or the nation— never for food.

Any animal able to cry out has a chance to be heard and left to live. Even among professed vegetarians, few feel the slightest qualm over eating the contents of a hen's egg that could have produced a chick if incubated properly; the early embryo has no audible voice. Our sympathies tend to stop too at the water line, for we are seldom aroused by the plight of a live lobster with its claws pegged shut, an oyster waiting to be swallowed, a hooked fish or one struggling in a net, or a whale harpooned for our nourishment or as food for pets. We like to believe that the slaughter of domestic animals is silent, quick, and as painless as possible.

With few reservations, our culture supports the policy that plants and animals can be sacrificed for scientific study. We try to assure ourselves that the scientists who conduct the research are well qualified, that their programs endanger no pets nor any type of life already threatened with extinction, and that they treat humanely any animal having, as Aristotle pointed out, "tongue and lung." Beyond the borders of India, it is hard to understand why Indians exempt cattle from scientific use, just as they would people. Because of popular demand, the Indian government has recently acted to block the export of rhesus monkeys destined for medical research, as though these primates were too nearly human—the very feature that makes them most valuable for testing drugs and treatments intended to benefit mankind, including Indians.

In most of the world, frogs are on the borderline of conscience, possibly because for generations fishermen have used these animals as fish bait. Now the British are wondering about their common frog, which is no longer common enough for fishermen. Perhaps too many are being caught to serve, alive or dead, in training scientists. No other reason has been found for this species vanishing in the wild. A matching fear applies to the coastal dogfish, which has for many years been popular under the name "rock salmon" in British fish-and-chips shops. Its scarcity has raised the price for edible pieces, and also for sale to educational institutions which buy this dogfish in preservative for classes to dissect.

No real census is kept on most kinds of animals. Ordinarily a few species are numerous or extremely rare without a known reason, either way. People notice when a change occurs, whether it is a previously inconspicuous animal that abruptly becomes common or a familiar one that disappears. Intuitively we know that the new combination of abundance and rarity is symptomatic of an upset in the established order. Temporarily it may be inconvenient. Over a longer time it can presage readjustments that more seriously affect our culture.

Scientists should be the first to investigate these changes and learn their implications. Often the most qualified men seem especially perplexed. A few years ago those at the famous Marine Biological Laboratory in Woods Hole, on Cape Cod, Massachusetts, were alerted because collectors for the supply department suddenly could find few live sea urchins for research. All of the usual areas of the sea floor near by seemed depleted, and many investigations on embryology in animals had to be shut down. No one knew what amenities a sea urchin needed, or whether a cause other than exploitation had led to the virtual disappearance of the species. A closed season was instituted to see if the population would recover naturally. New techniques were developed to use more thriftily all urchins caught in the future.

Of all the facets of modern culture that affect wildlife around the world, those on which opinion is most divided have to do with the setting aside of areas where the welfare of native creatures ranks higher than the presence or safety of any person, domestic animal, cultivated plant, electric transmission line, dam, highway, airport, or military installation. Almost as controversial are policies and enforcement of laws regulating the hunting of native animals for meat or entertainment, the trade in skins, plumes, horns, and other animal hard parts, and international traffic in live animals. Probably all governments should cooperate in prohibiting the commercial movement of any creature on the list of endangered species, and all parts of it that could be obtained through killing it on its native soil. Live animals destined for the pet trade and small private zoos, where normal reproduction is unlikely, need more protection too. Yet the lists of endangered species and subspecies compiled and documented since 1950 are incomplete. Often no cause for the rarity or recent decline in numbers is known. And still longer lists are accumulating of rare animals whose status is uncertain. Some of these creatures may already be extinct, for it is years since a living individual of many rare kinds was sighted reliably.

In the interaction of culture and wildlife, we would identify as the greatest threat today the uninformed unconcern of people who now form the majority. They are city people everywhere, with scant awareness for the natural world, and the country people in developing nations who have never been far from home or learned that the future is important—with wildlife in it. The second greatest threat may well be from the minority for whom economic gain outweighs any thoughts they might have about polluting the world with poisons, condemning productive land toward limited uses, and exploiting species whose future is already bleak.

We cannot regress to belief in a spirit inhabiting every river and stone, tree and animal. But we can progress toward a reorientation of technology and recreation. Professor Murray Gell-Mann, winner of the 1969 Nobel prize in physics, calls for "landmarks of technological renunciation"— things "we can do and don't do for environmental reasons." His recommendations extend the ethics of the great religions into realms of social relations at the most modern level, for they would benefit every form of life on earth in a lasting way.

Today's greatest hope for vanishing animals rests in people who, in growing numbers, discover how fast our living heritage from the past is dwindling, and who insist on protecting the remainder. Wildlife constitutes a resource with limitless potential, as well as an esthetic counterfoil to our predominantly urban existence. In reaching this point of view, culture completes a circle. It began with man's early uncomprehending fears of mysterious nature. It progressed through growing power and exploitation. Now it offers informed appreciation for the contributing role the human species can play as an inseparable part of the living world.

CHAPTER 5

PERILS
IN
OPEN
COUNTRY—
ON
GRASSLANDS
AND
SAVANNAS

IN ZULULAND, SOUTH AFRICA, we were visiting one of the two rhinoceros reserves and asking to see rhinos. "Hluhlue Reserve has only black rhinos," we were told, "and they're very dangerous animals."

"You mean you can't show us any?"

Our challenge to the chief ranger was as direct as we could make it.

"Well, yes, I can show you some. But it will have to be at dawn tomorrow morning when the wind will be steady. Be here at headquarters at 5:30, and I'll take you in the Land Rover to where we can stalk them on foot. Just remember, rhinos can't see well but their senses of smell and hearing are acute. If a rhino discovers our presence, we'll have to run for it. There are no trees to climb that a black rhino couldn't knock down. A full grown bull rhino weights about two tons."

The first red rays of the rising sun were behind us as we followed the ranger and a Negro game guard in single file up over the hill from the dirt road where the Land Rover was parked. "Not a sound, now," the ranger cautioned. "Watch you don't step on a stick and snap it. Or kick a stone. And don't mind the ticks, for they'll get all over you. You can clean them off when you get back."

Through the straggly tall grass between the thorny shrubs, we came over the top of a low hill and saw the rhinos feeding down slope ahead of us. The ranger whispered, "There are three of them, two females and a calf almost full grown."

"Can we go closer?" Through the field glasses and the telephoto lens on the camera the big beasts seemed almost insignificantly small.

"I can't risk your lives," the ranger whispered back. The game guard kept checking the wind, obviously ill at ease.

So we watched the rhinos using their V-shaped snouts to browse on the thorn scrub, wondered at the characteristic sores on their flanks and the oozing secretion from them that may rub off on branches and serve to mark a territory. The game guard wagged his finger. The wind was dying. We had to leave immediately, as silently as we had come. A black rhino will charge a strange sound or unfamiliar odor, rushing over the ground at better than 20 miles an hour, ready to use its two large conical head horns to toss a person in the air.

Back at reserve headquarters we thanked the men, cleaned ourselves of ticks, and had breakfast. If that was to be our only chance to see rhinos at Hluhlue, we might as well push on. Before noon, we were at the headquarters of the other rhino reserve, Umfolosi. Could we see rhinos? The ranger was sure we could, right after lunch. He would take us personally. On foot, we should see at least six of the world's last white rhinos, of which the total then was about 600.

The ranger, Mr. Ian Player, was as good as his promise. He took us in his Land Rover over some back roads in the reserve, then out into the bush, and finally under our own power along a narrow game trail where we had to bend nearly double to get under some of the thorny shrubs.

"Follow me," he cautioned in a soft voice, "and stay low, making as little noise as you can."

Soon he stopped and pointed. Among the small trees ahead, we could make out some dark shapes—rhinos resting in the shade. Mr. Player's eyes gleamed as he whispered to us, "Six, I think. Maybe seven."

Cautiously he gestured to one side, indicating that we should follow him in a circling movement. One of us (MM) tugged at his sleeve. "There are more that way," she warned. He grinned and continued his count, this time just holding up his fingers—eight, nine, ten. He made a sweeping motion with one hand and started over—eleven, twelve, thirteen. Then he saw another: number fourteen. We were almost at the center of a semicircle, half surrounded by sleepy white rhinos.

After a while, Mr. Player led us back and to one side. Just then a suspicious cow rhino and her calf trotted out into the open. Automatically they stood with tails together, facing out like the minute and hour hands of a clock. "That's the way rhinos do when they're uncertain which way to go," the ranger explained. "Sometimes six or seven will stand in just that radial pattern."

We gloried in the sight of this huge animal and her offspring, she the third largest kind of land animal alive today, weighing nearly four tons,

Relics from the fauna of Pliocene times, the black rhinoceroses of eastern and southern Africa can survive only where given spacious reserves and protection from poachers (photographed in northern Tanzania).

exceeded only by the two kinds of elephant. Square-lipped and a grazer, her gray color was due chiefly to the dust in which she had rolled.

"Isn't she beautiful?" Mr. Player enthused, proud as though he were a parent of the monster on the grassy plain, framed by the magnificent blue mountain scenery of Zululand. We wouldn't have chosen the same word, but our admiration was boundless. Here in Umfolosi Reserve, we hoped, the white rhino was safe.

In just two days we had met both of Africa's kinds of rhinos, out of five kinds in the whole world. Later, we found another small population of blacks on the broad grassy floor of the Ngorongoro Crater wildlife reserve in Tanzania. Black rhinos are still the most numerous of the species, but common only in a few localities, and surviving best in the dense mountain forest of Kenya.

We have no confidence that we will ever see alive even a solitary representative of the other three kinds of rhinos: the large one-horned rhinoceros of northeastern India and Nepal; the smaller sondai rhino, of which less than 50 individuals are believed to survive in a swampy jungle of western Java; or the smallest of all—the Asiatic two-horned rhino which, although protected by law, is still hunted surreptitiously over most of its range in dense hill forests of Southeast Asia, including Sumatra and Borneo.

The smallest of adult rhinos weighs over a ton, and seems to have reason to fear no natural hazard except man. For centuries these animals have been slaughtered by every means possible to gather their urine, their blood, and their solid keratinous horns for sale in the Orient. Few native people eat rhino meat when they can get it. Only the Somalis use rhino hide on their shields. The rest of these great animals is left for the jackals, hyenas, and vultures in Africa, or other scavengers in Asia. Just the few materials are salvaged for supposedly magical medicinal properties. In port cities, Chinese merchants pay about a dollar a pound for dried rhino blood. At almost $20 per ounce, each rhino horn brings about $2,500, all to produce a powder for sale in the aphrodisiac trade among the Chinese.

Faster than wildlife conservationists could arrange protection for the shrinking remnants of rhino populations, hunters and poachers have become better armed with strong wire snares, potent poisons, and powerful rifles. Rhinos are dying out faster than Oriental superstitions. Except for the white rhinos, which seem to be thriving on their South African reserve land, we fear the species in the wild are following into extinction the wooly rhinoceros of Europe, which vanished during the Ice Age as primitive man spread northward out of Africa.

North America has a comparable history of extermination. Long before the European explorers and colonists arrived, early Indians wiped out one species of bison that had withstood the great glaciers. Then the hunters reached a stalemate or ecological balance with surviving species (*Bison bison*), which became the most numerous large mammal the world has ever known. Over a territory extending from northern Mexico to Lake Winnipeg in Canada, and from the foothills of the Rockies to the western slopes of the Appalachians, thousands of separate bison herds made up a total estimated at between 50 and 75 million animals. Weighing 1,000 to 1,500 pounds as adults, they shared the western short-grass and the eastern long-grass prairies with a comparable number of pronghorns, which resemble antelopes and mature at 80 to 130 pounds each. Elk (*wapiti*) abounded on much the same area and beyond it. Together these animals provided most of the meat needed by some 30,000 Plains Indians, whose hunting methods did not permit them to make serious inroads on the hoofed animals, and for at least 30,000 prairie wolves, which brought down the old, the ill and unwary, and kept the bison alert.

Prior to the introduction of horses and firearms from the Old World, this prairie idyll rested on a generous supply of grama grass and buffalo grass. The greenery and the drought-dried remains and seeds also nourished countless prairie dogs, mice, seed-eating birds, and grasshoppers. All of these vegetarians benefited from the bison, which kept the grasses short, letting the smaller creatures see predators approaching before it was too late. Wolves and coyotes, foxes and badgers, grizzly bears, birds of prey and rattlesnakes took a tolerable toll. The wild meat-eaters and the Indians nourished themselves on grass at second hand.

At first, the Indians reveled in the new power they gained from Europeans. On horseback and with guns blazing, hunting parties stampeded the bison herds, driving them over steep cliffs where a few hundred died for the sake of choice cuts taken from a few dozen to supply one nightlong feast. Then the Indians began fighting the construction crews of the new railroads, who not only built the tracks westward but shot bison for food and shipped thousands of bison skins east to become lap robes and scatter rugs. Soon the train crews complained that bison herds crossing the tracks blocked shipments for hours at a time. Moreover, complaints from the stockmen who arrived were echoed in the *Congressional Record,* Volume Two: "They [the bison] eat the grass. They trample upon the plains upon which our settlers desire to herd their cattle and their sheep."

Worst of all, bison were the mainstay of the Indians who resisted the invading Europeans. To starve the Indians into submission, the bison had to go. Elimination of bison became Federal policy, as well as a practical necessity for the railroad men. The Union Pacific Railroad hired an American scout, William Frederick Cody (1846–1917), who later became a showman known all over the world as "Buffalo Bill"—largely because of his prowess in slaughtering bison. For audiences everywhere he described how he rode circles around the defenseless animals, shooting the fattest cows, to the recorded total of 4,280 in one twelve-month period.

Most of the carcasses were left for the wolves and vultures. The tongues of some were shipped to eastern markets. The timid pronghorns, which were not regarded as worth a bullet, fled westward as fast as the Europeans arrived. For a while the wolves and other predators did not miss the native hoofed animals that used to live on the plains. Nor did the grasses grow tall and make the prairie dogs more vulnerable. Instead, herds of placid sheep and cattle cropped the vegetation and attracted the more daring of the predators—the wolves and the last of the Indians. Stockmen regarded both as vermin. Gradually they cleared the Great Plains. In 1869 the last spike was driven in a transcontinental railway, linking the tracks of the Union Pacific to those of the Central Pacific. For a while the trains that could haul people and freight from coast to coast were carrying vast loads of sun-bleached bison bones, to be ground up as fertilizer.

After Indians and bison ceased to be a problem, scientists began to take an interest in them. John Wesley Powell collected Indian artifacts and compared the languages and cultures of different vanishing tribal groups. His trophies attracted attention in the exhibit halls of the Smithsonian Institution in Washingon, D. C., and led to a plan to display major animals of America prepared by taxidermist. Unfortunately, no suitable specimens of the American bison could be found. The Report for 1887 of the United States National Museum (a branch of the Smithsonian) carries an account by the distinguished zoologist William T. Hornaday, entitled simply, "The extermination of the American bison."

Actually a small herd remained in private hands on a ranch in the Flathead Valley of Montana. Through Hornaday's efforts, the Federal government purchased the animals and transferred them to the only national park in existence—Yellowstone—where the bison could share in the protection accorded all other kinds of life. At that time, a comparable remnant of the once-widespread European bison (the wisent) was being conserved in the huge parklike Bialowieza Forest of northeastern Poland. The last two species of bison were down to a few captives.

Explorers in northwestern Canada discovered a few more survivors of the American bison—animals that had taken shelter in a remote area of wooded wilderness along the boundary between Alberta and the Northwest Territories. The Canadian government set aside a reserve for these, the "wood buffalo," as Wood Buffalo Park, with an area half the size of Maine.

In captivity the bison, which (according to the *Congressional Record*) were "as uncivilized as the Indians," prospered with protection and plenty

Once numbering in the millions on the prairie heartland of North America, the bison survive today only in parks and zoos where their nomadic habits are controlled.

of room. When the Canadian herd seemed in danger of dying out, the United States government was able to send 6,673 of the plains bison to Wood Buffalo Park to revitalize the northern population. After the wisents in Poland and many in the zoos in Europe were mostly slaughtered for meat or destroyed by the tides of two world wars, American bison were shipped to Europe and crossed successfully with the remaining wisents. Apparently *Bison bison* of the New World and *Bison bonasus* of the Old were interfertile, and not so distantly related as had been believed. Today the national parks and wildlife refuges of the United States hold about 10,000 plains bison; another 14,000 roam Wood Buffalo Park. Both populations are held at a suitable level to match the food and space that have been set aside, mostly by deliberate culling and shipping of excess animals to zoos and parks on this and other continents.

Guidelines for making decisions about bison populations come primarily from research at the National Bison Range, 29 square miles near Missoula, Montana. We spent a while there, thrilled to see bison by the dozens grazing on the hillsides or silhouetted against the sky. Among them was an albino, pink-eyed and almost blinded by full sunlight. In former days, such a rarity received veneration from the Plains Indians. When an albino died, its white coat was saved to adorn an important chief. Today this respect has vanished. The albino is now just a statistic in the inheritance of pigmentation.

From 1886 to 1909 the bison were regarded as extinct or about to become so. It is easy to forget that they are still our contemporaries, for the bas-relief of the animal that adorned one face of the five-cent coins in the United States for 25 years was replaced in 1938 by the facade of a man-made building.

Last summer we dreamed again of the bison community as we sat in our car at the edge of a prairie-dog town. The nearest of these sociable ground squirrels kept popping out of their burrows to see if we had gone. The farther individuals became brave enough to bark at us. All of them were on the campus of the University of Colorado, in an area used for emergency parking—mostly at night when the prairie dogs were sleeping, out of sight.

These were black-tailed prairie dogs, the kind that Ernest Thompson Seton toward the end of the last century estimated as numbering five billion individuals, ranging over about 600,000 square miles of western short-grass prairies. A few years later Vernon Bailey of the Denver Museum reported a single megalopolis of these prairie dogs in a band across Texas, 250 miles long and about 100 miles wide. The abundance of the animals then could be attributed to their new freedom from predators, for the stockmen had killed off the wolves, the grizzly bears, many of the badgers and coyotes, the birds of prey, and rattlesnakes; and to the consistent overgrazing by cattle and sheep, too many of which were being kept on each piece of land. Weeds, roots, fruits, and insects, on which the livestock could not flourish, kept the prairie dogs fat and reproductive. The rodents even spread beyond their previous territory into former long-grass prairie because the domestic animals kept the vegetation low. The prevalence and plumpness of the prairie dogs on the same land where livestock remained lean and hungry irritated the stockmen, who soon calculated that 32 prairie dogs ate as much as a sheep, and 256 as much as a cow. Eliminating a billion prairie dogs should make room for four million more cattle. Without holes to stumble into, cattle might not break their legs so often.

We thought about the animals that were destroyed to make the prairies safe for cattle and improve them for prairie dogs: the bison, the elk, the wolves, the grizzlies. Wolves were the first in the New World to become objects of a bounty system: a penny per scalp, to be paid from 1630 onward by the Massachusetts Bay Company! Twelve wolves for a shilling, 280 for a pound sterling. Yet by 1717, gray wolves were still so numerous in New England that there was a proposal to build a wolf-proof fence across Cape Cod from Wareham to Sandwich, although it failed for lack of support by citizens on the mainland side, who could not benefit from the enterprise. Before 1800 the need for such a barrier had gone, most of the wolves having been trapped and shot. The last one in Maine died a violent death in 1860, and a few remained along the Canadian border of New York State into the early years of the twentieth century. An occasional wolf still strays south across that border.

Among the heirlooms we inherited is a gray wolf pelt made into a warm cover for a baby's crib, from an animal shot just north of Toronto, Ontario, on Crown Grant land in the early 1800's. But in 1843 John James Audubon was far west along the Missouri River between St. Louis and Fort Union before he noted in his diary that wolves, [grizzly] bear tracks, bison, elk, and pronghorns ("antelope") were abundant. At the end of the century, both wolves and coyotes were still so common in the American West that stockmen estimated a loss of 500,000 cattle and sheep annually and sent delegations to Washington, D.C., requesting free poison as their only hope to stay in business.

Today, to see a wolf in the wild, we would have to go into the wilderness west and north of Lake Superior, or to Alaska and adjacent Canada. The last ones in the Great Plains and Colorado were hunted like gangsters on the list of "most wanted," preferably dead. It is a tribute to wolf mentality that they outlived by a century or more the giant grizzly bears of the prairies, whose surviving descendants haunt the garbage pits at western national parks. To see these gargantuan bears scavenging where once they roamed so free makes us doubly dissatisfied with park policy in the New World. Parks are for people, not for wild animals, if a grizzly bear can be killed because it attacks a person. The program at Kruger National Park and other reserves in Africa seems more honest, for outside of a closed automobile by day or a fenced and patrolled camp area by night, a human visitor has no rights and the wildlife are wild.

We listened to the barking prairie dogs, but we thought of the birds that used to hear this sound all over the plains and into the foothills of the mountains: the long-legged little burrowing owls that let the prairie dogs do the digging for them and then moved in to find shelter and nest sites close to grasshoppers, crickets, and mice. Now we find these owls beside the airport runways—on artificial prairies, where they can hide underground while the mowing machine goes by. We dreamed of the grouse called prairie chickens, that are on the world list of endangered birds: the northern race of the "greater" species, now reduced to a few small localities in its former range from northeastern Colorado to central southern Canada and to Oklahoma; the southern race (Attwater's) of the same bird, now numbering less than a thousand individuals scattered over coastal prairies of Texas and adjacent Louisiana; and the lesser prairie chicken, a casualty of brush control in the semiarid high plains of southeastern Colorado, eastern New Mexico, the Texas panhandle, and western Oklahoma. Without tall grass prairies for the "greater," and large blocks of brushy grasslands (particularly sand sagebrush and shinnery oak) for the "lesser," the future of all three is bleak. The eastern race of the greater prairie chicken was the heath hen, officially extinct since 1930 from overhunting and loss of habitat.

The prairie dogs around our silent car ceased their alarmed yapping, their popping-up and out of sight, but showed their continued apprehension by disappearing down their holes, leaving us to bake in the summer sun. A quiet far more lasting had come to the Great Plains and the foothills when the Federal government responded after World War I to the stockmen's calls for help. First it was strychnine-soaked grain to be scattered near the holes of prairie dogs. Then came more effective poisons: thallium sulfate in 1928, sodium fluoroacetate (called "1080") in 1945. To clean up any surviving dogs, crews began pumping carbon disulfide fumigant into burrows from trucks with special equipment. By the early 1960's it became possible to list the few places in western states where substantial prairie dog towns continued. Scientists interested in animal behavior found difficulty in studying the social interactions among prairie dogs because, almost as soon as they began an investigation, Federal or state officials arrived to exterminate the colony. Perhaps this is why the biologists at the University of Colorado have put up no signs to show where their little dog town is located, and why the maintenance department office says "Yes, yes. Thank you for telling us," when visitors complain about the awful holes in the parking area—and then does nothing to fill them in. A few people still have a space in their lives for prairie dogs, and give them such affectionate names as "sod poodles" and "barking squirrels."

Probably it is a rare event anywhere in the world for a common herbivorous animal weighing a pound or more to shrink in numbers without a predator following it toward the vanishing point. On the North American prairies, the specialist in living with and on prairie dogs is the black-footed ferret, a counterpart of the widespread Eurasian polecat, which is the ancestor of the domesticated European ferret and the source of the pelts called "fitch." The black-foot is a handsome little animal about 18 inches long, with more conspicuous ears and a bushier tail than a weasel. Black of feet and tip of tail, it is mostly a yellowish brown on back and legs. Its face and underparts stay nearly white, but across its eyes is a thin black mask.

The black-footed ferret may never have been numerous. Naturalists even began to wonder if such a creature existed when the original specimen to be described and illustrated was lost in the early 1870's. A search through the U. S. National Museum turned up a tattered remnant of skin with yellow-buff fur and a black-tipped tail attached—just enough to confirm the earlier account. That first one was collected by a British trader along the lower Platte River in Nebraska during 1843, and sent by way of a taxidermist to John James Audubon. The famous artist and naturalist collaborated with the Reverend John Bachman in introducing "this handsome new species" from a poor specimen in a state of "tolerable preservation . . . stuffed with the wormwood [probably sand sagebrush] so abundant in parts of that country." It appeared on Plate 93 in the first (1849) volume of their monumental *Quadrupeds of North America*.

Encouraged by the museum specimen, scientists published in several sportsmen's magazines a request for additional information on the prairie ferret. In response, they received a number of skins. Yet today, in the collections of all the world's museums combined there are only about 100 of these animals represented. The records show chiefly that the animal was widespread over the Great Plains, from Alberta and Saskatchewan to Texas and Arizona, and to at least 10,500 feet elevation in the Rocky Mountains.

By becoming a specialist, feeding almost exclusively on the once-common prairie dogs of the Great Plains, the black-footed ferret is in danger of extinction now that prairie dogs are scarce. (LUTHER C. GOLDMAN, BUREAU OF SPORT FISHERIES AND WILDLIFE.)

A survey of black-foots made in 1954 established 60-odd individuals to have existed between 1946 and 1953 in ten states, about a third of them being animals found dead. Eleven more were picked up on highways between 1955 and 1967, after being killed at night by automobiles. Authenticated records of daytime sighting in this period, generally from clear photographs, came from 26 counties in South Dakota, and one each in North Dakota, Nebraska, Colorado, Wyoming, and Texas.

South Dakota has undertaken to learn more about the black-foot as part of the scientific activities in its Cooperative Wildlife Research Unit. The ferret is viewed, as are most other predators, as pouncing on favored prey whenever possible but scavenging on dead bodies too. It can travel easily through the underground passageways of a prairie dog town and find unwary inhabitants—perhaps asleep. When prairie dogs die in the open because of poison they have eaten, the black-foots devour the carcasses and may succumb in turn. Where prairie dogs are scarce, the ferret generally has chances to find poisoned horse meat set out for unwanted coyotes, or to feast on the bodies of dead coyotes that have been killed by a cyanide gun (a "coyote-getter"). So successful have been the combined programs recently against rodents and predators on private and public lands that the black-footed ferret is now listed among the most endangered species of mammals on earth—in the same category with the Asian rhinoceroses.

The only concession made so far by the Bureau of Sport Fisheries and Wildlife is to instruct its officers not to accord "damage suppression measures" to any prairie-dog town until it has been certified to be "ferret free." A few states within the animal's former range have made the black-foot a legally protected animal, one not to be shot by people hunting prairie dogs for sport. Recommendations for future action include capturing enough of the rare survivors to begin a breeding program in captivity, with a hope some day to release a healthy stock into sanctuaries such as national parks and monuments within the original territory.

North Americans who believe in having no undomesticated animals or plants that might conflict with their intensive use of private lands find no place for either black-footed ferrets or prairie dogs. Orientals who believe in the efficacy of rhino urine, blood, and powdered horn see no cause to concern themselves over the diminishing numbers of rhinos on their own continent and in Africa. A good many people, who see no cause for exterminating any living species for the temporary benefit of a few men, would question whether the Occidental attitude toward the natural world is any more intelligent and realistic than the Oriental one.

CHAPTER 6

DWELLERS IN FORESTS, SWAMPS, AND STREAMS

AS THE SPANISH conquistadores looked for gold and marketable gems among the treasures of Indian peoples in tropical America, they were mystified to be shown glorious green feathers nearly 3 feet long, soft as a ribbon and with a metallic iridescent sheen. No bird in their experience produced such plumes. Nor did explanations in a strange language, rich in a pagan mythology, help them understand how these feathers in the ceremonial garb of priests among the Mayan and Toltec tribes could represent the bird part of the feathered serpent god Quetzalcoatl.

Quetzal birds still seek fruits and mates and nesting sites high above the ground in the same tropical rain forests where the coatl, a poisonous pit-viper, lives among the undergrowth. Guatemala chose the quetzal, the plumed spirit of wildness, as a national emblem. The bird is shown perched on the official seal, and on many of the country's postage stamps and coins. But to see this feathered acrobat alive today, Guatemalans and others must go either into the remote highlands of adjacent Chiapas state in Mexico, or eastward to mountainous areas of Honduras, Nicaragua, Costa Rica, or Panama. In Guatemala itself the sacred quetzal is extinct, the coatl hard to find, and Quetzalcoatl—the promoter of peace and kindness, knowledge and happiness—all but forgotten.

To find wild quetzals in their native haunts we drove up the steep road from Zamorano, Honduras, toward the Rosario silver mine at San Antonio. Never are we likely to forget that trip, for it was the first on which we had to unload our expedition vehicle (a station wagon) and carry its luggage

81

load uphill by hand so that the lightened car could make the steep grade. Otherwise its motor roared, its wheels stayed absolutely still, while the automatic transmission churned all the energy into heating the fluid "drive." But we got there, into a high saddle where the sun shone and disappeared in flashes as a steady breeze blew dense clouds one after another up the windward slope.

Probably several quetzals were watching us all the time. Yet we saw none of them until a male bird ignored our silent presence and began courting his mate. Of a size halfway between that of a bluejay and a crow, he hurled his slender body through the air, his crested head and breast and upper parts flashing bright metallic green, his beak golden yellow, his jet-black eyes matching the long flight feathers on his wings and the central feathers of his tail, his outer tail feathers pure white, his abdomen flame red, and the few long green plumes from the base of his tail trailing like streamers as he twisted and turned in flight. No wonder many people regard this tropical trogon as the most beautiful bird in the world.

By comparison the quetzal's mate seemed dull. She sat quietly on a branch, one beady black eye following the aerial display in the clearing over the road and our parked car. With no crest and no long plumes, her head and breast were greenish brown, her wings and inner tail feathers a sooty gray, and the outer tail feathers merely barred with white. Even her beak was inconspicuous grayish black. Yet her slightest movement attracted the gorgeous male. Every so often he fluttered to a landing right beside her, panting from his exertions but flipping his tail and long plumes to alternately stand facing in the same direction she was and then turn about, facing into the forest behind her.

Almost no one persecutes quetzals, shooting at them or robbing their nests. In the forests where they live, people generally ignore them. No longer are their plumes treasured by Aztec priests, or marketed in the millinery trade. Laws have been passed to protect quetzals, but the legislation is largely irrelevant because it focuses on the physical bird rather than on a place for the bird to live. Every year the world has fewer quetzals because the high country above 4,500 feet elevation is being cleared of trees for homesites, for agricultural use (no matter how poorly the land can bear food), and for fuel. Guatemala lost its national birds by deforesting its mountain quetzal country.

We can appreciate why primitive agriculturalists, tilling the dry slopes below one of these mountain forests, might decide to work farther from the valley markets by felling the trees and clearing the mountain top for corn and beans. Obviously the moisture precipitates where the trees grow so densely, nourishing the low growths, the tree ferns, the tall broad-

Most spectacular of the trogons—birds of the New World tropics—are the quetzals. Long streamer feathers borne by the male arise above his tail and are left draped from the nest hole in a dead tree while he takes his turn incubating the eggs.

leaved evergreens of many kinds. Such well-watered land, with crumbly
soil rich in humus, should be ideal for agriculture. Yet the cloud forest is a
mirage. As soon as the trees are cut, the wind blows the clouds away,
leaving as little water on the summit as on the tilled slopes lower down. It
is the vegetation where the quetzels live that captures the clouds and produces the cloud forest. When these trees are cut, the destruction of the trap
for moisture is generally followed in a year or less by a drying up of the
springs and small streams on the lower slopes, which previously were fed
from the precipitation on the peak.

Today the cloud forests with quetzals are so isolated on mountain tops
that it is hard to imagine they were ever connected by continuous woodland at lower elevations. Yet we are willing to believe that the most
densely populated of the Central American nations, El Salvador, had quetzals too not so many years ago, although no one seems to recall when the
mountains (which are still there) had either cloud forests or these spectacular birds.

Both the extent and the pace of change, destroying the habitat and the
animal inhabitants, can be bewildering. We remember driving along one
section of the Pan American Highway in Costa Rica, through mountain
country beyond San José in the direction of Panama. The road remained
unfinished, although it had been open to traffic for almost two years. We
came to a temporary sign, telling us that we were entering the National
Park of the Giant Oaks. But the nearest tall trees stood several hundred
yards distant on each side of the road. We could scarcely see them for a
dense haze of smoke, constantly added to in new spirals rising from earthen
mounds close to the road. Until recently this had been a virgin forest, un-
reachable by any wheeled traffic. Now the trees were melting away from
the highway, being converted into charcoal as fast as unskilled laborers
could work.

The change was no government project. It was private enterprise, coordinated in the most casual fashion by men driving decrepit trucks along
the highway. At intervals they dropped off empty bags to be filled with
charcoal, picked up full ones and paid the workmen, sold axes and
shovels, and hauled the products to modern cities such as San José. The
woodcutters worked in ragged clothes, felling the trees with hand axes,
cutting the boles into pieces that a burro could carry. Other men dug with
rough shovels, preparing cavities in the forest soil close to the road, where
the wood could be heaped, covered with earth, and set afire to smolder
and turn to charcoal. As soon as it cooled, the porous black material was
ready for bagging.

Dismayed at this destruction of the noble trees, the national forest, the
resource that might have been harvested for timber on a program of per-

petual yield, we asked ourselves what the Costa Rican government might do to stop the workmen and the truckers before the whole area was bare of trees, the park sign a mockery. Suppose a patrol of enforcement officers rounded up the men, destroyed their shacks, confiscated their cheap tools and the ancient trucks; the penal costs would soon exceed the sale value of the equipment. What would the city people use for fuel if the supply of charcoal were cut off? Wealthy as the country is, it has no gas or coal or cheap petroleum, and no electric stove for every private home. The forest was not being burned by vandals, but exploited by poor men living barely above the subsistence level, who knew no other gainful occupation. They had no concept of what a national park should be, no idea of other ways in which the forest bonanza made available by the road could be utilized for their benefit.

We compared the situation with the one familiar to us in the redwood groves that have been set aside in California, and the national forests and parks elsewhere in the United States and Canada. In long straight lengths, a redwood tree may be worth $1,000 delivered to the sawmill. For charcoal or other purposes, it is virtually valueless. If woodsmen attempted to cut the park trees for profit, they would risk seizure of their giant saws, their expensive tractor-trailer trucks, their efficient sawmills, all representing capital investments that could not be risked on illegal enterprises. Consequently the forests remain almost untouched, although lightly guarded, on public land. The forest animals are far safer than in countries where charcoal is a major fuel.

The smoke made our eyes sting too much for us to choose to explore deep into the oak forests in Costa Rica. No one seems to have noticed what the charcoal burners have done to the native creatures there. Yet, as we think about the economics that affect the trees and the wildlife, we find it easier to deplore the depredations made by poor people than to suggest a constructive solution to their problems. A national park and the animals in it must be shown to be important before perpetuation of these resources can be realistic.

Almost certainly this is the reason why the emerging nations of equatorial Africa are taking such significant steps toward protection of the wildlife reserves they have inherited. No other asset brings them as much foreign exchange, or attracts so many visitors with money to spend. Only these nations, so far as we know, have attempted both to classify the available land according to its productive capabilities and to resettle native people toward improving the total economy. For the United States to do as much would imply closing the poverty-stricken parts of Appalachia and many marginal lands in the West to any human residents, declaring them national wildernesses in which visitors might stay for only a few weeks while on safari. It is one thing to urge people to move from unproductive lands, and another to forcibly settle them where the soil and weather make possible a good living for a larger population than has yet taken advantage of the resources.

Where these drastic moves have not been made, the spread of poor people on inferior soils is still endangering wildlife that has nowhere else to go. The largest of the world's primates is threatened in much the same way in Africa as the quetzals are in the New World. The similarity occurred to us as we were driving on a road in the eastern Congo, one that cut through many corners of the extensive Albert National Park, where supposedly no wild thing may be hunted. The park itself was established in 1925 through the efforts of the great American naturalist, explorer, and sculptor, Carl E. Akeley, whose exhibits of African mammals at the American Museum of Natural History set new high standards for lifelike accuracy.

Beyond a sign that read (in French) "Leaving Albert National Park" and the next one that would mark a re-entry point, we reached a little hotel with a familiar name—familiar from our reading of Akeley's books and those of his widow, Mary L. Jobe Akeley. It was the Mount Mikeno Hotel, obviously named for the volcanic peak on one side of a high saddle where the explorer had died and been buried in 1926. We went inside to find out what the connection was.

The answer was simple. The place where Akeley lay buried was no longer remote, to be reached only by a foot safari of many days, with black men in single file carrying everything that would be needed. Although our map did not show it, the hotel on the road was within two miles of Akeley's cairn. One of the employees could go with us the following morning as a guide to reach the burial site, if we would like to stay over.

By a different trail, the same guide could take us into a great bamboo forest, where we would have a good chance to see wild gorillas and their sleeping nests. To preserve those gorillas was Akeley's principal aim in getting the Albert Park established. Now the cornfields extended to the park boundaries, which used to be all wilderness. Walking through the fields, up the gentle slope, would be no hardship. The guide fee to either destination was negligible.

How long, we wonder, will wild gorillas tolerate being visited at bargain rates? We doubt that the bamboos will continue to grow, as they have on the slope of the old volcano for untold thousands of years, unless these powerful primates keep feeding among the thickets. In the balance of nature, it is likely that the bamboos need the gorillas pruning them just as much as the gorillas need the bamboos for food and bedding. A few years hence, if there are no gorillas there to make the guide and unarmed visitors walk circumspectly through the bamboo forest, surely no one will object to a thorough cutting of the vegetation to make space for enlarged cornfields. We suspect that cornfields endanger gorillas more than guns do, or than traps or curious visitors. Africa's gorillas are now seriously threatened and can vanish with no sign of a struggle, merely by losing their habitat to human uses that seem momentarily more important.

The heavy clouds that hid the volcanic peaks helped us make up our minds about staying over to stalk gorillas. A steady rain began, and threatened to continue indefinitely. We decided to stay on schedule and drive onward, south along the shores of Lake Kivu to the big research center built by the Belgians and known as IRSAC (Institut pour le Recherche Scientifique en Afrique Central). It is still operating, now under the Republic of the Congo. There to our delight the rain ceased. To our surprise, we could see wild gorillas—in huge palisade-like cages, where they were being studied and photographed.

A custodian led us up a ladder to a narrow catwalk suspended on cables above the penned animals. From this safe perch we could look down into several separate enclosures, each with a solitary full-grown gorilla. The females peered silently through gaps in the palisade. The big male beat on the walls with his fists, or drummed on his chest a fierce tattoo that should have frightened us away. Instead it saddened us to see these magnificent creatures so confined, so aware that they had lost their liberty at human hands. And we wondered whether in our lifetimes a day will dawn when the only gorillas in the world are penned, kept to be gaped at, while someone who has never seen a gorilla raises a poor crop of corn on the mountain slopes in the eastern Congo.

Other continents have bamboo forests, but no gorillas. We have explored some of these thickets in Costa Rica, not far downslope from the nationalized oak forests, but found no animals or signs of them among the maze of slender jointed stems. Western China has bamboo forests, which are the home of a famous vanishing animal, the giant panda. No one seems to know how they are faring. In 1959 nine of these big playful bearlike animals had a known address, five of them in the Peking zoo, the other four in far-distant cities. Now, just two survive outside of mainland China, one in London, the other in Moscow. Attempts to get them to mate in London have not succeeded.

In the early 1940's the Bronx Zoo of New York City had two giant pandas. We treasure some color motion picture records we made of them wrestling on their artificial rock ledge, between meals of imported bamboo shoots, common vegetables, rolled oats and milk, and cod liver oil. Who could have predicted that these popular animals, the gifts of Madame Chiang Kai-shek, would soon succumb to an infection and be irreplaceable? Before that decade ended, the Chiang Kai-sheks themselves were ousted from their native habitat on mainland China and given shelter on Formosa, almost like captive wildlife but able to dream of a return to a homeland that would never again be the same. We still wait for the day when friendly communication will let interested people around the world go where they choose and know how wild giant pandas fare, if indeed any more survive.

Taking the animals into captivity is a limited program at best, for the few that can be accommodated and cared for are individuals—unlikely to relax and adjust enough to reproduce their kind. Disappointment was the only outcome in the middle 1960's from long negotiations that led eventually to bringing the male giant panda from the Moscow zoo to visit the female in London. They failed to show any interest in one another, as though unwilling rather than unable to communicate. With no other pairing possible outside of China, the two adults were separated again, each to be kept alive as long as possible in solitary confinement. Even this maintenance requires far more care and cost than might be imagined from an uncritical reading of the story of Noah, who supposedly kept two of each kind of animal in close quarters for more than a month aboard a floating ark whose dimensions as translated suggest that it could fit easily inside a giant panda's cage.

As we think of the vanishing animals of the Old World, we realize how the forests dwindled because well-tended small herds of livestock were led through to feed on the undergrowth. After the trees were gone, replaced by cultivated fields of grain, young boys defended the crops against even the birds by having ready a supply of pebbles gathered from the eroding soil. This change, exposing forest land to the sun, spread gradually in the Near East, across North Africa, and through old Persia into the subcontinent of India. At the same pace, the Asiatic lions diminished in numbers. The emblems of Darius, of Xerxes, of Tiglath-pileser faded into history. Before the Roman Empire collapsed, there were few lions left to entertain the guests in the coliseums.

Today, perhaps a hundred Asiatic lions survive, all of them in the national Forest of Gir on the Saurashtra Peninsula of western India. They cannot find enough to eat, or even good places to hide, because herdsmen are continually driving little flocks of sheep, goats, and cattle through the forest. The domestic animals eat all of the young growth from plants that otherwise would have supported prey for lions. No young trees survive to replace the old ones as they die; the future of the national forest itself is threatened. Yet the aging trees can be expected to provide shade long after the lions are gone. Some of the olive trees along the Mediterranean coast, around the Gulf of Lions and elsewhere, are old enough to have shaded lions in Caesar's day. Now we think of lions as African animals, because the high savannas south of the great deserts shelter almost all of the survivors of this once widespread majestic cat. Incredible as it seems, most of this reduction in range was accomplished with little need to kill a lion with a trap, a spear or a gun.

In North America, similar destruction of the habitat threatens one of the smallest and most elusive of wood warblers, and the most magnificent of native woodpeckers, making both closer to extinction than the famous whooping cranes. The 4¼-inch warbler, named Bachman's warbler to honor the Reverend John Bachman of Charleston, South Carolina, who helped John James Audubon so much, formerly bred in the swamp forests from the Charleston region to southeastern Missouri, and migrated through the Gulf States to winter in Florida and Cuba. Now the virgin bottomland and swamp timber in these southeastern states have been cut, and no one can predict the warbler's future. The last few sightings of it have been along the South Carolina coast and near Lawson, Virginia, after the end of the breeding season.

The vanishing woodpecker is the ivory-bill, which once hammered on trees and uttered its single high-pitched note in great swamps from eastern Virginia to the tip of Florida, around the Gulf of Mexico to eastern Texas, and up the low plain of the Mississippi as far as southern Michigan. Bald cypress was the dominant tree, and the fact that this conifer shed its needles every winter meant nothing to the giant woodpecker. It could tell quite easily which bald-cypress was dead and contained edible insects and which trees merely appeared dead in season.

No one knows just how much territory each ivory-bill needs, or how many of them used to live in the Big Cypress swamp of southern Florida before the loggers got to work. Now the ivory-bills are gone from there, and a new road called "Alligator Alley" gives access to a wilderness tangle from which all of the big trees have been removed, and virtually every alligator too.

The hazard is the same, although slightly slower in reaching such critical stages, for the other two crested woodpeckers, each the size of a crow: the imperial woodpecker of the Mexican highlands, and the Magellanic of southern South America. All of them need extensive forests in which stand long-dead trees, full of insects that can be reached by a hungry bird with a strong beak and the power to use it.

Lumbermen take an entirely different interest in tall trees. They count as lost any tree that dies and rots, with insects boring in its wood and woodpeckers chipping away to reach the insects or to make nest cavities. As fast as roads are built to dry-land forests, or means found to harvest the mature trees in the great swamps, the number of dead trees shrinks rapidly and with it the number of large woodpeckers.

One of our personal continuing regrets has to do with a second-growth forest track near our home, within the natural range of a slightly less magnificent bird—the pileated woodpecker. Only 15 inches long instead of 18 or more, it has the same requirements in food, but needs less undisturbed space than the more southern giants. Occasionally we see or hear one in the woodlands. Often we find the rectangular holes these birds cut into dead and dying pines and hemlocks to reach carpenter ants and beetle larvae. But we did not try soon enough to save a grove of trees on university land, along a favorite path. We saw the ribbons of blue plastic fastened around the trees by staff and students of the forestry classes, and should have inquired promptly as to the significance of these markers. Had we known that an outside contractor was being hired to cut those trees and haul away the valuable parts, we would have offered to buy every one of them within fifty yards of the path as a living delight—to stand until borers and woodpeckers and fungi took it down naturally. The conservation gesture would have been modest, but might have taught the forestry class more about forest values than all the piles of logs and confusion of slash they were brought to see.

Sometimes we wonder if there is an unrecognized law of nature that decrees for every large species of any type of animal either its progressive extermination when man arrives or an abject adjustment to domestication. The gigantic cave bears (*Ursus spelaeus*), which were 3,000-pound contemporaries of early man in northern Europe, vanished with no descendants in the forests or in captivity. The smaller Eurasian brown bears managed to stay away from human communities for centuries, inhabiting open forests perhaps as far south as in the Atlas Mountains of North Africa. They supplied characters for fairy tales, animal clowns for circuses, powerful monsters to be baited in bear pits, and the "Russian" bear, which is able to learn how to shuffle on its hind legs in the tempo of martial music. In the wild it is no longer common, chiefly because so few areas of the Old World offer it fruits, roots, insects, burrowing rodents, bee trees with free honey, and other favorite foods.

In the New World, brown bears that may be of the same species (*Ursus arctos*) grow to far larger size and are known as Alaskan brown bears and grizzlies. Formerly widespread from deep in Mexico to the arctic

Once widespread across the Great Plains, the grizzly bear proved too dangerous a neighbor for man and his livestock. (W. J. SCHOONMAKER FROM NATIONAL AUDUBON SOCIETY.)

tundras, they have survived only in some Mexican forests (from which they recently vanished), in Yellowstone National Park (Wyoming) and Glacier National Park (Montana), in the forested mountains of Alberta, Canada, and northward to Alaska—and in secure cages at the larger zoos. Biggest is the race on Kodiak Island, in Alaska, beasts growing to a weight of as much as 1,500 pounds, standing 4 feet tall at the shoulder and 8 feet long from snout to stubby tail. None of them seems willing to dance to any human tune. In consequence they seem likely to become a memory as thin as the emblematic bear that waves on the state flag of California.

The plight of this largest American carnivore may be just about 700 years later than that of the world's heaviest known birds, the "elephant bird," which became extinct just about the time that the earliest Negro pioneers reached the coast of South Africa and crossed to the big island of Madagascar. Right up to the present century, the Madagascan natives continued to use empty eggshells of these forest birds as water jars. They substituted other containers only after museums bid up the price of eggshells, for by then it was obvious that the birds that had laid them were gone forever. The number of eggshells broken and discarded in so long a time is beyond estimation. But since each one in a museum today has a small hole at one end, through which the original contents were removed, it seems certain that every water jar cost the life of an "elephant bird" chick that might have hatched. Apparently the monstrous bodies of the parent birds were eaten too, for skeletons from village middens have been dug up and reconstructed, showing eleven different extinct birds of this one type. At least one (*Aepyornis maximus*) stood over 9 feet tall, must have weighed a full 1,000 pounds, and laid eggs 13 inches long. The two-gallon capacity of such an egg would accommodate seven ostrich eggs.

Today the tallest bird is the male of the African ostrich, which may weigh 200 pounds and stand 8 feet high. We have no fear that it will go extinct, for ostriches breed in confinement on special farms, such as those around the town of Oudtshoorn in the Cape Province of South Africa. In a grocery store there we found ostrich eggs for sale, each egg containing as much nourishment as two dozen hen's eggs and not noticeably different in flavor when scrambled in a buttered pan. Ostriches are raised in big flocks, yielding also large plumes for feather dusters and stage costumes, skin for decorative leather goods, and flesh that can be dried to become a favorite South African kind of jerked meat known as ostrich biltong.

Wild ostriches range in lion country, over many of the highland savannas and into the fringes of the desert, where their sharp eyes can see danger at a great distance and their long powerful legs carry them from it faster than a horse can run. We wonder whether, long ago, the flightless ostrich was a forest animal whose natural habitat was felled and burned. If so, it survived by being adaptable—just as in modern times.

In North America, place names in regions that once were virgin forest commemorate animals that have vanished locally, or forever everywhere: Pigeon Lake and Pigeon River, along the boundary between the United States and the Canadian province of Ontario, reminding us of passenger pigeons in their former multitudes; Salmon Falls River, dividing New Hampshire from Maine, where no salmon have run for longer than anyone can remember; Beaver Falls on the Beaver River in western Pennsylvania, where the beaver were trapped out and their dams destroyed soon after the colonists settled.

Three centuries ago the salmon spawned in rivers flowing into the ocean all around the North Atlantic from Portugal, past Iceland, to the state of Connecticut. New Englanders developed the tradition of eating fresh salmon steak on the fourth of July, as part of the holiday celebration. Now their salmon must be imported from the Maritime Provinces of Canada, and the supply shrinks each year. In New Brunswick and provinces fronting on the Gulf of St. Lawrence the continuation of salmon fishing rests on a difficult decision: whether to favor forest industries or fishing. Effi-

ciency in one requires the regular spraying of insecticides from aircraft for control of the spruce bud moth or other pests. Salmon fisheries require prevention of pollution in the spawning streams. For a while, the forest exploiters seemed to have most of the votes, because their operations paid more taxes than fishermen and canneries could. Their lobbyists are still vocal and solvent. Currently the balance swings in favor of fish, because Atlantic salmon in the New World are becoming a sportsman's prize—caught in swift streams where fishing rights are rented out, just as in much of Europe. Recreation has plenty of money to spend, which impresses the legislators.

Pacific salmon have other man-made troubles. Unlike *Salmo salar* of the North Atlantic, the six species of *Oncorhynchus* follow a behavior pattern that brings each adult fish only once in a lifetime to the spawning grounds—in some specific river from California northward and down the Asiatic coast to China and Japan. Whereas the Atlantic salmon is generally a 10-pound fish, the pink or humpbacked salmon ranges from 3 to 6 pounds, the sockeye or red salmon 4 to 7, the silver or coho salmon 7 to 10, the chum or dog salmon 10 to 12, the cherry salmon of Japan about the same, while the giant is the king or Chinook salmon averaging 23 pounds but sometimes attaining a weight of as much as 80. Sockeyes still ascend the Fraser River for more than 700 miles to spawn east of

Alaska's panhandle; chum and king salmon struggle up the Yukon River fully 2,000 miles from the sea, to spawn in its headwaters.

Bears, both black and grizzly, used to be the principal predators on Pacific salmon ascending the rapids and tributary streams. Indians took a reasonable share. Commercial fishermen made the first real inroads on the salmon populations and, when their take threatened to deplete the supply, accepted international regulations—albeit reluctantly. To open their nets on specified days to let spawners through meant smaller profits for the good of unknown competitors who might be in business when next the life cycle of the fish came full turn.

Designers of dams for hydroelectric power, flood control, and navigation took great pride in the fish ladders they incorporated in their plans, wherever the river served commercial runs of salmon. At some of these installations employees keep a continuous tally of each major kind of fish ascending the ladder, and report the total as a measure of its success. We took a photograph of the score board at Bonneville Dam on the Columbia River:

With spectacular leaps, the Pacific salmon surmount rapids and low waterfalls to reach their traditional spawning beds among the tributaries of fast rivers. (GEORGE B. KELEZ, BUREAU OF COMMERCIAL FISHERIES.)

	Average Annual Total Since 1938	Total This Year, to Date	Total Yesterday
Salmon	466,974	308,947	2,558
Steelhead [trout]	142,021	21,768	867
Other fishes	336,007	119,015	5,460
Total all fishes	945,002	449,730	8,885
Human visitors	510,286	1,934,610	3,457

The Bonneville fish ladder cost about $7.5 million to construct, and serves fewer than two fish per human visitor in an average year. Even so, the comparatively small number of mature fish that ascend the gently flowing steps of the ladder and reach the waters above the dam might make it worthwhile if the future were bright once they found their home stream, reproduced, and quietly died. Unfortunately their young seldom find the fish ladder from above. Instead, as they descend the river, they tend to go through the turbines and be killed.

Each dam is a drastic change in the environment of salmon and other fishes. We look for better ways to minimize the obstacle, while each year the fishes that might benefit are fewer and the commercial catch is poorer. The day comes closer when fishes that can navigate for thousands of miles at sea and return to their home streams after years of absence will vanish forever, carrying with them the secret of their remarkable direction sense and many other heritages that might make ours a better world.

The excessive cropping of the Pacific salmon on their spawning runs has long been a big factor in their declining numbers. Now, pelagic fishermen —chiefly from Japan—are contributing to the shrinkage by harvesting immature fish on their long circuit of the high seas. Studies in search of compensatory ways to improve the habitat during the freshwater phase of each life cycle have revealed more cause for concern than the expected kinds of pollution: industrial wastes that affect the fish directly; insecticides that kill the insect larvae and crustaceans that are their normal food; waste heat from factories and thermonuclear electric installations that raise the river temperature intolerably high. Additionally, as never before, the natural predators (especially fishes) in fresh water are depleting the young salmon, seriously diminishing the number that reach the stage at which they will descend the streams to complete growth in the ocean. Formerly these predators were kept few by the sequence of a big salmon run and then a small one, and a spectacular run was possible once or twice in a five-year cycle. Now that the runs have been evened out by adjusting the number of mature fish allowed upstream to reproduce each year, the canneries have been provided with a reliable supply and so have the predators.

The fish ladder at Bonneville Dam on the Columbia River allows ocean-going fishes to reach spawning grounds upstream. Unfortunately the young fish rarely use this route to reach the sea. (BOB WILLIAMS, BUREAU OF COMMERCIAL FISHERIES.)

As man strives to regulate the outdoor world as though it were a factory to serve his needs, the wild denizens of forests, swamps, and streams lose their homes first, their lives second. The pace is simply faster than that shown by the history of the Nile Valley, which has lost its fauna throughout Egypt. The sacred ibis, whose head adorns portraits of the great god Thoth, is gone. So is the hamadryas baboon, sacred to the ancient Egyptians as an attendant of Thoth, the god of letters and scribe for the supreme Osiris; hundreds of these baboons were carefully mummified and entombed with the mortal remains of Egyptian kings. The crocodiles and hippopotamuses no longer soak in the shallows. No cheetahs pursue antelopes and ostriches along the dry margins. To see the animals depicted on the ancient monuments, an Egyptian now must go to wilder territory along the upper Nile, nearer to the Equator, farther from civilization, where the Ethiopians, the Kenyans, and Ugandans, like the Sudanese, have not yet destroyed their natural world.

CHAPTER 7

ANIMALS
ON
REMOTE
ISLANDS

DAY AFTER DAY we climbed one of the volcanic mountains on the West Indian island of St. Lucia, peeled a ripe banana, and placed it conspicuously atop the cut surface of a tall tree stump. Before the next morning, every trace of this fruit regularly disappeared. We could not be sure if our bait was attracting the kind of bird we so much wanted to see, for the island has many different feathered creatures that enjoy a ripe banana. Then our patience got its reward. Hardly had we stepped back after setting a fresh offering in the same site when a rainbow-colored parrot flew down to enjoy the fruit. Big as a crow, brilliantly green above, with a violet-blue head, violet on the wings, and a red patch on its chest, this was Jacquot —the St. Lucia parrot—a bird found nowhere else in the world.

Greedily the parrot grasped the banana in one clenched foot and tore at the fruit with its powerful black beak. We could see the bird's firm gray tongue shifting the pulp around in readiness for swallowing. Yet as it ate, the parrot watched alertly in all directions. Carrying the last bite in its mouth, it flapped off into the shadows of the trees, leaving us thrilled to have stood so close to a rare creature free on its native soil.

Looking away from the forest that was home to the parrot, we could see to the north the distant, larger island of Martinique. If we continued our walk around the mountain, we might see to the south the near island of St. Vincent. Both islands lie within easy flying distance for a St. Lucia parrot, yet never does one of these birds stray from its isolated peaks. Martinique has no parrots; it had a different kind, and a macaw, until

The native parrot of the island of St. Lucia in the West Indies visits neither Martinique to the north (where the parrots are now extinct) nor St. Vincent to the south (which has a different parrot), but gambles its future on finding suitable habitat at home.

The brown owl of Jamaica is often abroad by day, catching small reptiles as well as insects and mice. The bird flies well, but is native to no other island and no continent.

they were exterminated in the seventeenth and eighteenth centuries. St. Vincent has a still different parrot of about the same size, with a body mostly golden brown, but white and yellow on its head and variegated wings. It is another of the strong-flying members of the big genus *Amazona,* but a homebody that never visits St. Lucia or island-hops down the necklace of little islands—the charming, wooded Grenadines—to the next big one, Grenada. Each of these parrots is a self-isolated bird, an endemic, indigenous to one small piece of land and, on it, to the mountain forests that have not yet been cut. "Not yet been cut" are the magic words that save these parrots from extinction.

To become acquainted with animals that exist only on specific islands, we have traveled many thousands of miles. As we find time and opportunity, we will willingly go again, and farther. Island animals provide a special challenge because they have become so much more vulnerable than their ancestors, which managed to reach the isolated bits of land, from the nearest continent. Generally the course of evolution on an island is quick, far faster than on the mainland. The ancestral colonists had to adapt themselves to unfamiliar resources, but in doing so against a new background of limited competition, they lost much of their earlier versatility. This made them less able to cope with new changes that might come later to their island sanctuary.

The distance from the mainland may not be great, or the barrier that confers isolation anything particularly impressive. On a few of the intermediate islands in the string of Florida keys, a distinct race of the white-tailed deer evolved, maturing to a body size comparable to that of a collie dog. Known as *Odocoileus virginianus clavatus,* instead of *O. virginianus virginianus,* they remain remote despite their ability to swim for long distances from island to island, buoyed up somewhat by air trapped among the hairs of their brown coats. They travel about four miles an hour, and reach small uninhabited keys where they can find browse.

In 1960, when a census was taken of Key deer, less than 100 could be found. To help them survive, the U. S. Fish and Wildlife Service leased a considerable part of Big Pine Key and prohibited hunting. We visited this Key Deer Wildlife Refuge in 1962 and found the local residents incensed over the conservation measure. So far as the people could see, no one except themselves would lose if the Key deer became extinct. The animals were scrawny little things, anyway, poor venison but good targets. Hunting them was fun, where other fun was hard to find. The residents resented the game managers as intruders, almost like soldiers of a foreign government. Thinking of these people as potential jurors, we understood how a poacher who shot the egret warden was acquitted.

On islands off the arid southern coast of Australia live the rare Cape Barren geese, each almost the size of a turkey. If run down-wind, when they cannot take to their wings, they are easily captured. They are said to be good eating, and prove easily domesticated.

We mentioned that scientists regard the Key deer as a separate race of white-tail, a line of inheritance with special features in addition to small size. To the residents we talked to, this seemed downright fraud at their expense. But they did admit that the little deer had become scarce. They blamed a hurricane. We could see that a violent storm might kill a dozen deer in a few hours, drowning some while crushing others under fallen trees. There seemed no way to guess whether full-grown deer or young ones would be more likely to perish in a hurricane. We saw no point in arguing that two or three hurricanes in a decade would reduce the deer herd less than even two or three hunters active several times a month over a comparable number of years, shooting only animals old enough to reproduce.

The only Key deer we have seen at close range was a seemingly docile three-point buck that had been crippled by a car speeding along the highway. Nursed back to health at Refuge headquarters, hand-fed and tame, it could no longer find a place for itself among the elusive wild deer on the island. To the threatened herd, the little buck was just as much a loss as though it had been killed.

At the last census, the number of deer had not risen much. And landowners on the key are torn between renewing the leases on their holdings

This yearling buck, raised in captivity by Warden Jack Watson, was rescued after being struck by a speeding automobile, and later grew good antlers. (COURTESY OF RALPH TINGLEY.)

to the Fish and Wildlife Service as a deer sanctuary, and selling to real-estate developers who are bent on transforming Big Pine Key into a vacation village, like a far-flung outpost of tailored suburbia. Leasing is a holding action, speculating on a continued rise in sale price. Although the valuation is high, the Federal government has been able to secure a tract sufficiently large to be a sanctuary.

Even without people, the plight of these little deer might be perilous. Few of the keys are more than four feet above mean high tide and, while they have coral platforms under them, most of the coral is dead. The limy material can dissolve away, or fragment with erosion. As navigators must know, if they are to take boats of moderate draft through the waters among the keys, islands appear and disappear so often that new charts are constantly essential. Neither man nor deer can count on finding land and vegetation where it used to be. No computer can predict the pattern that will be followed in the next decade, or reach a reliable conclusion based on recorded history to show whether the future will offer more habitable islands or fewer.

The mountainous northern islands of the West Indies seem more permanent because they have a firm volcanic base. Yet on them, six out of fourteen different kinds of small rodents have become extinct in the last few centuries. All known as hutias and related to the South American nutria, the remaining eight are on the endangered list. Puerto Rico and the

Isolated on a few Florida keys, the diminutive local race of the white-tailed deer struggles for survival despite hurricanes and hunters. A wild doe watches, ready to run. (COURTESY OF RALPH TINGLEY.)

Virgin Islands no longer harbor any, nor do the Bahamas. The big island of Hispaniola, shared by Haiti and the Dominican Republic, had two species at latest count, from a former assortment of seven. Jamaica, which once had three kinds, now has one. Cuba supposedly still has three, and the adjacent small Isle of Pines has one of these and a unique species.

No fur trade contributed to the disappearance of hutias, for their pelage is harsh, never soft and thick like that of a nutria. In most parts of the world they would be overlooked as a source of human food because they are the size of guinea pigs or large rats. Yet in the West Indies they have been trapped systematically, introduced from one island to another for their meat, and even kept in semidomestication because on these remote outliers of the Americas, nothing larger and more tasty is native. People of the West Indies have always hungered for more animal protein in their diet.

Several of the extinct kinds of hutias are known only from what are called "subfossils," meaning bones gathered and assembled into skeletons from the remains of aboriginal campsites. Apparently all hutias, like those existing now, had robust bodies, short ears and legs, and strong claws, used in digging for plant foods and in holding whatever edible lizard a hutia catches. Unfortunately, hutias reproduce slowly, usually one young at a time. Before man and exotic mammals were introduced, this habit sufficed. It predisposes hutias to be wiped out by hunters, or by dogs and Asiatic mongooses that hunt on their own.

With some dry corn begged from the animal keeper at the Institute of Jamaica, we once baited a wild hutia into showing itself at sunset where the corner of a sugar-cane plantation, some forest, and the road were close together. Day after day we set out the corn among the sugar-cane stems where birds would be less likely to find it. Then we waited, concealed in our parked car, hoping to see whatever animal was coming regularly to the bait. Would it be just a rat, with which the plantations are plagued? The creature we finally saw left no doubt in our minds. The size of a cottontail rabbit, it was blackish brown above and paler below, with a stubby, furry tail no more than two inches long. No rat in Jamaica comes in these dimensions.

Our color movie record is as good as could be expected in fading light, but it proves that at least one hutia was present in a moderately populated part of the island. There must have been more. And Jamaica is a big island. The question no one has answered yet is whether Jamaican hutias have adjusted to the presence of dogs, rats, mongooses, and people too. If they lack this ability, their future will be short, for the animals and human beings from the Old World have come to stay.

Ground-nesting birds on West Indian islands and various kinds of reptiles, particularly snakes and lizards, have suffered as much as hutias

The short-tailed rodents known as hutias colonized the northern islands of the West Indies and some of the Bahama group long ago and evolved separate species, all now endangered or extinct. This is the Bahama hutia. (A. W. AMBLER FROM NATIONAL AUDUBON SOCIETY.)

have from the introduced predators. More species, in fact, have vanished from this one archipelago in the last four hundred years than from all the continents of the world in the last four thousand. Additional species have become restricted to offshore islets too tiny to be attractive for human occupancy. The famous yellow boa, a Jamaican snake of modest size, has simply retreated into the Blue Mountains. Apparently this keeps it far enough from plantations that rats and mongooses have not followed. For people who distrust snakes, this change seems to make the island more attractive. Yet the croplands suffer seriously from pests that the snakes previously kept under control.

On Cuba at the present time, the fate of at least three kinds of local birds is bound up in the continued existence of a big swamp on the Zapata Peninsula along the south coast. The Zapata finch, which resembles a large sparrow, has short rounded wings and weak flight—just enough to get about in the swamp and marshlands in search of insects and seeds. It conceals its cup-shaped nest in hummocks of sawgrass, and is not found anywhere else in the world. Similarly weak flight keeps the Zapata wren among dense scrub, where it can hop instead of using its feeble wings; it too has never been seen alive beyond the borders of the swamp. On the ground below, at least in the part of this dense, bush-covered area to the north of the heavily wooded higher ground known as Santo Tomás, an al-most flightless bird scurries between the plants. Resembling a coot or gallinule in shape, it is the Zapata rail, with body about a foot long stand-ing on bright red legs and feet. It is olive-green above, gray on the head and underneath, except for a white throat patch and a red base to the beak. So nearly impassible is this territory to a man on foot that no one has yet discovered where this rare rail nests.

Scientists enthuse over these three birds of the Zapata swamp because each belongs to a genus otherwise unrepresented in the West Indies. They try to account for their presence, without real knowledge of how long each has been there. We wonder how long the Zapata swamp will continue to offer these birds the only refuge they know. To our way of thinking, the critical time will come when the Cuban refugees who have become familiar with the greater Miami areas of Florida can go home and rebuild their na-tive land. It seems likely that large numbers of these Cubans will go back to the island once they feel safe to return, and that they will take along with them new ideas gained where Miami and its suburbs are spreading up and down the coast, and out onto filled land that formerly was man-grove swamp and shallow water. Suppose the exiled Cubans choose to build bedroom suburbs near Havana, across the narrow island to the south shore. Beyond the bay is the Zapata swamp. As the crow flies, its heart is less than 80 miles from the center of Havana. Presently it would be viewed as useless land—useless except to birds, including three kinds that cannot fly away. These feathered Cubans of the Zapata are less well adapted to survive elsewhere than the human refugees in Florida.

Of all the islands in the world where wildlife is presently endangered, the most famous are the thirteen clustered in an area about 200 miles across, straddling the Equator in the Pacific Ocean some 600 miles west of the Equadorian coast. Spanish explorers named them the Galápagos for the giant land tortoises found there in large numbers, they are the eroding re-mains of lava piles and volcanic cones whose geological age has never been established reliably. Chilled by the northbound Humboldt Current, in which the water temperature is around 63 degrees Fahrenheit, they have arid shores, few springs or streams, and misty highlands where tree ferns grow. Closer to the steep rocky cliffs and few sandy beaches, cacti of large size bush out wherever the tortoises now are few. Only the big reptiles seem able to prune away the lower branches and cause the plants to assume a treelike form.

Despite the lack of harbors and the inhospitability of the islands, sea captains regularly called there to let the crew bring dozens of the giant tortoises aboard. Even when stored without food or water in the hold for weeks, these animals stayed alive and could be slaughtered as needed for meat and fat. On land, the eggs of the tortoises and their young fell prey to free-ranging dogs and pigs when these were introduced. Gradually the numbers of tortoises decreased, particularly of old ones weighing 500 pounds or more.

When Charles Darwin visited the Galápagos in 1835, during his voyage aboard H.M.S. *Beagle,* he found a different, distinctive race of giant tortoise on each of the major islands. He also noticed that the future for these animals was bleak. Today they are extinct on some islands, and only a few remain on others. Dogs and pigs have interfered also with the reproduction of the flightless cormorants which are unique on the Galápagos, and of the indigenous penguins—the most northern of all penguins. These birds feed on the many small fishes and squids in the cold waters offshore, but no longer have a safe place to hide their eggs. The three-foot lizards known as land iguanas are in similarly desperate straits. Strangely, their kin—the only marine iguanas in the world—seem unaffected; they continue to clamber confidently down the lava rock into the surf and swim to kelp beds near shore, to feed on the coarse seaweeds.

Darwin noticed that each island also had its own peculiar mockingbird, and certain distinctive small sparrowlike birds now known as "Darwin's finches." Fortunately, the finches are still there, all twelve kinds of them. Each finds its own types of food without much competition from the others. Of the four seed-eating finches, one stays in humid regions, while the others in coastal arid zones seem to divide up the seeds according to size: small, medium, and large. A "vegetarian" finch eats buds, small leaves, and fruits. A "cactus finch" takes flowers of the prickly-pear cactus as its special domain. A kind called the "warbler-finch" acts like a flycatcher, snatching insects in flight. Three other insect eaters specialize in finding insects on foliage, but stay separate in their hunting grounds, none conflicting with the mangrove finch that stays in mangrove thickets when seeking a mixed diet. A "woodpecker-finch" uses cactus spines as tools with which to extricate insects from holes it pecks in tree bark.

Apparently these finches greatly puzzled Darwin, and he did not feel ready to formulate his thoughts about them until the 1845 revised edition of his *Journal* of the voyage, when he described "the perfect gradation in the size of the beaks in the different species" for the first time. He concluded:

> Seeing this gradation and diversity of structure in one small, intimately related group of birds, one might really fancy that from an original paucity of birds in this archipelago, one species had been taken and modified for different ends.

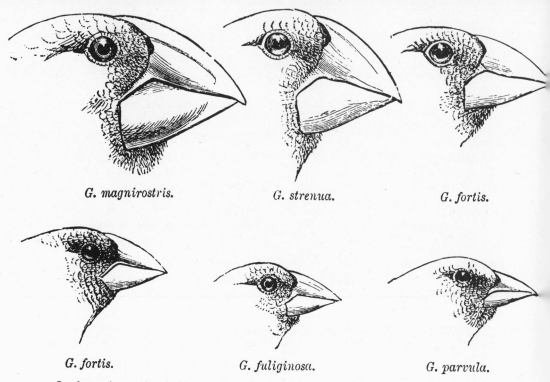

G. magnirostris.   *G. strenua.*   *G. fortis.*

G. fortis.   *G. fuliginosa.*   *G. parvula.*

On the various volcanic islands of the Galápagos, Charles Darwin found similar finches with dissimilar habits and specialized beaks, dividing the food resources and shelter with a minimum of competition. (FROM NEWTON'S *Dictionary of Birds,* COURTESY OF THE AMERICAN MUSEUM OF NATURAL HISTORY.)

By then he had also written his thoughts to his friend Joseph Hooker (11 January, 1844):

> I was so struck with the distribution of the Galapagos organisms . . . that I determined to collect blindly every sort of fact, which could bear any way on what are species. . . . I am almost convinced (quite contrary to the opinion I started with) that species are not (it is like confessing a murder) immutable.

Today, scientists are much less hesitant about estimating that the arrival on the Galápagos of one exotic species in each 10,000 years would account for the evolution and presence of every kind of life known there.

Darwin was well aware that the giant tortoises of the Galápagos (*Testudo elephantopus*) differed little in size but considerably in the pattern of their shell plates from similar giants far off on islands in the Indian Ocean. Originally the Old World had two species of these monsters, but the one on the islands of Mauritius, Rodriguez, and Réunion became extinct in the 1700's. The remaining species (*Testudo gigantea*) was native to Aldabra Island, a coral atoll some 260 miles northwest of Madagascar and 400 east of the African mainland. Through Darwin's efforts in 1874, Aldabra was informally set aside as a sanctuary under British protection, to preserve a safe environment for giant tortoises and for a considerable number of highly special animals of other kinds and plants living on the remote bit of land.

Today, between 1,000 and 2,000 of the Aldabran tortoises survive on their island, and another 50 or less in zoos elsewhere in the world, where they have little inclination to reproduce their kind. One venerable individual, in the garden of Government House on the island of St. Helena in the mid-Atlantic, is said to be the only animal still alive that could have seen Napoleon as he paced the paths during his exile.

Thinking back much farther, it is difficult to imagine how these plodding tortoises could have reached such widely separated places as Aldabra and the Galápagos. Almost certainly the ancestors that came to the island in the Indian Ocean found their new environment a volcanic peak with a fringing coral reef. Now the top of the volcano has eroded away completely, and most of the coral is dead, elevated by land movements to a height of 20 to 80 feet above sea level. Much of the dead coral is strangely vitrified, and rings when struck. The rest is porous, holding a thin soil, in which some 170 different kinds of plants grow, 18 of them native nowhere else in the world.

Amid the separate islands of Aldabra atoll, a shallow lagoon fringed with mangroves stretches in an oval 18 miles long. Flamingos, which may

The giant tortoises have been eliminated from most of the remote islands in the Indian Ocean, partly as provisions that could be carried away on shipboard, and partly as victims of rats, dogs and men that colonized the islands (photographed near Zanzibar).

be a distinctive race, feed in the lagoon. Great sea-going hawksbill turtles migrate to it every year to mate and lay their eggs. South Island is the biggest area of land. On its eastern end the Aldabran tortoises live, close to the mangrove area where one of the few nesting colonies of sacred ibis known still raise their young. Smaller Middle Island is the only home of a flightless rail, a unique kind of marsh bird found nowhere else. Aldabra also has nesting boobies, seabirds related to gannets, differing from other boobies in the Indian Ocean in having pink instead of red feet, and in other distinctive ways. Only a few of these creatures inhabit West Island, where less than a hundred people live. Almost all the people are contract laborers who harvest coconuts, cut mangrove as directed, eat mostly fish and turtle meat, and dream of returning home to the distant Seychelles Islands from which they came.

Early in 1967 the British Government announced new plans for this dependency. With the help of the United States, a major air base would be built there, including a radio and radar tracking station for jet aircraft and space surveillance. The 9,000-foot runway would go on the east end of South Island. The central lagoon would be dredged as a harbor for naval vessels. A big dam and circuiting highway would link all parts of the atoll. Work could start at once, despite the announced British policy to withdraw all installations east of the Suez Canal.

Immediately scientists all over the world protested vigorously, individually and through the Royal Society of London, the National Academy of Sciences and the Smithsonian Institution in America, and other centers. Never had such concerted resistance been expressed to any military or engineering project. The British Broadcasting Commission sent a survey party to Aldabra, including Dr. David R. Stoddard of Cambridge University, one of the principal protesters in Britain. Upon its return, the party reported that the jet runway was to be exactly where the giant tortoises were making their last stand, and would require clearing all the mangroves in which the sacred ibis nest.

Nor could takeoff and landing of jet aircraft be risked except at night until the thousands of frigate birds which nest on Aldabra were destroyed. They soar 30 to 3,000 feet above the ground daily there for much of the year. Eliminating the adults would not promptly solve the problem, since juveniles now at sea would be returning in new waves every nesting season for the next seven years. By then the air base might well be obsolete. Why build it?

Dredging of the lagoon would clear it of hawksbill turtles, a living resource that already is in serious difficulties. The circuiting road, moreover, would be used quickly by house cats, which have gone wild on

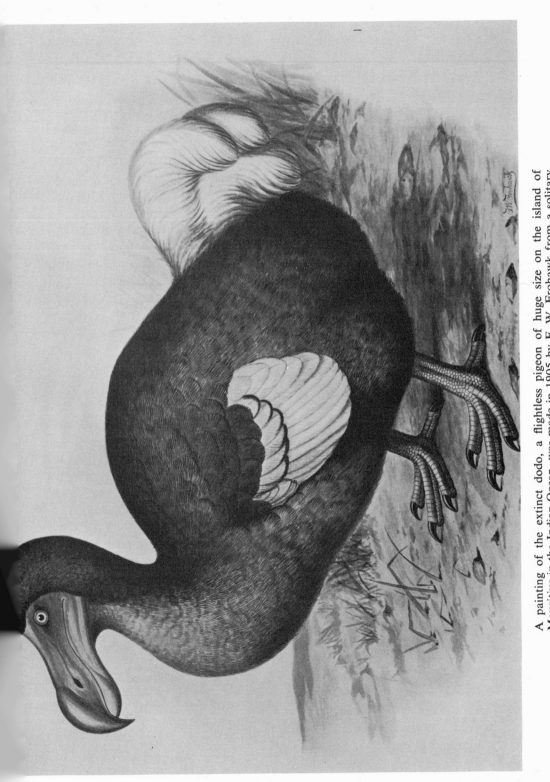

A painting of the extinct dodo, a flightless pigeon of huge size on the island of Mauritius in the Indian Ocean, was made in 1905 by F. W. Frohawk from a solitary specimen preserved in the British Museum (Natural History) in London. (COURTESY OF THE AMERICAN MUSEUM OF NATURAL HISTORY.)

South Island as well as West Island. As soon as they could reach Middle Island, they would destroy the flightless rails, perhaps the nesting boobies and flamingos, the native doves and white-tailed tropic birds as well.

During the heated discussions, the opponents of the proposed construction reminded the proponents and the world at large of the sad history on three similar islands in the Indian Ocean, from which the English language added the phrase "dead as a dodo." This large flightless pigeon became the symbol of vulnerability in 1681, when sailors landing on the island of Mauritius clubbed the adults to death and introduced dogs and hogs that destroyed the nests and young.

Dodos comprised a little family, the Raphidae, with three or perhaps four species, the others being on the adjacent islands of Réunion and Rodriguez. They were not alone, however, in being exterminated. Scientists could list a whole series of extinctions, with the dates at which each bird was seen alive, and add to it five kinds of endemic birds on Mauritius, four on Réunion, and one (a warbler) unique to Rodriguez among the species presently rare and seriously endangered. Most people had not even heard of the losses on these isolated islands in the same ocean as Aldabra, but were duly impressed by the statistics:

Mauritius	*Réunion*	*Rodriguez*
Yellow rail, 1638	Pink pigeon, 1669	Flightless night heron,
Broad-billed parrot,	Bourbon parakeet, 1669	1730
1638	Réunion solitaire, 1746	Blue rail, 1730
Dodo, 1681	Réunion fody, 1776	Little owl, 1730
Blue pigeon, 1830	Ring-necked parakeet,	Rodriguez parakeet,
Scops owl, 1837	1800	1760
	Mascarene parrot, 1834	Rodriguez solitaire,
	Crested starling, 1862	1791
		Leguat's starling, 1832
		Rodriguez pigeon, 1867
		Ring-necked parakeet,
		1875

For months, the Secretary of State for Defense would give no assurance that the Aldabra plan would be dropped. Then the British pound underwent a financial crisis, and all participation in the expensive scheme had to be set aside. Said Dr. Stoddard, who felt relieved but not really satisfied, "It is a little sad that it was a sterling crisis and not scientific opinion that made the government change its mind."

From London to Aldabra atoll is more than 10,000 miles, almost halfway around the earth. To a signpost we photographed on the South Island of New Zealand it is 11,820 miles to London—and from that point to the South Pole only another 2,998 miles. New Zealanders have every right to feel isolated. They are also determined that, with no native terrestrial mammals, they will do all in their power to prevent any more endemic animals from following into extinction the famous moas and four other birds now regarded as lost forever. Nowhere else in the world, perhaps, could people drum up such enthusiasm for protecting wildlife known by Polynesian (Maori) names—kiwi, weka, pukeko, takahe, kotuku, kea, kaka, kakapo, tieke, and tuatara.

In their folklore the Maoris have always maintained that the moas were almost extinct when their ancestors arrived as colonists from Polynesia, bringing along cultural skills and domesticated plants. They disclaimed any connection with the earlier inhabitants of the two big islands, insisting that the "moa hunters" were primitive castaways who survived only until the supply of flightless moas gave out. This history, handed down orally for generations, gained real support recently when the carbon-14 method of dating organic debris associated with or incorporated in fossils was applied to the kitchen middens and moa bones the archeologists had collected. Possibly one small species of moa, not much bigger than a turkey, survived on the South Island until 1773, four years after Captain James Cook circumnavigated New Zealand and his official naturalist, the explorer Joseph Banks, made the first systematic studies of both Maori culture and native wildlife. The skeletal remains of the other 21 species, including the tallest (*Dinornis robustus*), standing 12 feet high, date back much farther —before 900 A.D., when the principal influx of Polynesians occurred.

Right down to the present, the Maoris treasure ceremonial capes made of feather-covered skins of the moas' small kin, the three different kiwis that are equally local and flightless but carnivorous and strangely nocturnal. Kiwis hide by day in the dense "bush" country, and roam only in darkness to probe with their long beaks for worms, insects, and snails deep in the forest soil. New Zealanders like to call themselves "kiwis," and show a remarkable awareness of their birds. But the future of feathered kiwis depends partly upon the continued existence of dense native bush, which has little value since it produces neither sheep nor lumber, and partly on the birds' own abilities in concealing and defending their eggs against introduced predators.

The biggest of the kiwis, from the South Island, is only about 2½ feet long and weighs less than 4 pounds. Yet the hen bird, which is the larger in each pair, lays the biggest eggs in proportion to body size of any bird known—a one-pound egg, one-third the weight of the largest an ostrich can produce. When a hen kiwi lays two such eggs as a clutch in her under-

The kiwis of New Zealand have managed to survive despite their inability to fly. Nocturnal probers of forest soil, in which they find worms and edible insects chiefly by smell, kiwis run through dense underbrush or, as a last resort, defend themselves by kicking with their strong legs. (COURTESY CONSULATE GENERAL OF NEW ZEALAND, N.Y.C.)

ground nest hole, the eggs she incubates weigh more than half as much as she does. They are nourishing trophies for any predator that can find them and break them open before being driven off with well-placed and vigorous kicks by the parent bird.

We turned over a great many large pieces of rotting wood before we found a kiwi's bedroom occupied. The sudden light of day confused the bird, and it peered about with tiny dazed eyes before running into the underbrush. Its tailless body and sturdy legs give it a strange gait. Its wings have failed to grow to more than an inch in length and seem utterly useless, although each bears a strong gray claw which must be important to the bird in some way. A kiwi's feathers lack the microscopic hooks that hold into a vane the feathers on other birds; consequently they more nearly resemble coarse branching hairs of an earth-brown color.

At the Mount Bruce Game Farm on the North Island, the conscientious director Mr. Colin Roderick showed us the large enclosures in which kiwis and other native rarities are being protected by high fences and given the best living conditions the country's scientists can devise. The kiwi pen, for example, had a great many low shrubs under a canopy of trees to keep the soil moist and penetrable by a beak. Plenty of fragments from dead trees were scattered about for the birds to use as shelter. Food supplements were set out each evening, all to induce the kiwis to relax in their facsimile native bush and reproduce. The game farm is far more than a specialized zoo, since breeding and scientific observations are the sole purposes to be served.

We had previously visited constructive centers of this type in South Africa, where endangered animals on government game farms have not only escaped extermination but produced many offspring. The young, when independent, were used in restocking outside reserves, where supervision would be far less extensive. To us, the most magnificent aspect of these efforts in both countries has been the recruitment of men who devote themselves so knowledgeably and selflessly to the projects.

Each of these curators is faced with difficult decisions, such as how large a portion of the game farm should be allocated to each individual animal, or pair, or species, to match its inherited territorial needs. What factors are missing from the pen that would be present in the natural environment? Even more trying, at times, is to find ways to ensure privacy for the wild animals. So many people within the country, and visitors like ourselves from elsewhere, are eager to glimpse the rare creatures for which the game farm has been established. Repeatedly the curators are tempted to transform the sanctuary into a display area. From discussions with these men, we have come to appreciate that animals able to tolerate seeing people on the opposite side of the boundary fence are more likely to give the game farm a good reputation, and also to multiply within its confines.

Others of the rare and endangered native birds with unfamiliar Maori names proved to be extremely local in distribution and elusive in the wild. A weka turned out to be a flightless rail, which wags its short tail and dashes through the grass, defending itself successfully against dogs and often killing rats. Four different races of wekas fight for suitable living space on the North Island, the east and west coasts of the South Island, and on little Stewart Island still farther south.

A pukeko would be just a gallinule in Africa, or Europe, or America, not very different from the purple gallinule that is so widespread in the Northern Hemisphere, although perhaps a little less ready to fly. The flightless takahe is obviously a larger bird of the same type. Yet few birds in New Zealand have had such an exciting history. This bird is the one that was described from subfossil bones of four specimens collected in the southwestern part of the South Island in 1849, 1851, 1879, and 1898, all presumably the remains of an extinct contemporary of the moas. No one even hinted that it might have been alive a century before when Captain Cook first charted New Zealand's shores.

Found only on New Zealand and islands close by, wekas are large flightless rails which flick their tails as they walk. They run rapidly, swim without hesitation, and are most active at dusk. (COURTESY CONSULATE GENERAL OF NEW ZEALAND, N.Y.C.)

Then, in 1948, a Dr. Geoffrey Orbell on holiday from his dental practice saw a live takahe while hunting for other game west of Lake Te Anau in the Murchison range of mountains. He alerted other dedicated bird watchers, organized a search party, and located a few more of the rarities. When shown photographs of the bird, Maoris recognized it as the takahe—a creature their ancestors had enjoyed eating in days when it was common. But as suddenly as the fossil *Notornis mantelli* had come to life, the live ones disappeared; all were feared lost again.

A later expedition turned up nearly 200 takahes in a remote valley floored with tussock grass at an elevation of 2,000 to 3,000 feet in the Murchison range. It was named Takahe Valley and set aside as a wildlife preserve. Today, so far as the wardens know, every takahe alive wears a numbered identifying anklet. The question is whether they can be induced to breed elsewhere. New Zealanders fear to have all their takahes nest in one valley, because a wildfire could sweep through and again make this navy-blue bird with the big red beak and feet extinct.

The kotuku surprised us, for it is the same species (*Casmerodius albus*) as the bird we call an American egret, that Europeans know as the "great white heron," and Africans have named the "great white egret." It is fairly common in Australia, and occasionally makes the long flight of nearly 1,500 miles eastward to New Zealand. There it is a rarity, nesting in only one known site on the west coast of the South Island. It takes a person accustomed to the Maori names of birds and plants and places to understand a New Zealand field guide that identifies this one site by a town, a "white pine" tree, and a river as "near Okarito in a kahikatea swamp through which the sluggish Waitangi-roto crawls." Every New Zealander knows the Waitangi from the treaty signed in 1840 along its banks with the Maori chiefs, officially annexing New Zealand as part of the British Empire.

The kea, the kaka, and the kakapo are all parrots, big olive-green ones 18 to 23 inches long. Biggest is the kakapo, which early colonists called the "owl parrot" because the feathers around its face and its arched beak give it an owllike appearance. Formerly widespread on both big islands of New Zealand in the forests of antarctic beech, this flightless bird is now one of the country's rarest. The only known individuals survive in a remote part of the rugged Fiordland country on the South Island, where they escape persecution by introduced animals and can still find their favored assortment of fruits, fungi, tussock grasses, and roots, nectar-bearing flowers and sleeping lizards—for the kakapo is strictly nocturnal. It pains us to know that among the curiosa in the Zoology Department at the University of New Hampshire is a kakapo, mounted by a taxidermist no one knows how long ago, a specimen without a tag or much appreciation so far from its native land.

The kea and the kaka are closely allied, but well able to fly and in no great danger. The kea emerges from the forests of the South Island mountain country where it lives, and is daring enough to steal our picnic lunch if we leave it unguarded. Keas are scavengers, and have earned a reputation as sheep killers, using their sharp, narrow, curved beaks to cut through the back flesh and reach the kidney fat they crave. Apparently they were educated to this by sheep raisers themselves, who slaughtered sheep in kea country and discarded the unsaleable entrails for the waiting parrots to pick up. To a kea, it seems to make little difference whether a sheep has been slaughtered at the meat camp or is too sick, injured from a fall, or trapped in snow to resist a hesitant attack. For a healthy sheep to be killed by a kea seems to be a rare event.

We saw several keas but no kakas during our exploration of New Zealand. But then, we spent only a comparatively short time in the large tracts of native forests where kakas live. If kakas saw us, they made no sound that attracted our attention. Perhaps their silence by day and eerie calls at night mean that they are partly nocturnal and less likely to be molested.

From 1848, when the flightless New Zealand rail *Notornis hochstetteri* was described from a subfossil skull, until 1949, only two live birds of this kind were seen—and [...] 1907 book on extinct birds. (COURTESY OF

Once common enough on the main islands of New Zealand for the Polynesian Maoris to eat and know as tuataras, these old-style reptiles cling to life on offshore rocky islets as the sole representatives of the order Rhynchocephalia—the "beak heads" of Mesozoic times.

Different subspecies live on each of the big islands, seemingly unaffected yet by the spread of civilization.

The tieke is logically called the saddleback, for across the black feathers of its 10-inch body it wears a bright chestnut saddle. Although its shape suggests that of a small crow, it actually belongs to a family found only in New Zealand: the New Zealand wattlebirds, with three different kinds known—one (the huia) believed extinct, and the other two (the tieke and the kokako) extremely rare and feared to be diminishing in numbers. A fine tieke came to an apple that we speared on a short branch in a woodland, and we had a chance to admire its large sharp beak and orange wattles, its short powerful flights and determined hopping along the tree limb to the bait.

For a while we thought the tieke had a mate, a smaller yellowish green bird that came to the apple every time it was unattended. But the interloper was a bellbird, named for its loud ringing call, one of the brush-tongued honeyeaters of the South Pacific area that went through a period of near extinction for no known cause at the turn of the last century. We hope that the handsome saddleback, the tieke, will make a like recovery.

The final rarity we journeyed far to see while in New Zealand, the tuatara, is a lizardlike reptile that depends upon birds, and certain shrubs, as well as solitude for survival. It takes refuge for the day in the nesting burrows dug by shearwaters, relatives of the albatrosses known locally as "muttonbirds," which roam the far reaches of the Pacific Ocean when not raising young on New Zealand's offshore islands. All of the shearwaters had gone by the time we arrived, leaving the tuataras in complete possession of the deep burrows in the steep island slopes. On sunny days the 2 foot reptiles come to the burrow opening to bask, their sensitive eyes protected by vertically slit pupils like those of a crocodile or cat. By night the tuataras stalk the slopes to catch large wingless crickets and slow-moving snails that share the island sanctuaries. Whether, in season, a tuatara takes an occasional shearwater egg or chick to eat underground has not been proved, although suspected.

Probably this partnership is of long standing, perhaps since shearwaters appeared on earth. The tuataras have a still more ancient ancestry, since they are the last survivors of a group of reptiles called Rhynchocephalians ("beak heads") that were contemporary with the extinct dinosaurs. The third member of this partnership is an evergreen shrub with shiny stinking leaves that somehow appeal to goats. It grows well on the windswept coasts in the soil kept loose by burrowing shearwaters and fertilized with their droppings. The shrub (Coprosma), in turn, gives some anchorage to the slopes and solid shade that prevents the summer sun from baking the soil to a hard crust through which a shearwater cannot dig. If man's goats destroy the shrubs, the shearwaters are shut out and hunt elsewhere for nesting sites. The tuataras then cannot find shelter for the day, and soon disappear. Anything else that interferes with the nesting of the sea-birds has a similar effect on the ancient reptiles.

Before we made our trip by plane, car, fishing boat, and on foot to visit tuataras in their burrows, a friend warned us never to handle one of these reptiles carelessly. He had a deep scar in one arm where a tuatara had bitten out a piece of flesh. The animal can move quickly and powerfully if necessary, although most of its actions seem sluggish. Yet its way of life leaves it vulnerable. According to Dr. W. H. Dawbin, a New Zealander who has been making a special study of live tuataras, their eggs take about 12 months to hatch—all this while they are inviting morsels of food in the soil for any animal that can find them and dig them out. After hatching, a tuatara needs nearly 20 years to reach maturity—longer than any other rep-tile known and longer even than our own species. Thereafter a tuatara may survive to be 100 or older, no one knows for sure. The Maoris, who en-joy a meal of tuataras at least in retrospect, claim that these reptiles can get to the two-century mark, as some of earth's oldest animals.

Despite the protection now given to tuataras on offshore islands around New Zealand, they may be in danger in a way that no single government can control. The shearwaters, which share their burrows with tuataras, are caught up in a worldwide decline affecting the reproductive success of all pelagic birds, due apparently to DDT and other pesticides related to it. Since the middle 1940's these and radioactive wastes have been accumu-lating—devastating genii from the technological bottle. We know the form-ula to turn them loose, but no way to make them harmless to kinds of life with which we have no cause to war.

As peace-loving land-dwellers our terror grows to see the whole planet poisoned, to face an increasing threat in a poorer world for the temporary benefit of people in their battle with insect pests. To the natural hazards for life, technological man has added a new one. It calls to mind on the one hand the scientific quipster who said "Dilution is no solution to pol-lution," and on the other the pessimistic answer to the question Shake-speare put into lines for Lady Macbeth, "Will all great Neptune's ocean wash this . . . from my hand?" To so contaminate the oceans that the effects are felt on every continent is such a global calamity that we dread the ecological carelessnesses that can come next.

For the toothed whales and the savage sharks, as for more than 150 different kinds of birds that feed exclusively on animals from the open sea, man-made poisons pose a greater threat than anything in their millennia of evolution. What can be done to help the 17 kinds of penguins, the 14 of broad-winged albatrosses, the 56 of shearwaters and fulmars, the 22 of auks, murres, and puffins, the 3 of tropic birds, the 9 of boobies and gannets, the 5 of frigate birds, and the many terns that flit and feed over the open oceans so gracefully that we call them "sea swallows"? Only for one, so far, has a program of counterbalancing improvements been started. The others, like the seals and sea lions, are on their own, in an increasingly hostile world with nowhere else to turn.

The one petrel species receiving special care was already a rare bird before DDT became a problem. Apparently exterminated on the isolated islands of Bermuda in 1631, it was rediscovered and studied just in time to trace a progressive decline in reproductive success. For a variety of reasons, including insecticides picked up in food at sea, the Bermuda petrel or cahow has raised to the flying stage about 3 percent fewer chicks each year over the last ten years. The total population of about 100 birds of this kind is expected to shrink to zero by 1978 unless spectacular improvements are made in their nesting performance.

Following up a gracious invitation from Mr. David Wingate, conservation officer for the Bermuda Department of Agriculture, we spent a while in Bermuda during April recently, mostly to understand the scientific, humanitarian ways he tries to save the cahow from extinction. Despite stormy weather, we accompanied him on the perilous rounds he makes every day or two from the end of October to the beginning of June, to check on the welfare of the remaining birds of this vanishing kind. We ducked the spray whipped by gusty winds as we bounced across the wave tops by motorboat to offshore islets along Bermuda's southeastern fringe. Our guide knew from years of experience how to minimize exposure to the full violence of the waves sweeping into Castle Harbour through the deep water of Castle Roads. He could judge within inches the correct place to drop anchor before backing the boat into the lee of the jagged, rocky islets. At exactly the right instant he stepped from the stern—swaying atop the highest wave—onto the shelving limestone, and helped us to disembark at equally critical moments. After securing the tie line, he led us up the almost vertical cliffs that William Beebe once described as "effectively arranged, serried ranks of pins, daggers, needles, half-opened scissors, knives, nails, fish-hooks, arrows and bits of broken glasss . . . tempered to marble hardness, and sculptured and whetted to razor sharpness by the waves."

These are the bastions that protected cahows for 300 years while the world of science believed them extinct. It is on the storm-wracked summits of these islets that there is still a chance to improve conditions for nesting cahows in ways these sea birds will accept. Fortunately, the Bermuda government and David Wingate are determined that this chance, which may well be the last, will not be missed. By tightening the birds' defenses locally, it may be possible to tide them over until the poisons that cahows meet on the open seas diminish in some natural way.

Most of the past hazards met by cahows no longer threaten them. No ship captain, in order to have a supply of fresh meat on future visits, is now likely to leave a few hogs ashore to feed and breed freely, destroying the ground-nesting birds. The "great abundance of Hogges," mentioned by the chronicler after the wreck of the *Sea Venture* on Bermuda in 1609, disappeared without a survivor. Even in those days, when the leader of the party, Sir George Somers, hunted hogs "to the number of two and thirty at one time," it is unlikely that any of these animals swam through the turbulent waters to the outlying islets on which cahows still nest. Although there is evidence that a cedar forest once shielded these outlying rocks, they are too small and rough to have supported a population of introduced hogs.

People and cats are no longer a problem. Bermudians who cross the rough water by boat are kept well aware of the need to protect the cahows. Only historians now quote the words of Nathanial Butler, first governor of the islands, who wrote in 1619 that the cahow

> is a night bird, and all the daye long lies hidd in holes of the rocks, whence both themselves and their young are in great numbers extracted with ease, and prove (especially the young) so pleasing in a dish, as ashamed I am to tell how many dosen of them have been devoured by some of our northern stomacks, even at one only a meale.

Conspicuous signs at every landing explain that pets, even on a leash, are strictly forbidden. Visitors too must get special permission from the warden to go ashore where cahows are nesting.

The black rats, which arrived with the first colonists, swim well. Norway rats, which reached Bermuda later, occasionally make the hazardous crossing. We could see rusting cans lying among the bushes, as though left by a generation of litterbugs. Each can conceals from the rain a few wafers containing warfarin, a poison that rats cannot taste. Even so, during the 1969 breeding season rats did reach two cahow nests on one islet and destroyed the parents as well as the young.

Two different seabirds might be expected to compete with cahows for nest sites, but one of them—Audubon's shearwater, which is at its northern limit of the cahow's range—is now too rare to matter. Fossils on Bermuda show that it once was abundant there. Probably it lived amicably beside the cahows for thousands of years. Elsewhere in its nesting range, which extends from the Bahamas to the Grenadines in the West Indies, Audubon's shearwater is famous for producing weird cries—like a laughing witch—on its nesting grounds at night. This has led to wide use of the French *diablotin* (little devil) for Audubon's shearwater.

What simpler explanation could be offered than that these birds were responsible for the "clamor," the "shrieking and din" at dusk recorded by men shipwrecked on Bermuda? After finding themselves aground on "the dangerous and dreaded Islands of the Bermudas, feared and avoyded by all sea travellers alive, above any other place in the world," the marooned people from the *Sea Venture* discovered that "all the Faries of the rocks were but flocks of birds, and all the Divils that haunted the woods were but heards of swine."

The loud and terrifying cries described by sailors shipwrecked on Bermuda seem not to have come from the cahows, whose call during their courtship period is a drawn-out, ghostly *oooooh* or *aaaaaw*. After mating, so far as human ears can detect, cahows are silent, even in the nest. Yet they resemble Audubon's shearwaters enough in size, shape, and coloration as to be confused by uncritical islanders; even their eggs and chicks look much alike.

It was not until the destruction of the main island's inland, soil-burrowing population of cahows by man and domestic animals that the Bermudian petrel came into competition with other, more numerous and aggressive seabirds. The cahows were forced to accept natural cliff holes and crevices on exposed islets, where the soil had disappeared because of seaside erosion and undermining by land crabs.

These nearly vertical cliffs, with their holes and shelflike limestone strata, having long been the nest sites for slightly larger fliers which Bermudians call longtails; elsewhere they are known as white-tailed tropic birds. By nesting in these inaccessible places, longtails remained numerous during the great famine caused by an overpopulation of rats from 1614 to 1620. By contrast, the cahows and Audubon's shearwaters disappeared under the combined onslaught of hogs, hungry people, and swarming rats. After 1621, cahows were mistakenly regarded as extinct.

The conflict between longtails and cahows continued unsuspected, preventing any appreciable increase in the numbers of the rare petrel. Actually, cahow eggs are laid in January and hatch in early March. The longtails do not return to Bermuda before mid-March. But although each cahow chick in a longtail nest has about two weeks to grow before competition appears at the door, neither the chick nor an adult cahow is any match for a tropic bird. The newcomer simply enters and removes any occupants it finds,

usually killing them in the process of eviction. Indeed, the battered specimen of a cahow now in the collection of the Smithsonian Institution
shows just the sort of damage a longtail might inflict with its sharp beak.
The specimen was collected in 1945 by Fred T. Hall, an American Army
officer who was stationed on Bermuda during World War II. He found it
among beach drift near Kindley Air Force Base, which is quite close to the
islets where cahows still nest.

Cahows are special to Bermudians, who know that these birds breed nowhere else. Longtails, by contrast, are numerous and widespread in the
West Indies and on islets of the Indian and Pacific Oceans. Everyone
favors biasing the island world for cahows.

A first step seemed easy and humane. Wherever cahows adopt a longtail nest site and start a family, the conservation officer can install a piece
of plyboard fitted to the entranceway. The *first* doorframe tried has a large
hole, letting the parent cahows come and go easily. With little hesitation
they accept the change. Then the board is replaced with others having
progressively smaller holes, until the cahows can just squeeze through.
Theoretically, when the plumper-bodied longtails arrive they will be
fenced out.

But when a pair of tropic birds returns to a nest site they have used before, they show far more determination than anyone expected. Compress-
ing their bodies, they force themselves through any hole a cahow can manage comfortably. As long as the pair live, no tight door frame will keep
them out. On the other hand, longtails that are *prospecting* for a new site
will make no such effort. Consequently, the only longtail nests offering a
secure place for cahows to breed are ones from which an established pair
of tropic birds has been eliminated.

In the long run, it is better to take still more time and prepare nests for
cahows in their traditional breeding site—atop islets where soil would
normally be present. David Wingate showed us where he had used a metal
tool to cut a groove almost horizontally in the limestone, ending in a shallow cavity about 15 inches in diameter. After covering this channel and
cavity with wire mesh to make an artificial entrance tunnel and nest
chamber, he had applied thick cement and roofed it permanently—except
at the tunnel entrance and at an observation hole above the chamber. He
had concealed his construction work with earth, rocks, and vegetation,
even dropping a handful of plant debris atop the fitted concrete cap which
closed the observation hole and kept out rain.

With justifiable pride he lifted the cover from one of these artifical nests
that had been discovered and used by a pair of cahows. We peered in and
could barely see the downy, slate-gray chick on the sandy floor about a

A pearl-gray and enormously obese chick of the Bermudian petrel in the darkness of its underground nest chamber. When its parents cease bringing the chick food by regurgitation, it will become slim, fully feathered and capable of emerging from the burrow to fly and swim and feed itself.

foot below the hole. Under its feet, a scattering of still-green sea purslane stems and leaves provided a semblance of a nest. But the chick itself, viewed from above, was so roly-poly, so fat from repeated feedings by attentive parents and from no exercise, that we could hardly tell head from tail. A small black beak stuck out at one end. A whitish rump patch marked the other. Its eyes were hidden completely by its fuzz.

Using a compact electronic flashgun, we photographed the chick, disturbing it as little as possible. Conservation policy forbids any handling of cahow chicks, for fear the excitement will cause them to regurgitate their last meal and then go hungry for hours or days until the parents bring more food.

Just as among human families, cahow parents differ considerably in the amount of attention they give their young. Some arrive nightly with food and continue to feed their offspring until its program of development calls for it to slim down and be able to creep through the long tunnel to the open. Other parents seem more casual, arriving with food every other night or so, and commonly deserting their chick long before it can emerge. Chicks vary, too. Generally they emerge night after night to exercise their wings for perhaps a week before actually flying away. A few depart after only two or three nights of exercising.

As yet there are no good answers to the questions we asked about how long young cahows roam at sea before returning to nest, or how long mature cahows live. With these birds so few, the slight risks from attaching a numbered metal anklet seem too great; no cahow is yet banded. A shiny marker might attract a hungry fish, leading it to seize a cahow resting on the open sea. Probably the common aluminum leg bands would corrode to uselessness anyway, exposed so often to seawater, before the wearer returned to be tallied again on Bermuda. Everything is being done to safeguard each cahow, to improve its chances of survival. If the persistent pesticides the birds are certain to get in their normal food from the open sea are to be counterbalanced, Bermuda's offshore islets must be made ideal.

With 26 nesting pairs in 1968, only seven chicks were expected to survive beyond two weeks after hatching. Instead, eight passed this critical age in places where longtails were unlikely to interfere. In 1969, from about the same number of nests, only 5 or possibly 6 youngsters reached the flying stage. They disappeared into two solid weeks of southeast gale. The sample is still too small to prove that the downward trend in reproductive success is being reversed. Yet it gives some hope.

It is followed by the dream that cahows will become so crowded on their tiny islets that some will spread as colonists to nearby Nonsuch Island. Nonsuch is part of Bermuda's wildlife sanctuary system, kept ready for petrels and shearwaters to use. Its 14¼ acres are covered with deep soil, set out with blight-resistant cedars and other native trees in the temporary shelter of Australian pines and tamarisks. An estimated 10,000 pairs of cahows could nest there; Audubon's shearwaters could too, if once they got a start.

At present, the only sign of a cahow on Nonsuch is a white skeleton hanging in the doorway of the main building where William Beebe worked from 1928 to 1931, and where David Wingate now resides for much of the year. The bones were collected from crumbling burrows where cahows once nested in large numbers. Digging those bones, cleaning and assembling them painstakingly, were minor parts of the far-reaching studies that are yielding more information every year about this rare, gentle, threatened bird.

From the windows of the big house and from the porches outside, most of the landmarks in the recent history of the cahow are plainly visible. In

A skeleton of the Bermudian petrel—the cahow—assembled with great care by David Wingate, the Conservation Officer who has done so much to protect this endangered bird.

the distance is the forbidding pinnacle of Gurnet Rock, which seems to have been too barren of soil or crevices to have been useful to cahows in recent times. Nearer, and to the right, are Castle Island and the islets where cahows now live. The original specimen was collected from a rock crevice about 20 feet above high water on the southeast side of Castle Island by Louis L. A. Mowbray in February of 1906. But the mounted bird, now in the collection of the American Museum of Natural History, was not recognized until 1916 to be a kind of petrel unnamed by science. It received full description as *Æstrelata* (now *Pterodroma*) *cahow*.

To the smaller islets in 1951 went Louis S. Mowbray, his son, the present director of the Bermuda Government Aquarium and Museum at Flatt's Bridge; Dr. Robert Cushman Murphy, curator of birds at the American Museum of Natural History, and his wife; and a keen schoolboy, David Wingate. They discovered nesting cahows, confirming that the supposedly extinct bird still lived. Miraculously, they realized, it had clung to its offshore rocks even though these had been used during World War II as bombing targets for the air force!

From visiting these same islets, we could easily conclude that the sea itself threatens the cahows more than anything else. Constantly it hammers

The Hawaiian goose, known locally as the nene, became endangered in its sole habitat —the wet places among the lava fields where, while molting and flightless, it could not escape from introduced dogs. (REX GARY SCHMIDT, BUREAU OF SPORT FISHERIES AND WILDLIFE.)

at those porous rocks, undermining them, causing their collapse, shrinking the area to which cahows still cling. Yet now the sea threatens less for its violence than for its poisons, because of the invisible insidious pollution it has received and still is receiving from distant continents.

Most island-dwellers, which include more than half of the world's endangered wildlife, have not yet had to react to anything as subtle as poisons. Nor has erosion due to natural causes destroyed their world. Their peril, instead, is from people and introduced predators or competitors. Directly or indirectly, they are victims of recent changes. So seldom has a way been found to help them that each success shines with special splendor.

The little Hawaiian goose, now chosen as the state bird and known locally by its Polynesian name of nene (pronounced nay-nay), is one happy triumph of recent years. Presumably its ancestors were a pair of strong-flying geese that somehow found these islands in mid-Pacific. About the same size and weight as a Canada goose, they found food and nesting sites high on the slopes of big volcanoes, such as Mauna Kea and Mauna Loa on the major island of Hawaii. Gradually they became adept at running over the lava, seldom taking to their wings. With no native predators to trouble them, nenes lost most of their wariness and, at molting time, their ability to fly. Unlike most geese, they shed all of their flight feathers at once. Until new ones grow to useful length, the birds are grounded. Their only shelter is in ill-drained pools among the lava fields.

Men with dogs and guns found Hawaiian geese easy targets and delicious eating. The introduced mongooses from continental India spread into the lava country in search of almost anything edible. Against these new hazards, the nenes could not maintain themselves. Even when their volcanic territory was set aside as a national park in 1916 and hunting supposedly ceased, the exotic predators continued to reduce the goose population. In 1950, less than 30 survivors could be found.

In desperation, the Hawaiian park managers caught three of these rarities and shipped them to England, accepting an offer from Commander Peter Scott to try breeding them under complete protection on his experimental waterfowl sanctuary, known as The Wildfowl Trust. By 1957 he had succeeded in raising 30 young birds. In 1964 and 1965, he sent 100 nenes to Hawaii for release—and still had almost an equal number retained as breeding stock. Those still on English soil at Slimbridge charmed us as they paddled around the marshy ponds and begged visitors for food. This includes a special whole wheat bread developed to match their needs. Gentler and more lovable geese we could not ask for. Now that successful nesting has been reported again from Hawaii, the survival of this species appears secure.

Life is not all uphill. But to every kind of animal, time brings challenges that must be surmounted as the price of progress. In recent times, our own species has carelessly and increasingly provided for life on remote islands most of the barriers in the path toward the future. Carefully we can give the extra help that puts these animals over the top. Indeed, we are the only part of nature able to do so deliberately. Therein lies our uniqueness, our cultural adaptation, and our greatest challenge. In what better way could we earn our self-respect and prove our full potential? It is our world, as well as theirs, that we would keep rich by becoming stewards instead of despoilers. Today, as never before, we have the knowledge to impel us. We realize fully for the first time our own isolation on an inhabitable earth, as though it were an island in the universe, separated from any other by vast spaces we cannot cross. The plight of island life is ours as well.

CHAPTER 8

ANIMALS
OF
THE
HIGH
PEAKS

THE FIRST TIME we drove over Logan Pass, crossing at 6,664 feet elevation from the western to the eastern slopes of the Continental Divide, we left our car in a parking space and hiked the well-marked trail to better than 8,000 feet above sea level. This close to the Canadian border and halfway through July, we walked in a delightful alpine meadow considerably higher than tree line. Glacier lilies and other delicate flowers grew lush in the soggy soil where little rivulets trickled, bringing cold meltwater from snowfields slightly farther up the slope.

Despite the steady breeze, butterflies of several kinds flitted gently back and forth. Sparrow-sized birds we recognized by their tail-wagging to be pipits had arrived from their seashore wintering grounds to find nest sites among the granite crags.

Through our field glasses we scanned the higher ground, particularly one distant area where the steeper cliffs had shielded the land from snowstorms and the sun had already cleared the load of ice from over a clump of willows. All winter the yellow-green withes had been held flat against the frozen ground. Now they were leafing out at the same time as they regained their upcurving, nearly upright stance.

Among the willows, snow-white animals moved as a small herd. We recognized them as Rocky Mountain goats, the North American counterpart of the chamois in alpine parts of the Old World. Including adults of both sexes and young, nearly a dozen nibbled at the greenery. At the same time they progressed in a direction that would take them before long into the

Mountain goats, with their spiky horns, are chamois-like animals that avoid winter snows by descending the slopes from craggy heights where they find food and safety all summer. (DAVID L. SPENCER, BUREAU OF SPORT FISHERIES AND WILDLIFE.)

shade of the massive mountain. Could we climb close enough to photograph them before they passed the sunny area? We decided to try.

Across risky snow bridges over the larger streams of meltwater, from one rock outcropping to the next, we hurried—always upslope, bent double so as to be least conspicuous to the feeding goats. Haste, excitement, and the thinner air of the high altitude to which we were unaccustomed, combined to make our breathing fast and a little difficult. When at last we got within 50 feet of the herd and rose up into plain sight to steady the camera on a rock, we could not hold it still. Our movie record shows the surprised goats and the mountain rising and falling in time with the photographer's quick breathing, jiggling in tune with a racing heart! That was once we regretted not having lugged our sturdy tripod. Never again have we had so fine an opportunity to film these wary animals at such close range.

The little herd made no attempt to run. Had they been skilled mountaineers, with nothing to fear from human hands, they could not have moved on more graciously, confidently, or with greater dignity. In less than a minute, all reached the shade, continuing around the steep side of Logan Peak. It was we who were apprehensive as we retraced our steps over the slanting snowfields and melting ice bridges, to the meadow of alpine flowers and the parking place where we had left our car. Gravity seemed to pull at us more on the descent than it did while we climbed.

Before we left this beautiful pass, we thought about some of the difficulties the mountain goats and similar animals face around the world. According to season, they climb higher or lower on the slopes, finding pathways across exposed cliffs on ledges only an inch or two in width. To reach the edible plants at these elevations and to escape danger among the high peaks, they must constantly be ready to move. A newborn kid, in fact, stands up when 10 minutes old, nurses 10 minutes later, and is off with its parents, jumping from rock to rock at 30 minutes of age.

No doubt many goats fall to their death, for the hazards of the heights are horrifying to contemplate. Gusts of strong wind come without warning. Hailstorms and pelting rain beat frequently against the mountain and everything on it. In good weather, foxes and mountain lions follow the goats as high as they dare, trying particularly to separate a kid from its protecting mother. Eagles learn to swoop at them, and feast when a frightened kid reacts in the wrong way. Yet, for millenia, the mountain goats have survived between bare rocks and harsh elements above and the predators below. Perhaps the goats were never numerous. Today they are getting ever scarcer and, in the United States, are virtually limited to national parks along the Rockies and coast ranges, where they have protection from hunters.

In North America the bighorn sheep seldom go as high as the mountain goats and, in winter, show a greater readiness to spread out into the valleys and even adjacent prairie land to forage. This brings them into competition with domestic sheep and cattle and lets mountain people keep closer count on the number of bighorns. Winters take a terrible toll, for the bighorns have special needs we can easily forget. Safety is foremost. Always they must stay in terrain that offers plenty of quick escape routes in case predators, whether wolves or hunters, should appear. Secondary is their choice of south- or west-facing slopes, which may be less subject to winter gales and deep snow, or just the area where winter is shortest and the bighorns' favorite vegetation grows. In their diet they are highly selective, and on their winter ranges often find little that is digestible because domestic sheep have been grazing there all summer. Ranchers who take compassion on starving mountain sheep report that giving them hay does no good; the bighorns cannot digest it. They grow weak from hunger and fall prey to diseases and parasites, even when no predators attack.

In the craggy region around East Kootenay in southern British Columbia, the bighorn sheep suffered from three bad winters in a row, beginning in 1964. Six herds, on which game wardens kept a census by light air-

The massive horns of the ram, which are used in contests over mating rights, seem out of proportion to the slender legs of the agile bighorn sheep. (CHARLES G. HANSEN, BUREAU OF SPORT FISHERIES AND WILDLIFE.)

plane, shrank from a total of nearly 3,000 animals in 1964 to less than 650. One herd diminished from 200 to just 3. Yet so inborn and decisive is the choice of winter rangeland for bighorns that the animals passed by areas in which they could have found food. Instead, they went to traditional territory where escape was surer—and so was starvation. During the two centuries or less since white men arrived in numbers along the western mountains in North America, changes in the hazards for bighorns have come faster than could be matched by adjustments in the animals' way of life.

So often we too are readier for yesterday's challenges than those we meet today or that will face us tomorrow. A century—three generations of people or ten of sheep—gives too little chance to verify the value in some cultural or inherited trait. Conditions now change so fast that former choices become invalid. Modern hazards can rarely be matched by a new behavior among animals of the peaks. The sheep that escaped from wolf and eagle might teach their young or inherit the ability to learn quickly. But how can the wild sheep cope with the tame sheep that have fattened in the mountain valleys and been driven off as soon as the food grew scarce? Or with the hunter who never shows himself, while his bullets speed up the mountain faster than any eagle flies?

We think of the klipspringers that formerly thrived in rocky mountains across Africa from northern Nigeria to the southern Sudan, south to the very tip of the great continent. On their little round hoofs these "cliff-springing" antelope leaped from crag to crag, often clinging as though with suction cups. They learned to escape from leopard and lion, wildcat and constrictor snake, by climbing to lookout points and watching with sharp eyes for any movement that might betray a predator. Silhouetted against the sky, they made perfect targets for gunners. Their meat tasted enough like venison and their back hair was springy, suitable for stuffing saddlebags, that klipspringers fairly invited attention. And native people, who had not been able to reach these animals easily with spear or arrow, took little time to acquire and learn to use a rifle—less time than was needed to learn not to shoot the last klipspringer.

Only a fraction of the former population survives, almost all of them in rocky terrain forbidding to any man lugging a gun or a carcass weighing 30 pounds. This is why our friend, Dr. Douglas Hey, who is Director of Nature Conservation for the Cape Province in South Africa, had to say to us sadly on one field trip, "There used to be klipspringers among these rocky outcrops when I was a boy. But I can't show you one today."

Essentially the same answer awaited us in Europe, when we reached the Swiss alps and expressed a wish to get within camera distance of some wild animals of high country: the chamois, the ibex, and the alpine marmot. "There are plenty of marmots," an experienced field naturalist told us. "But you would be surer to see chamois and ibex if you go to our Swiss national park, in the easternmost corner of our country, or cross into the fine Italian park of northwestern Italy, or to the French alpine park just across the border from it."

Italy has chamois and ibex too in the Parco Nazionale d'Abruzzo in the Apennines. Chamois survive elsewhere in the wild mostly as rather small animals, weighing up to 90 pounds, in the Caucasus, on remote peaks of Greece, and in the Pyrenees. Larger specimens roam the wild Carpathian Mountains of Czechoslovakia and Rumania, where bucks weigh as much as 135 pounds. Chamois suggest to us the ewes of mountain sheep in western North America, except that their horns curl backward into hooks near the sharp tips. These animals hurl themselves across chasms for distances as great as 20 feet, stopping without accident on flat rock surfaces no bigger than a dinner plate. Or they jump more than 10 feet straight up or down, from ledge to ledge. In early winter, however, snow forces these animals lower on the mountains, to the zone of evergreen coniferous trees. Apparently many chamois perish by starting upslope too early in spring and being cut off by storms or killed in avalanches as they try to reach their craggy peaks.

The ibex is now even rarer outside protected parks, although it retreats still higher on the mountains into dizzy crags, where it must have difficulty finding enough of the right kinds of vegetation to satisfy its appetite. A full-grown ram of this kind of goat weighs 200 pounds, of which about 30 pounds are inert massive horns that curve obliquely backward for as much as 60 inches. Less than 2,500 are believed to survive in northern Spain. A few inhabit the Pindus range in northern Greece or find privacy on Greek islands and on Crete, where they have a history dating back 30 centuries to days of the Minoan civilization.

The ibex's predicament became evident more than a century ago, when Europeans suddenly realized that only about 60 individuals remained, all of them in the northwest corner of Italy on a spectacular area of alpine country known as the Gran Paradiso. King Victor Emmanuel II proclaimed this a royal hunting park in 1856, effectively closing it to exploitation. In 1922, when it became a national park, the ibex population was found to have grown considerably and spread across the border into the mountains of adjacent France. By 1938 the herds in this area totaled about 3,000 animals. But during World War II they were hunted wantonly and, in 1945, only 419 ibex could be found. Given prompt protection, their numbers rose again. Counting the animals that were transported from the

Gran Paradiso and released in the 64 square miles of the Swiss national park, an area established primarily as a sanctuary for ibex, the present population in parks is approaching 3,000 again.

Even the lovely high valleys near tree line and above in the lofty Himalayas no longer afford much safety for the animals that, although unfamiliar, are best fitted to live there. As of April, 1966, these endangered kinds of wildlife included the red goral, a chamoislike animal of high Tibet, Assam, and Burma, the goatlike takins of Bhutan and alpine parts of adjacent China, the sheeplike Nilgiri tahrs of India, and the markhor goats of forbidding peaks from India to Afghanistan. So few scientists have had an opportunity to explore these parts of Asia that far too little is known of the agile cud-chewing animals now becoming scarce there.

Only in zoos have we seen alive these goatlike and sheeplike animals of the Old World. Zoo keepers tell us that they all adapt readily to confinement, except for the ram ibex, which never seems to lose his readiness to come on the run and bowl over his keeper. Men who have been butted insist that it is all in fun for the ibex—never malicious. Yet behavior of this kind is unsuitable in a domesticated animal. Were these the criteria that led our ancestors among the Stone Age Eurasians to choose the sheep and goat they did, from the various kinds available? The domestic goat may be an outcome from a cross between a tame ibex (*Capra ibex*) and a bezoar goat (*C. aegagrus*), which is native to the old Persian area of the Middle East. Perhaps its ancestry is further diversified by an admixture of the Caucasian wild goat (*C. cydricus*), an animal that is now a rarity both in zoos and in its native haunts. We wonder whether the advantage seen in the domestic goat (now known as *C. hircus*) was its versatility in food, its willingness to climb a tree instead of a crag. Herded about in Mediterranean countries, goats have become destroyers of forests, creators of deserts, a plague upon the land. How did our ancestors make such a mistake? None of the wild goats cause comparable damage. Instead, where they are protected from human interference and some predators, they come into a natural balance with the land. They adjust the size of their populations automatically to match the food supply, devastating nothing.

No one knows where domestic sheep originated either, for no closely similar animal lives wild. But the butting habit persists in all, and is most spectacular among the bighorn sheep of North American mountains. These are the magnificent creatures that wildlife photographer Cleveland Grant captured on movie film as the "Rams of the Rimrocks"; they choose opponents, walk apart like duelists on some narrow ledge, and then race to bang their heavy horns together and somehow settle ownership of territory and meek ewes.

We remember a domestic sheep that gave us trouble with this butting habit. She was several years old and had had lambs of her own, but was still known as "Lambie" from the days when she was practically a house-pet of the postmaster in a tiny community far north in the Canadian province of Ontario. From our summer cottage we hiked over the hilltop once or twice a day to fill pails with fresh water from the postmaster's spring. Lambie always came running to have her head scratched, and pushed headlong against us to get attention. With a pailful of water in each hand, we could not continue scratching Lambie all day as she would have liked. Then she butted, spilling the water if not the water carrier, who was trying to follow a narrow, twisting sheep trail up the hill.

The wild sheep and goats, alone or with their near kin such as chamois, are far from alone on the rough and precipitous high country where they seem so much at home. This is eagle land, affording nesting eyries for the larger birds of prey and the giants among vultures and condors. Today almost every one of these big birds is endangered.

Biggest among these birds in the Old World is the bearded vulture, whose pointed wings and feeble talons help identify it as a true kite. On pinions spreading 8 or 10 feet tip to tip, it soars most of the day on the updrafts from mountain valleys, cocking its head to study the land below, searching for the carcass of an animal—preferably one that other vultures have already picked clean. The bearded giant gets its name from a tuft of spiny black feathers that droop below its nostrils like an Oriental mustache. A mask-shaped marking across its eyes gives the bird an appearance of fierceness. Yet, like the smaller kites of Europe and the New World, it is unfitted for clutching any struggling prey larger than a small lizard, a big snail, or an insect. The bearded vulture specializes, instead, on swallowing whole the small bones from carcasses it finds and carrying larger bones aloft, dropping them on rocks that will break the bones into manageable fragments. Marrow from long bones is the bird's favorite food.

Formerly, the bearded vultures scavenged over the peaks from the Pyrenees to the Himalayas and south almost to the Cape of Good Hope. But sheepherders, impressed by the wingspan of the giant birds, began calling them lammergeiers ("lamb killers") and persecuting them, even accusing them of carrying off children from mountain valleys. Now only an occasional bird of this kind is seen over the Atlas Mountains of North Africa, the Alps, and the Carpathians. The remainder stay near the Himalayas, soaring like sailplanes on set wings, steering by slight movements of the long dihedral tail, and tending nests with a solitary egg or youngster high on some vertical rock face.

With the increased use of poison to get rid of nuisance animals, such as the alpine marmots that compete with domestic sheep for summer forage,

The Central America tapir climbs and swims to roam the mountainous parts of the wet tropics, crossing streams or plunging through dense undergrowth to stay alive where jaguars and pumas are a hazard.

a new peril for the scavengers has appeared. The vultures of all kinds, large and small, die of the poison they get in carcasses. Even the marrow of the bones can contain enough toxic material to be deadly, if not in one dose, then in repeated doses. In this respect, the animals that prey upon the herbivores or scavenge for their remains are in greater danger than those that eat plants directly.

The birds of the mountain peaks are free to come and go as they choose. But animals on the high ground, isolated through their inability to cross the surrounding barrier of unsuitable lowlands, may be as vulnerable as any on a remote island. Any feature that makes these creatures worth hunting, such as edible meat or attractive skins, or even rarity alone, is enough to direct them toward oblivion.

Above 10,000 feet altitude in the Andes is the territory of the wooly or mountain tapir, whose trails often ascend to the thin grasslands above tree line. Weighing 500 pounds or more, these animals normally choose a moderate grade, one so easy for a man to follow that mountain roadbuilders are often accused of letting tapirs do their engineering. No doubt this habit occasionally helps a jaguar creep up on a tapir to within pouncing distance, or a spectacled bear vary its herbivorous diet with an occasional meal of tapir meat. Human hunters stalk both the bear and the tapir, and keep the numbers of both animals so small that less is known about their habits than those of bears and tapirs elsewhere in the world.

Tropical America has two other kinds of tapirs at lower elevation, one in Brazil and the other ranging from Ecuador and Colombia to Guatemala. One more is an endangered animal in rain forests of Southeast Asia. All are the remnants of a once-numerous group of animals known from fossils in Eurasia and North America, where none survive today. Those that live along both sides of the high Andes offer almost the only hope that this evolutionary experiment will lead on to greater variety and additional adaptations in the future. For the sake of some meat, which is generally decomposing by the time it is dragged down to a human community, it would be a pity to lose the mountain tapir forever.

Remote as most animals appear in the high Andes, and little as they produce that offers food to mankind, they are raided repeatedly by hunters and trappers who make quick trips to the treeless heights and lofty slopes. There, at between 10,000 and 18,000 feet elevation in Chile, Bolivia, and Peru, men recently came close to exterminating the small animals that have, for size and weight, the most valuable pelts in the world. Chinchillas are colonial rodents, each 9 to 15 inches long, with a 3- to 6-inch tail which twitches from side to side when the animal is nervous. Apparently monogamous, chinchillas dig in among the rocks of mountain slopes, staying higher than most predators go and tolerating the cold within a coat of silky-soft dense fur.

During the early 1900's, Chile alone exported more than 200,000 chinchilla skins annually. At that time, a coat made of the best quality "royal" wild chinchilla sold for as much as $100,000. Soon the hunters could find no more. Captive animals, raised with great care where the weather never reached temperatures intolerably high for them, contribute almost all of the chinchilla fur sold today. Now in the Chilean mountains, where the little rodents have been given legal protection, enforcement is letting the survivors make a slow comeback. Once again chinchillas can be seen in the sunshine, nipping off vegetation among the rocks and holding it in their paws while they sit on their haunches, eating away in plain sight.

No one in these countries seems to care if the rodent neighbors of the chinchillas disappear. These are the mountain vizcachas, whose large ears and hopping gait give them the appearance of long-tailed rabbits. They cluster their colonies and underground burrows near streams all the way up the slopes from 3,000 to 15,000 feet elevation, and come into competition with domestic animals for the scanty grasses and other plant foods on the semiarid hillsides.

At still higher levels, on the loftiest of grasslands, law enforcement fails almost completely to protect the shrinking population of little camel-like animals, the vicuñas. Weighing 80 to 150 pounds and standing about 30 inches tall at the shoulder, they run from danger at better than 35 miles an hour. This is fast traveling in the thin air of high elevations. At close range, they spit in self-defense. None of these ancestral habits saves them from being hunted and shot for the fine silky fleece they bear. Lowland legislators and conservationists point out how easy and logical it would be to harvest only a reasonable number of male vicuñas each year, leaving the pregnant females to reproduce and the young to grow up. Hunters in the uplands are far more practical. Any vicuña of saleable size that they fail to harvest on one hunting trip is likely to be taken by someone else before they can return. No game warden stays at these heights to see that the laws are obeyed. Vicuñas and hunters are on their own.

How different this is from the situation the Spanish conquistadores found when they first reached the high Andes! Then the vicuñas were royal property, defended by every loyal subject of the Inca realm. Each year a few were taken on a ceremonial hunt, and their fleeces turned into robes for state occasions. Any Indian who killed a vicuña in other ways was tried for his crime and put to death. Only the low rainfall and consequent barrenness of the land limited the number of vicuñas that roamed the altiplano.

No comparable civilization in the past protected the mountain animals in central and northeastern Asia. There the rains come frequently, supporting a forest at 8,000 feet elevation, and brushy vegetation to nearly 12,000 feet. Trappers ascend the slopes many times a year to catch musk deer. These strange little animals stand about 2 feet tall, but rest like a rabbit in a "form" all day, feeding warily only in the early morning and late afternoon. Both sexes of musk deer have a downcurved tusk on each side from the upper jaw, and no horns. Trappers catch and kill both sexes and young ones too, merely to get from mature males the special collecting pouch full of a brownish waxlike substance, secreted from a gland in the abdomen. The substance is a musk, which commands a high price in the perfume and soap industries. Getting each ball of secretion, and the valuable pouch as well, costs the lives of many musk deer. Only the small size of these animals and their secretive habits appear to save them from extinction, for thousands are captured and slaughtered each year.

A like danger threatens the most spectacular birds in the world: the 44 different kinds of birds of paradise that inhabit remote valleys of New Guinea, high in the mountains but still within the dense rain forest. Hunting cannot be supervised in country of this kind. Consequently the survival of the birds depends mostly on prohibition of any market for their glorious plumage, and of export of living birds at a rate that would deplete the isolated populations. Scarcely anything is known about the breeding habits of birds of paradise. But what has been discovered shows that each kind has its highly special acrobatics, in which the handsome male courts a plain prospective mate by displaying his distinctive plumes.

Largest and best known of the birds of paradise is the one called simply the "great" bird of paradise (*Paradisaea apoda*). The expedition under the Portuguese navigator Ferdinand Magellan brought back a few feathered skins of it to Europe in 1522. With these trophies and from later expeditions came the story that birds of paradise lacked feet, spent their whole lives on the wing—even mated and incubated their eggs in flight. The fact was simpler: natives of New Guinea prepared the skins for sale by cutting off all parts of the legs, since these contributed nothing to the glory of the feathers.

Around the middle of the nineteenth century, when communications between New Guinea and European markets improved, more of these amazing bird skins were imported for millinery use, reaching a rate of 50,000 to 100,000 annually in the years between 1880 and 1910. Fearing that the birds would be exterminated by such intensive hunting, scientists finally got the traffic stopped completely in 1924. Steps to legalize it again were taken as recently as 1965 in the Papual legislature, to provide employment for native people now emerging from the Stone Age. Although the latest attempt failed, more can be expected. Meanwhile the birds of paradise live on.

The mountains of New Guinea still seem remote, although some of them can now be reached by determined travelers in ordinary passenger cars. In Europe and North America, valleys and peaks that are almost as high (although never so lush) are visited annually by thousands of tourists. In some of these places, we have encountered small animals with a long history of isolation despite their evident ability to get around. Many of them show patterns of evolution that are natural consequences of slow change, due to variations in land form or weather during the Ice Age or more recently.

One of these events dates back to millennia before Mongoloid people spread into North America and affected the lives of animals in coniferous forests along the old meandering Colorado River in northern Arizona. Just north of the river, close to the present border between Arizona and Utah, geologic forces caused the plateau to bulge upward. As rapidly as the land rose against the river, threatening to dam it, the water cut through and maintained its channel. Higher and higher the strata buckled, while the Colorado kept to its former course. Today the river is still in place, flowing steadily through the winding Grand Canyon. The north rim is now a mile higher than the river, and a thousand feet above the south rim. Occasional rains and meltwater from winter snow drain from the north rim into the canyon, eroding its side until the chasm now averages 14 miles across. By contrast, moisture falling on the south rim drains away from the river, leaving the canyon wall incredibly sheer.

Geologists come from all over the world to marvel at the successive strata exposed in Grand Canyon, where the fossil record can be traced back to Cambrian times. Naturalists are equally impressed by the difference in climate due to elevation between the two rims, the lower south one being much more arid and clad in lower trees including piñon pine, while the north rim is moist and supports a fine forest of tall western yellow (ponderosa) pine interspersed with Gambel oak. This green forest covers the whole dome of rock, an area of more than 2,100 square miles known as the Kaibab Plateau. Bounded on the south by the Grand Canyon, by deep Marble and Kanab Canyons to the east and west, it slopes into the semi-desert lands of Utah to the north. Since the climate changed at the end of the last major glaciation, this plateau has been isolated for any land animal that could not cross many miles of arid country.

This isolation has been long enough to allow a black tree squirrel with hairy tassels on its ears to evolve specific differences, including an all-white tail, distinguishing it from the more widespread Abert's squirrel, which formerly lived along the south rim of Grand Canyon. The Kaibab squirrel seems well supplied with its special food, which is the cambium layer of yellow pine trees and, in season, the acorns of Gambel oak. Yet its numbers have shrunk to their lowest ebb in half a century without obvious reason. A fourth of its territory is land of the Grand Canyon National Park, where all wildlife and native plants receive complete protection. The remainder is Kaibab National Forest, which is maintained as an equal sanctuary for squirrels.

The Kaibab Plateau is historic soil. Once the Navaho and Piute Indians used it as a favorite hunting place and meeting center. They called it "Buckskin Mountain," because its deer furnished them with so many valuable hides. The field surveyor for the U. S. Geological Survey, C. E. Dutton, waxed enthusiastic about it as a forested and grassy oasis in the midst of the desert. In the *Second Annual Report* (1882), he wrote:

> There is a constant succession of parks and glades—dreamy avenues of grass and flowers winding between sylvan walls or spreading out into broad open meadows. From June until September there is a display of wild flowers quite beyond description.

Teddy Roosevelt, while President, visited the plateau and fell in love with its magnificent herd of mule deer. Seeing that these handsome animals were suffering from intense competition by introduced horses, cattle, and sheep, he created in 1906 the Grand Canyon National Game Preserve. The stockmen were moved out, but the program they had begun to protect their animals by destroying predators was given greater impetus—now to favor the mule deer. Between that time and 1931, when this effort belatedly ended, professional hunters, by trapping and shooting on the Kaibab Plateau, eliminated 30 wolves, 816 cougars, 863 bobcats, and 7,388 coyotes. In response, the deer herd began increasing by about a fifth each year.

Never before had the consequences of damage to a web of food relations been seen so clearly. By 1916, the Forest Service reported damage to the understory of the Kaibab Forest, due to browsing by the deer, which numbered about 40,000—one deer to each 17 acres of land useful to them. By the summer of 1924 the herd included about 100,000 animals. The famous naturalist George Shiras III recognized the signs of impending disaster and rushed an urgent memorandum to the Forest Service. Responding to his forecast that deer would soon be starving, the Service issued emergency hunting permits for use in the part of the plateau under its jurisdiction. License holders removed only about 1,000 deer. Sixty times that many died the following winter, unable to reach enough shrubs and branches to eat. Again in 1926 the Forest Service encouraged hunting, and got rid of another 1,000 deer. Fully 60 percent of the herd died for lack of food before spring of 1927. Repeated disasters shrank the population to an estimated 20,000 animals by 1930. Still this was too many for the carrying capacity of the damaged forest on the Kaibab Plateau. Not until 1939 did careful control measures bring the deer herd to about 10,000—one deer for each 68 acres. Held at that number, the deer have regained their health and the Kaibab recovered much of its original charm.

The numbers of Kaibab squirrels was greatest during the 1930's, as though the crash of the deer population favored changes in the vegetation helpful to these isolated, bushy-tailed rodents. Since then a good many have been found dead from being struck by automobile traffic, and a smaller number from obvious disease. Now the custodians of the National Park area on the north rim and of the Kaibab National Forest are beginning to wonder if predators are needed in greater numbers, to weed out the diseased squirrels before they infect others, and if the long history of complete prevention of forest fires on the plateau is having adverse effects on the habitat—subtle changes that no one has yet detected. Fewer than 1,000 Kaibab squirrels remain in this glorious sanctuary, which seems to be the lowest number for at least 50 years. Their trend toward rarity alarms many thoughtful visitors to the pine forest, for if an animal admired and protected in a national park can be threatened by extinction for no known cause despite study, what hope is there for the rest of the animal world?

The hazards for animals on the peaks and rocky eminences are just now becoming appreciated from new research on alpine and arctic life. Not until about a century ago had anyone suspected what America's first professional naturalist, Louis Agassiz, proved: that his adopted New England, like his native Switzerland, had been scarred by the ice of tremendous glaciers. Still nearer modern times, other scientists dated these events as between 2,000,000 and 15,000 years ago. The latest decade has revealed, by other methods, that the warmest time since the glaciers melted took place about 7,000 years ago. It was then that trees grew highest on the mountain peaks.

We had occasion to review some of these changes recently while field-tripping with the distinguished poet Mark van Doren in the mountains above Boulder, Colorado. Flitting around us conspicuously were 3-inch butterflies with distinctively rounded wings. Each had a sparse pattern of short streaks and polka dots on creamy white, the few dots red and encircled with black and the streaks plain black. "Those are *Parnassius* butterflies," we commented, "named for Mount Parnassus in Greece. They are high-altitude fliers and very limited in distribution. To us they're rather special."

"None in Boulder?"

"None east of the Rockies. Today they live only on our western mountains and in Eurasia at similar heights."

"You imply that once they were more widespread."

"Supposedly these butterflies lived all across both the New World and the Old some 20,000 years ago, along the margins of the great ice sheets that still remained from the Ice Age. As the weather warmed and the ice retreated northward and up each major mountain, the butterflies followed the chill where their food plants grew. On the peaks they became isolated, and no longer able to visit back and forth. Today the famous mountains of Greece have their own species of *Parnassius*. Different kinds, we're told, are in the Alps, the Himalayas, and here in the Rocky Mountains."

Together we wondered about the comparative altitudes of Mount Parnassus, the sacred mountain above Delphi, and where we stood in Colorado. Later we looked up the measurements: Mount Parnassus, 8,068 feet; Mount Olympus, the highest in Greece, overlooking the Thessalian Plain, 9,753 feet. The butterflies around our poet companion and ourselves flew at an intermediate altitude, but on higher peaks they ascend right to the edge of the snowfields. Their black caterpillars, strangely flattened like

Parnassius butterflies visit paintbrush flowers in the mountains of western North America. Insects of the same type live amid the peaks of Eurasia, as relics from a wider distribution before the Ice Ages.

leeches, spread their bodies to capture heat from the sun and then creep among the low-growing stonecrops and saxifrages to feed on these alpine herbs.

From watching butterflies flit about, especially on a mountain top, it is easy to believe them aimless. They take no obvious direction, or rest in any particular kind of site: now on a flower of one kind, now on a different one, or perhaps a stone. Gusts of wind carry them aloft like lifeless leaves. We hardly notice when they reappear, after a remarkable amount of tacking back and forth.

On many a western peak the *Parnassius* butterflies manage not to be distracted by day-flying sheep moths (*Pseudohazis*), of similar size and comparable shape of wing. The markings on sheep moths are bolder and their flight stronger, faster. Often we have kept watch on individuals and observed them traveling crosswind first to the right, then the left, then right again, advancing into the breeze not more than 10 or 15 feet between one traverse and the next, even when each cross tack took them 100 yards or so. More systematically than most people would search for a lost possession, they were surveying the mountain slope for something important to a sheep moth. So rarely did they pause, perhaps to place an egg when they found the right kind of plant, that we could never discover what reward the alpine area held for all this effort. Nor have we been able to learn that these insects ever put their strong flight and considerable abilities in navigation to use in travel to distant peaks.

The sheep moths and *Parnassius* butterflies may well have been lowland insects in the days when the Great Ice spread around the Northern Hemisphere and alpine-arctic vegetation fringed its southern edges. We wonder what, then, dislodged them from the highest peaks of New England where the land extends above tree line, and north of the trees on the arctic tundra of Canada.

Other, somewhat smaller, browner, and less conspicuous butterflies show that the arctic and the alpine are much alike today, affording the particular amenities they need—as nowhere more temperate does. Butterfly collections are enriched by specimens of *Erebia* species, known colloquially as "alpines," and of *Oeneis* species, called "arctics," although there is no real distinction according to the places these insects live. Their caterpillars eat grasses, freeze solid most nights, and thaw again by day above tree line on mountains and north of the trees on the tundra. There the weather is still as harsh as any that formerly spread coast to coast around the edge of the Great Ice.

One called the "White Mountain butterfly" (*Oeneis semidea*), with leaf-brown wings that are thin and semitranslucent, flies also in Labrador and over the tundra northwest of Hudson Bay; it is closest to our home around the summit of Mount Washington (6,288 feet) and along the adjacent Presidental range in New Hampshire. Another, the "Katahdin butterfly" (*O. katahdin*) with paler pinkish wings irregularly smudged below with dark brown, is now restricted to the alpine meadow at the top of Maine's highest peak (5,288 feet). We climbed to find it one day in late June, when patches of deep snow still dotted the treeless summit. Perhaps two dozen of the butterflies were active each time the sun shone warmly. They sat on the ground, with wings closed, whenever a cloud passed by. We found a flat stone to sit on, for the soil was wet, and we watched these insects, realizing that they are more restricted in distribution than almost any other animal on earth. The whole world, for them, was a few acres of thin soil among the upthrust rocks on a single peak.

After a sudden brief snowstorm, the sun blazed hot again. We sat and thought about the hazards of life above tree line on Katahdin or any other mountain. If the climate cools, they can go lower. Everything else will grow lower, leaving them a living space to which they are superbly fitted. But if the climate gets warmer, what then? Everything on the mountain slopes will move a little higher. The tree line will be nearer the summit, and the alpine garden smaller. The grasses in that garden hold the whole future for Katahdin butterflies. If trees shade out the grasses, the butterfly will become extinct.

In the years since the Ice Age, trees have grown higher on our country's mountain slopes. Recent studies of the bristlecone pines along the boundary between California and Nevada have revealed that the oldest known living things, pines 4,600 years of age, grow only so far up the mountain. Beyond that, for nearly another thousand feet, are the eroding but undecomposed carcasses of bristlecone pines that died thousands of years ago. Using computers to compare the thicknesses of successive growth rings in living trees and dead carcasses, Dr. C. W. Ferguson, Jr., and his co-workers at the University of Arizona have been able to establish that the bristlecones farthest up the mountain grew there about 7,000 years ago. At that time the climate was substantially milder than at present or at any other time since the retreat of the Great Ice 15,000 years ago.

Where, we wonder, was tree line during this warm period on Maine's Mount Katahdin? Surely it was higher, and the Katahdin butterfly was in greater peril than it is today. This warm period may have wiped out the stonecrops and saxifrages upon the peaks, but not the grasses, eliminating the *Parnassius* butterflies and the sheep moths, but not the "arctic" butterfly that now lives nowhere else.

In a very real sense, animals on the peaks keep their backs turned toward the harsh weather higher up. Few other kinds of life can tolerate the cold, the wind, the snow that hides the food, the ice that forms every night. For eons, the predators and competition have come from lower elevations, and this pattern of alertness is now part of the behavior the mountain animals inherit. They have little to fear from higher slopes. Many a hunter has discovered this while stalking mammals near the peaks. If he can bypass his quarry and approach it from above, he need not take such pains to hide himself. The animal will largely ignore him.

Only the slow crumbling of the mountain or a progressive warming of the climate is likely to leave the undefended rear exposed. Until the present decade, no one had a reliable measure of the rate at which a mountain eroded naturally from under the living things that inhabit its upper slopes. Now it is known that the rocky soil around the roots of bristlecone pines is blown and washed away about one foot every thousand years. On peaks that remained unglaciated all through the two million years of the Ice Age, the isolated relict plants and animals had to adjust to erosive loss of the earth's surface amounting to perhaps 2,000 feet in elevation. Their world and the climate that high altitude produced changed at a steady pace.

We think of those two million years of arctic and alpine conditions as pressing upon the native kinds of life, molding the animals of the peaks, directing the evolution of their tolerance for physical hardships imposed by extended winter and a short annual growing season. In meeting this harsh challenge from their environment, these animals largely lost their ability to compete successfully with the greater variety of life in more temperate climates. This made them doubly vulnerable—pressed upon by creatures from the warmer lands below and threatened by any warming trend in weather. Isolated on the crumbling peaks, they find progressively fewer places in which their spectacular specialties will save them. Unless the world soon grows colder again, they have nowhere to go except to oblivion.

CHAPTER 9

IN
LANDS
OF
THE
SLANTING
SUN

OF THE MIGRANT birds we know, most travel poleward to their breeding grounds in time for summer solstice. Those that cross the Arctic Circle include hordes of shorebirds and arctic terns, as well as smaller numbers of barnacle geese and whooper swans, heading for nest sites where the sun is melting the last of the winter snow. In the Southern Hemisphere, their counterparts are penguins and shearwaters homing to remote islands, the penguins swimming and cavorting in the cold water, the shearwaters flying low over the waves as though to cut the crests. By equinox, most of these birds will be away again, heading for the Equator or even crossing it.

At summer solstice the polar lands and latitudes as low as 40 degrees from the Equator are glorious with light and life. At midnight the sun is less than 18 degrees below the horizon, although on the opposite side of the earth. In the direction of the pole the sky stays bright, giving twilight illumination that banishes true night. Beyond the polar circles the sun circuits the sky, staying in sight unless concealed by clouds. Yet the rays from the sun slant down from no higher than 45 degrees above the horizontal at midday. The closer to the pole we go in these "lands of the midnight sun" the lower is their slant at noon.

Automatically we compare these conditions with those at our own home, which is halfway between the North Pole and the Equator. Twilight at summer solstice squeezes night into less than three-and-a-half hours, although the sun vanishes at 7:50 and does not rise again until 4:13. Like the migrant birds, we can gain daylight by traveling poleward.

153

Six months later, we're ready to follow the birds to or near the tropics. At winter solstice, the sun at home sets at 4:20, not to rise again until 7:35 the next day. Winter twilight leaves us with more than twelve hours of night. Yet at noon near winter solstice, our shadows are never 30 feet long as they could be if we lived in western Canada or Labrador, Scotland or Scandinavia. At this season the lands of the midnight sun have no sun at all—just a midday twilight and penetrating cold.

For arctic animals that cannot migrate for hundreds or thousands of miles, polar winter is the season of severest trial. Storms come frequently, bringing winds that drive snow and hail into crevices, sweeping clean the rounded tops of rocks polished by glaciers millennia ago. Food disappears and is not renewed, because most land plants die and shrivel in the waning light, leaving only spores and seeds to confront the bitter cold. Where rocks shield from the wind a shallow soil under a blanket of hard-packed snow, a few trees spread out, mere inches tall, as though espaliered against the earth. Any twigs that project beyond the snow are devoured by an arctic hare, a musk ox, a reindeer, or a hungry bear, or are pruned away by the wind.

Hidden beneath the snow in many places are gray-green lichens that rank among the best-adapted plants for tolerating long winters and bene-

In southern Alaska, musk oxen sometimes find vegetation far more luxuriant than any on the northern tundras. (FRANK DUFRESNE, BUREAU OF SPORT FISHERIES AND WILDLIFE.)

fiting from fresh air, moisture, light, and warmth when spring arrives. With an almost rubberlike flexibility while moist, they change little when the temperature falls; only when very dry do they become crisp, brittle, and combustible. Some, known as *Cetraria,* are irregularly fan-shaped, almost like tattered cloth. Others, called reindeer moss (*Cladonia rangiferina*), branch as though miniature leafless shrubs. Both form arctic ranges particularly well suited to tame reindeer and their wild counterparts (the caribou), which scrape through the snow to reach them.

Lichens serve importantly as food for lemmings too, both the four different kinds of true lemmings that remain brown or gray all winter and the five types of collared lemmings that change to a white coat during the months when snow is on the ground. All of these rat-sized rodents have short tails, legs, and ears, which conserves their body heat. In autumn they grow longer claws on their front feet, the better to dig for lichens and edible roots. The special claws are only on the thumbs of true lemmings, but on toes of a collared lemming that correspond to our fourth and fifth fingers.

As much as possible, the lemmings stay out of sight in their shallow burrows. No other animals of the tundra are so efficient at transforming plant foods into meat attractive to polar predators. Where lemmings are plentiful, snowy owls and arctic foxes easily survive the winter. Arctic wolves prey on lemmings when caribou are scarce. Bears eat any lemmings they can catch. Even a caribou will eat a lemming if it has a chance. Despite these dangerous neighbors, the lemmings multiply as though their food supply is endless. For about four years the population increases in each area and then, for no known cause, suddenly collapses. Scandinavia's true lemmings make forced marches to lower ground, and often end by swimming to their doom at sea. The predators on the lichen ranges go hungry and turn to a starvation diet of plants. The snowy owls fly south. Usually the lichens have time to renew themselves.

The long-term need to conserve the lichen ranges is matched also by the normal behavior of caribou. These arctic deer follow many different routes between the northern coasts in summer, where greenery is plentiful and flies are few, and the fringe of the taiga in winter, where the evergreen trees offer protection from gales. Laplanders, who caught and trained these animals to work in harness guided by reins (hence reindeer), learned to be equally nomadic and to notice when their domesticated herds were depleting the lichens. This became their signal to move on, not to return until the lichen range recovered. Eskimos merely observed the irregular trekking of the caribou, and camped where they expected herds to come by. Where caribou abounded, this casual practice succeeded. But it left

A European reindeer introduced on St. Paul Island, Alaska, to augment the food resources of native people in this part of the Pribilof group of islands. (V. B. SCHEFFER, BUREAU OF SPORT FISHERIES AND WILDLIFE.)

them in serious need of meat, bones, sinews, hides, and other useful parts when the animals failed to arrive.

The lichen ranges and the number of caribou have shrunk, and with them the population of Eskimos that can live in the old ways. Much of the change has been due to fire toward the end of the summer growing season, just before new storms soak the land or cover it with thin snow. The tundra has always been at its driest in late summer, but electrical storms with lightning that might start a blaze are rare then. The greater incidence of fire is a consequence of careless people, who regard the combustible lichens as of no importance. Once burned, a lichen range may need a century to recover. In many places the bared land has been hospitable to grasses, which can tolerate a fire every autumn. But even when unburned, the dry dormant grass cannot replace lichens in the diet of caribou and lemmings. An arctic grassland offers little to any animal all through the long winter.

In the Canadian Northwest Territory, the Yukon, and parts of Alaska, bears that are extraordinarily tolerant of cold and versatile in food requirements are finding less to eat. The barren-grounds race of the grizzly bear is on the danger list, perhaps headed for extinction. So is the glacier bear of mountain slopes, a gray-blue form of the American black bear found nowhere else. These powerful animals dig for lemmings and ground squirrels, skillfully flip salmon and other fishes from the tumbling water of river rapids, devour whatever carrion they can find, eat quantities of virtually every kind of vegetation, and for the most part stay out of man's way. Yet none of their adaptations fit them for surviving the effects of fire and firearms, which have changed their polar world so much in this century.

Around many of the arctic coasts the annual disappearance of the sun does not interfere so much with the supply of food for native animals. Bivalves continue to filter particles of food from the water. Assorted snails and echinoderms engulf nourishing detritus on the bottom. Fishes feed on the shellfish. Walruses use their tusks to pry animals out of the sea floor. Squids catch the fishes. Seals fatten on both fishes and squids. Polar bears, which are the most aquatic and cold-tolerant of all bears, take seals and any fish they can capture in shallow water. All of these animals benefit from a phenomenon that has no equivalent in the Southern Hemisphere: the Gulf Stream. The warm current brings a wealth of live and dying creatures of small size, as well as heat, from lower latitudes. It floods this bounty into the Arctic Ocean between Greenland and Scandinavia, adding all year to the supply of nourishing ooze on the bottom and particles in the water, and causing an outflow through Bering Strait and between Greenland and Labrador.

Polar bears are denizens of arctic coasts, and never travel far from the pack ice among which they live mostly on seals and fish. Commonly they bear their young on floating ice, and teach them to swim at an early age. (COURTESY OF THE AMERICAN MUSEUM OF NATURAL HISTORY.)

Around the time of spring equinox, the pregnant polar bears have their cubs on remote ice floes. At the same season the surviving grizzly bears dig shelter in the frozen tundra, in which to give birth. Both will nurse their young until the long days of June, when the migrant birds arrive from the south, and the seals and walruses haul out from the cold waters to reproduce. The number of newcomers is enormous by comparison with the predators. Consequently the waterfowl, the shorebirds, and the seals are amazingly unwary; the chance that any individual will be destroyed is so slight. Bears, foxes, wolves, and skua gulls that have feasted merely stand or rest, waiting for their meals to be digested. They rarely risk a close approach to a mother walrus or a bull seal, although they ordinarily find an opportunity to remove any dead or unprotected young.

The normal rate of reproduction among the seals, walruses, and bears, and the alertness with which these animals react to the approach of anyone on land, sufficed for millennia against Eskimo hunters armed with homemade weapons. Nor did men in individual skin-covered boats pose a serious threat. But when Europeans arrived with guns and sturdier craft, the populations of these animals began to shrink. Only an international agreement in 1911, prohibiting all pelagic sealing and regulating the annual harvest of skins, saved the fur seals in Alaskan waters from extermination. Now the Atlantic walrus is in danger in Canada, Greenland, Norway, and the western U.S.S.R. The polar bear is threatened in these same regions and in Alaska and Siberia too, which complete the natural circle of its range.

Since 1956 the Soviet Union has led the world in protecting polar bears, forbidding all hunting of this animal. The other four countries began estimating the number being killed each year: about 300 each in Alaska and Norway, nearly 500 in Canada, and 100 in Greenland. In Canada and Greenland, only residents (chiefly Eskimos) are allowed to hunt these animals, under regulations intended to limit the number taken to those actually used by aborigines for food and fur. Norway's bears are almost all in the vicinity of the Spitsbergen Islands, where trophy hunters in small boats cruise along the edge of the pack ice each summer. In Alaska the Eskimos with their dog sleds and skimobiles have almost given up hunting polar bears, unable to compete with affluent white trophy hunters from farther south who pay the high license fee, hire an authorized guide, and charter an airplane from which to pick out the big animal they want on an ice floe far from land. Meanwhile scientists are trying, with tranquilizing darts and metal tags or radio transmitters attached to individual bears, to learn how far these polar animals travel by walking and swimming and how fast they reproduce and grow, and to make a census of the bears from which to estimate their danger of extinction. At present no one knows what proportion of the total is represented by the 1,200 bears killed each year.

A program of international cooperation on polar bears began in 1965, with Canadians aware that their shores were the most hazardous for these animals. In April, 1968, a Polar Bear Provincial Park of 7,000 square miles was established in Ontario, fronting on James Bay and Hudson Bay. Within the park, no commercial development will be permitted. Nonhunting, non-fishing visitors will be welcomed when they come by air; other means of access are lacking. No Indians or Eskimos live in the park, which will also conserve walrus, bearded seal, arctic fox, and a seasonal herd of caribou. It is known to be an important breeding area for both snow and blue goose, and for willow ptarmigan.

The willow ptarmigan at low elevations and the rock ptarmigan on mountain slopes have snowy owls as winter neighbors. Only a few cormorants remain along coasts with open water in all seasons while the other arctic birds migrate to warmer regions. Many of the travelers are away, in fact, southbound long before the approach of autumn. As soon as their parental duties of the year are done, they fly off, in some cases leaving their young to follow with only inherited guidance. Varied as these patterns of behavior are, we can scarcely see in them a reason for three species of northern nesters to be presently in danger of extinction, or for three others to have already disappeared.

The endangered ones are all North American. Most famous is the whooping crane, which was once widespread, breeding from its present range in the central southern Mackenzie district of Canada south through the prairie sloughs to Iowa. Its present southern destination, close to Aran-

The reddish brown chick of the year has followed its parents on the long flight from the breeding grounds of all whooping cranes to their established refuge on the Texas coast. (LUTHER C. GOLDMAN, BUREAU OF SPORT FISHERIES AND WILDLIFE.)

With the cooperation of the Canadian Wildlife Service, this chick and a few others have hatched from eggs taken by helicopter from whooping crane nests in Wood Buffalo Park, northwestern Canada. (LUTHER C. GOLDMAN, BUREAU OF SPORT FISHERIES AND WILDLIFE.)

sas Pass on the Texas coast, is a remnant from former time when it wintered from the Gulf Coast of Louisiana to northern Mexico. During the summer of 1968, ten occupied nests (the largest number seen in any year to that date) were observed in two areas of Wood Buffalo National Park. In addition to the 20 parents tending these nests, another 28 wild whooping cranes presumably were somewhere in this northern region, while 19 others in protective custody matured toward the day when their offspring might be freed.

It is easy to become distracted by the publicity aimed at saving whoopers on migration from hunters' guns, and to marvel at the efficiency with which a few eggs each year are whisked by helicopter and jet airplane from nests in the north to incubators in the U. S. Fish and Wildlife research center at Laurel, Maryland. But the fact is that whooping cranes have been exterminated over all the good nesting areas their ancestors occupied, and now must survive with help—expensive help—on marginal northern fringes of the normal breeding range. Luck, rather than intelligent management, left of this endangered species a few birds that had in their heritage a tie to national park land at one end of their annual trip and to an undeveloped area along the Gulf Coast that could be set aside for their winter sanctuary. That the national park had been set aside for the welfare of another vanishing species was coincidence, and a happy one.

The Hudsonian godwit and the Eskimo curlew are the other two northern nesters now tottering on the edge of extinction. Both are long-beaked sandpipers that swing eastward from the arctic wetlands and travel down the Atlantic coast to spend the winter in southern South America, then return by a different route, crossing the Gulf of Mexico and flying northbound between the Rocky Mountains and the Mississippi to their nesting areas. The Hudsonian is the larger bird, but both have suffered since the 1880's everywhere except on their breeding grounds.

One change in their fortunes came gradually, reducing the amount of food the birds could find. Marshes were drained or filled along the Atlantic coast, and grazing lands used previously by native wildlife in South America and the central United States and Canada were transformed into efficient fields of cereal crops. On their wintering areas, hunters had always taken a significant toll. Abruptly this hazard increased as market gunners in North America turned to shorebirds, which seemed in limitless supply, to satisfy their hungry customers, since passenger pigeons were getting scarce. So rapidly did this combination of calamities afflict the shorebirds that by 1900 extinction seemed inevitable for all except the smallest species.

Possibly the Hudsonian godwit was the least common of the shorebirds even before 1880. It vanished completely during the great slaughter, and did not reappear when given protection in North America. Official bird listings published in 1936 indicated it as being extinct or almost so. But a few survivors continued the species. Since 1950, small numbers of this rare sandpiper have been observed traveling north through the Mississippi Valley. Apparently their southbound route now takes them out over the Atlantic Ocean. They can rest on the water along the way, but probably get no food until they reach South America. Since their winter quarters remain unknown, it may be that they have found some haven still overlooked by both agriculturalist and hunter. This godwit seems likely to be endangered until South Americans too take an interest in leaving it a place in the world.

The Eskimo curlew stirred far more controversy when it disappeared, partly because it had been such a delight to epicures. Even Thomas Nuttall's *Manual of the Ornithology of the United States and Canada*, published in 1832, comments that "the small, or Esquimaux curlew, is very fat, plump, and well-flavoured." A fat one, ready for migration, might weigh a pound. To get them, gunners journeyed to Labrador, where these curlews congregated before making their long overwater flight.

When Dr. William T. Hornaday, Director of the New York Zoological Park, listed the Eskimo curlew along with the passenger pigeon as extinct in 1914, no one questioned his statement. Sight records before and after that date could easily have been whimbrels or Hudsonian godwits, despite the fact that both are slightly larger birds. Then a real Eskimo curlew was collected in the Argentine. In March, 1945, a pair of these birds—apparently mated—were seen by a competent observer on Galveston Island, Texas. Others have been sighted nearby, generally singly, in 1950, 1959, 1960, 1961, and 1962—but not in 1963 or 1964. During the fall of 1963, one was shot in the West Indies on Barbados, and the specimen reached the collection of the Philadelphia Academy of Natural Sciences in Pennsylvania. No one can tell at present how many of these curlews remain, where they winter, or whether somewhere in their vast former nesting grounds they are contributing to the future of their kind.

The extinct Labrador duck, last seen alive in 1875, formerly appeared each autumn along the Atlantic coast as far south as Chesapeake Bay. Never common, it was a member of the scoter tribe, but equipped with a strangely flared beak tip as though adapted to special feeding habits. No one ever learned what foods it ate, before that final one was shot off Long Island, New York. It may already have been in difficulty, unable to find suitable nourishment.

So often, the candidates for extinction seem to be the highly specialized animals. Both of the other birds that vanished from northern nesting areas fit this category because they dispensed with the ability to fly. Best known was the great auk, standing 20 inches tall, and the original penguin, after which the Antarctic birds were named—despite a lack of any true relationship. The auk remained at sea, diving for fishes and squids in the cold waters of the North Atlantic, except at nesting season. Then it clambered clumsily up the steep shores of rocky islands to lay its single egg and brood its chick. Fishermen took a holiday from their nets at this season, to seek out the auks—the adults for their feathers and the young birds for the oil that could be rendered as a substitute for kerosene. Auk bones by the ton still lie in the soil atop Funk Island, just north of Newfoundland. But records show that the last pair of great auks died a violent death at the hands of a fisherman on Iceland in 1844.

The spectacled cormorant of the Commander (Komandorskiye) Islands off the Kamchatka coast of Russia was discovered in 1741 when the explorer Vitus Bering and his naturalist George Wilhelm Steller took refuge there from a violent storm. By 1852, when a scientific expedition landed to seek more specimens, the birds were gone and have not been seen since. Probably hungry Aleuts, sheltering on the islands during the intervening years, ate the last of this species for lack of other food.

Today the Commander Islands are like the Aleutians in being bleak as ever. They lie along the southern fringe of the Bering Sea, beyond the normal limit of pack ice. We think of them as remote, and so they are from any major city of the Old World or the New. Yet they are at the same latitude as the British Isles and the north coast of Germany. They are polar for lack of a Gulf Stream to warm them, and because a cold current flows in their direction through Bering Strait out of the part of the Arctic Ocean known as the Chukchi Sea. The Chukchi and the northern portion of the Bering Sea provide poor shelter to three-quarters of the world's remaining walruses. Most of the outer quarter comprises an Atlantic race at comparable latitudes in Hudson Bay, and between Baffin Island and Greenland, where they must contend with pack ice every winter.

Perhaps the walruses were always arctic animals, but their winter wanderings in former times brought them down the Atlantic coasts frequently to Boston Harbor, occasionally to Chesapeake Bay, and at least once up the Thames River to London. Upon rare occasions they still turn up along the shore of Japan's northernmost island, and to Kodiak beside the Alaskan coast. Until 1641 the members of a herd hauled themselves ashore regularly in breeding season on Sable Island near Nova Scotia. In that year, twelve men who landed there managed to harvest "four hundred pair of sea-horse teeth, which were estimated worth three hundred pounds sterling," in addition to a barrel of oil apiece rendered from the walrus fat. *Sea horse, whale horse, walrus* are among the names given to these strange creatures, which have the disconcerting habit of coming up alongside a small boat and hooking their powerful tusks over the gunwale while taking a close look at the occupants.

Walruses carefully guard their tusks when clambering out on rocky shores, but use them to get a grip on cakes of pack ice, to cut breathing holes in winter time, and to grub in the bottom for shellfish. Since a walrus must come to the surface at frequent intervals for air, it cannot dive routinely more than about 300 feet to feed. This limits its distribution to the vicinity of coasts and small islands. There, from the seventeenth century on, whalers sought out the animal for ivory and oil. Between 1830 and 1930, close to three million were slaughtered in the Bering Sea alone, and the world population of walruses had shrunk to less than 100,000. Fortunately, the survivors were able to take refuge in commercially inaccessible ice fields and escape the extinction that faced them everywhere else. During the last 15 years their numbers may even have increased a little.

Curiously, at the opposite end of the world where a major continent surrounds the South Pole, the only animals that frequent the pack ice and are now endangered are the rare endemics called Ross seals or big-eyed seals. These 7-foot swimmers are seen singly or in small groups, sometimes in company with the most abundant seals of antarctic waters—the so-called crabeater seals which actually use their remarkable cheek teeth to strain shrimp and krill crustaceans from the plankton. Ross seals catch some crustaceans, but feed mostly on squid and fish. No one knows why they are so uncommon. Prior to World War II, fewer than 50 Ross seals had been seen. Postwar explorers, aided by improved equipment, have discovered 500 to 1,000 times as many, sparsely distributed around the long perimeter of the southern continent.

So far, no living inhabitants of the ice-clad continent have been found valuable enough to invite risking ships, aircraft, or human lives to harvest and then haul away the products for the immense distances to major markets in the Northern Hemisphere. Seemingly in consequence, no mammal or bird that frequents antarctic coasts and offshore waters (except whales) has been hunted close to extinction. The scattered scientific centers maintained by many nations have not changed the south polar landscape, except locally.

One introduced animal that can survive outdoors in southern winter remains a hazard, as Dr. Robert Cushman Murphy pointed out after a visit to Antarctica. The sled dog or husky, brought from North Polar regions, has already demonstrated its ability to escape and survive until recovered. No stretch of the imagination is required to think of them going wild, living where no four-footed predator has been known before. All through the antarctic summer they could live well in the nesting areas of Adélie penguins and skua gulls, and then transfer their gastronomic attention to emperor penguins through the night of winter. Today the mechanized vehicles, such as skimobiles, snow cats, and aircraft, have completely displaced the huskies from any significant role in transporting men or materials. The remaining dogs are kept for sentiment, as pets of lonely men, despite the continuing hazard they offer to native life.

Far as the Antarctic is from any agricultural land or insect pests, it is within the range of DDT and derivative insecticides that travel as airborne dust and in ocean currents. The bodies of penguins and their eggs have contained measurable amounts of these toxic substances. Sea leopards, which prey on penguins, are the peak predators in the Antarctic. So far no one knows how they are faring, or what the future will bring to this south polar world.

CHAPTER 10

HAZARDS FOR ANIMALS OF THE ENDLESS SEAS

WHEN WE PICK up a handful of soil and crumble it between our fingers, we hold part of an island, whether part of a small one or a land of continental size. But when we dip ourselves into a river or the sea, we enter a great continuum because the aquatic world, which spreads over nearly three-quarters of the earth's surface, is confluent. It isolates the terrestrial world and gives us a special view of the planet. We stay close to shore, whereas an energetic, long-lived and hardy sea creature might swim down through either the Atlantic or the Pacific Oceans from the Arctic Ocean to the shores of Antarctica, and still have extra space to move in the Indian Ocean, the Mediterranean, the Gulf of Mexico, the Caribbean, and the dark depths into which the sun can never penetrate.

Few marine animals actually follow a migratory course that takes them, according to the season, through the middle latitudes to waters south and north of the tropics. Herman Melville wrote enthusiastically of one that does—the "white" sperm whale he called Moby Dick. He based his story on the beliefs of experienced whalers, among whom he had worked. Scientists did not accept such casual observations until they had recovered from captured whales hundreds of individual darts of stainless steel, bearing identifying numbers. Months or years had passed since these markers had been shot into the back blubber of the same animals elsewhere on their travels. Now we can feel confident that the freedom of the sea is real, and that Moby Dick might have traveled as the story tells, feeding along the way on giant squids and lesser animals in the open sea.

Sperm whales, like most other whales, remain remote from coasts. For this reason, no one is sure whether the estimate of 250,000 still in existence is high or low, and what proportion the 25,000 killed each year actually represents. Of the big species, only the humpback and the gray whales are likely to be seen from land. All but the gray seem doomed if stranded in shallow water by a receding tide, for the great bodies tear apart or the animal suffocates if not buoyed up. Grays as much as 50 feet long generally keep their distance visually, "spy-hopping" by raising their heads vertically out of the water, as they follow Pacific shorelines south from Bering Sea in autumn and north again in spring. Grays are unusual too in finding refuge in lagoons to calve and mate during the winter months. Those that seek such places along the coast of Baja California swim close enough to the steep shore at San Diego to be counted from a park lookout. Other whales reproduce just as successfully in the broad reaches of the oceans, although usually in waters that offer temporary warmth rather than abundant food.

Gigantic as some of these animals are, only a male sperm whale (which may be 63 feet long) has a gullet big enough for a man to slide through whole, as in the story of Jonah. The sperm whale is the largest of the predatory species, which have teeth instead of whalebone (baleen) plates in the mouth. It commonly feeds 100 to 300 feet below the surface and has been known to dive as deep as 3,500 feet, getting caught there in a transoceanic telephone cable. The smaller-toothed whales include the dreaded killers, which whalers often know by their proper name orca (*Orcinus orca*).

Other whales of this and larger size, such as the right whales of northern and southern waters, the Sei whale of the far south, the finback whale, and the great blue (or sulfur-bottom) whale, all remain near the surface, filtering out small fishes and smaller crustaceans by means of the whalebone plates that hang inside the mouth from the upper jaw.

The North Atlantic right whales were the first to attract man's attention. They were the "right" kind to kill for oil, because their bodies do not sink at death, as do those of other whales. Beginning in the fifteenth century, European fishermen began pursuing right whales, first off the Bay of Biscay, and then all the way to North America. By 1700 they had decreased the number so far that whaling expeditions no longer proved profitable. The Greenland right whales, which found some refuge among the icebergs of waters farther north, proved an elusive substitute until a century later when they too became rare. The blubber of these animals can be rendered to yield 50 to 80 percent of its weight in oil; the bones contain 10 to 70 percent according to sex, age, and season; and the muscles too can be processed to obtain from 2 to 8 percent of their weight as a saleable fuel. Today we need to be reminded that whale oil, and candles made from whale fat, competed on the market with olive oil to be burned in lamps. Not until later did chemists learn to distill kerosene ("coal oil") as a cheaper substitute.

Yankee whalers from the New England coast put new life and romance into the whaling industry, starting about 1712 with ships and equipment especially designed for pursuing sperm whales in Atlantic waters. By 1846, when their operations became unprofitable and essentially ceased, they had 729 whaling vessels in action every season. Sperm whales have an extraordinarily large storage cistern in their heads, a "case" for pure oil. From it, they appear to use oil at every dive to mix with air and produce a stiff foam in lungs and middle ears. It is believed that this keeps these organs from collapsing under the great pressure of water which, at 3,000 feet below the surface, amounts to nearly a ton per square inch. If whaling reduced the number of sperm whales, no one noticed. The gain from pursuing them shrank before the living resource showed signs of depletion. Sperm whales were saved by the discovery of petroleum in 1809, and by progressive reductions in price as ways to refine the raw material were improved.

Some of these refining techniques were applied to whale oil, yielding new products. Whalebone for corset stiffeners continued to find a market. Extracted bone found use as fertilizer, for its lime. Whale meat became an important commodity for pet food, or ground and dried as a supplement in the diet of poultry and livestock. Gradually the whalers adjusted their methods to match their sales, and to find whales farther from home. Pacific gray whales lasted from around 1750 to 1830, when they almost became extinct. The right whales of South Atlantic, South Pacific, and South Indian Ocean areas supported the industry from about 1800 to 1900, when severe depletion struck them too. North Pacific right whales, called bowheads, went into disastrous decline even faster, between 1843 and 1908.

During the early years of the present century, technological advances allowed whalers to invade the last sanctuary of the big mammals of the endless seas—the Antarctic. A harpoon cannon was invented, and steam-powered whaling vessels took the place of those that had operated under sail. Huge factory ships soon went along, to allow complete processing of whales captured by a satellite fleet of small fast whale-catchers. Efficiently the whalers brought the great blue whale, largest animal known ever to have inhabited the world, to the edge of extinction and then turned to smaller whales with a formula for rating their annual catches in "blue whale units." One blue whale equals two finback whales or two-and-a-half humpback whales, or six Sei whales. Discussions of conserving the remaining resource and setting aside a large area as a sanctuary occupied delegates to an International Whaling Commission, but made little progress because a few whaling nations refused to accept any limitation so long as there was profit to be made. Voluntary curtailment, starting in 1930, did not suffice. Total protection for blue whales and humpbacks, begun in 1963, merely antedated the virtual end of pelagic whaling in 1968. Agreement came too late, when there were almost no more whales to either catch or save.

The plight of whales and of whalers is a consequence of greed, incredibly poor judgment, and failure in international respect. Whaling companies in each nation urged their engineers to design more efficient factory ships and related equipment, as though the whales were a limitless resource to be strip-mined by whichever operator got there first. Neither the directors of the companies nor the investors who advanced the money paid attention to the live whales or the possibility of managing them as a self-perpetuating crop. Whalers of the "other" nation could never be trusted to show restraint for the good of all. And now that the factory ships are rusting in their home ports while whalers young enough to learn new skills are trying other occupations, the engineers are offering to design pilot models of harvesting machines—imitation whales—to gather plankton from the surface layers of the oceans and dehydrate it into compressed cakes that some land animal would eat. Whales that had evolved this ability and perfected it over a period of 60 million years seem obsolete.

In New England towns such as New Bedford, Massachusetts, where museums display mementos from whaling days, the trade has turned to shellfish. Men who might have sailed the farthest seas to harvest a share of the world's whales now travel weekly just 150 miles east of Nantucket to dredge for sea scallops on Georges Bank. We wonder what they will turn to when the scallops cannot reproduce fast enough to maintain the commercial supply.

A few years ago we accepted the invitation of a Maine lobsterman to go along with him on his circuit as he replaced traps that had been working with others freshly baited. Good fortune brought us near a live whale, a humpback, cruising parallel to the shore past the lobsterman's line of buoys. His curiosity matched ours, and he took time off to bring his boat within a dozen yards of the monster, to match its speed and direction. For minute after minute we gaped as the whale alternately raised its head awash, mouth gaping, then submerged shallowly, closing its mouth to press the captured plankton from between its whalebone plates like so much toothpaste down its throat. Irregular knobs as big as two clenched fists studded the top of the animal's head and appeared like huge warts also on the extraordinarily long flippers with which the whale seemed to steady itself in the water. Behind the low dorsal fin, which remained in the air, the enormous tail sculled up and down, propelling the great body at a leisurely pace. Occasionally, when the whale's head came up, we could make out its eye below the water surface. If the creature was apprehensive of our company, it gave no sign. Every few minutes its paired blowholes opened briefly and closed again for a change of air; they made no sound we could detect above the noise of the boat's engine.

On other occasions, off the California coast, gray whales delighted us. Some we saw at a great distance, swimming in groups, spouting at intervals a mixture of air, oil, and water. Experienced whale-watchers informed us that grays benefited from World War II, because in 1946 Japanese whalers ceased to approach the American coast, and few Canadian or United States fishermen ignored the protection ordered for these animals from 1938 on. Without interference, the population increased. Now about 6,000 are counted each year on annual migration.

One whale, supposedly a gray, swam repeatedly around the oceanographic research ship M/V *Stranger* on a night we were aboard. Seemingly the anchored vessel piqued the whale's curiosity. But although its *whoooosh* of breathing sounded extremely close, we never succeeded in getting the ship's searchlight to show us the whale.

We prefer to remember these live cetaceans, rather than a dead one with which we made an appointment by telephone in Durban, South Africa. The managers of the land-based whaling company had sold their principal ships, and continued to process only the few whales that could be caught in the Indian Ocean near shore. If we hurried to the whaling station, they told us, we would be in time for their third and last whale of the day. Right then it was being loaded onto their private railroad train, to be hauled to the flensing platform.

Although we raced we were still politely, tactfully sipping tea with the management when along the railway from the shore came a locomotive and single car—not a flat car but a salver-shaped one, bearing the dead Sei whale, tail first. It chugged past the end of the building and out of sight. Later, we caught up with it alongside the flensing platform, where all operations had been ordered stopped pending our arrival.

Around the monster's tail just forward of its expanded flukes, a heavy chain had been secured, leading by cable to a powerful winch. Without delay, the machinery began to grind and clank, hauling the blue-black carcass off the train and onto the platform. The whale rolled on its side, its white belly facing us, which let us see that its forward third—below the cavernous mouth—bore about twenty lengthwise red creases. In life these serve the animal like the pleats of an accordion, letting it dilate its mouth

Although South Africans no longer engage in pelagic whaling, they do capture a few whales with shore-based equipment. Here a Sei whale, 52 feet long, is being flensed near Durban on the Indian Ocean coast.

cavity enormously to capture food from the surface waters. Norwegians call any whale with these creases a rorqual ("red creases"), applying the term equally to six different whales: the rare giant blue, the fast-swimming finback whale, the ponderous humpback, the Sei, and two lesser kinds called the Minke whale and Bryde's whale.

As soon as a man with a tape measure recorded the total length as 50 feet, workmen moved in with great curved knives on poles. Skillfully, speedily, they separated the body into manageable pieces. At a matching pace, steel cables from the winch machinery were hooked to each piece, letting the winch operator help with each step and then haul off the whale fragment to its appropriate chute in the flensing platform. More than forty tons of animal were cut and neatly sent on their way to the digesters, as though a surgeon had deftly performed the operation. In twenty minutes it was finished, with a minimum of lost motion, waste fragments, and none of the gore or stench our reading had led us to expect.

Half a world away in Newfoundland, shore-based whaling continues, primarily to obtain pilot whales no more than 28 feet long, from which up to 1,500 pounds of meat can be taken for sale to raisers of fur foxes. Like sperm whales, the pilots have teeth and dive for food. Their heads contain oil, although far less in proportion to body size. But the market for blubber oil, head oil, and bone oil is too limited to support the whaling industry if, for any reason, fox furs went out of style.

Some of the sharks grow to be larger than any pilot whale. The most monstrous are the whale shark and the basking shark, either of which may attain a length of 45 feet and a weight of more than two tons. Both have evolved feeding habits similar to those of baleen whales, cruising slowly in surface waters while filtering out a diet of small fishes and smaller plankton animals. The giant manta rays of the tropical Pacific Ocean, which measure as much as 22 feet across and weigh almost as much, are plankton eaters too. Yet no fishery has ever developed to harvest these sea animals, and their numbers are believed to remain unchanged.

The great white shark, which is a man-eater as big as 36 feet long, patrols the open seas, ranging from the surface to at least 4,200 feet below. Capable of smashing in the side of a lifeboat or overturning a life raft to reach anything edible aboard, these giants are the terror of anyone shipwrecked or surviving an airplane crash at sea. White sharks, and the smaller tiger sharks that are full grown at half their size, are the ever-hungry peak predators in the pyramid of food relations. Tigers often follow ships, or congregate in the shipping lanes for garbage thrown overboard. Those caught there sometimes still have undigested remains of people in their stomachs, from feeding on bodies that have fallen into the water. Probably these big sharks are too few to be put to human use. For this reason they are likely to continue undiminished, unchallenged in the open seas.

For a few years during World War II, when fishing for cod in the North Atlantic became too dangerous because of prowling submarines and floating mines, fishermen along the Pacific coast of North America got rich by catching sharks of almost any size, from the largest to dogfishes less than 3 feet long. Usually all parts except the livers were tossed back into the water, to be devoured quickly by uncaught sharks, for they are eager cannibals. The liver of a shark is extraordinarily large and oily, serving not only as a reserve center for food but also in place of a gas-filled swim bladder to give buoyancy to the streamlined body. Sold to factories along the coast, the livers were extracted of "fish liver oil" as a substitute for cod liver oil in diets needing a supplement of vitamin D. This competition with cod liver oil continued in the immediate postwar years until 1950, when ways were found to synthesize this vitamin with greater purity and potency at a lower price. Shark-catching for profit virtually ceased. Neither a vogue for tanned sharkskin as an imitation shagreen leather for ladies' shoes, belts, and handbags, nor the gain that might be realized from reducing the number of small- and medium-sized sharks attacking fish caught in nets, has led to any concerted effort that might be regarded as a hazard to these voracious swimmers.

Not quite a century ago the pioneering research vessel H.M.S. *Challenger* set out to sea on an expedition lasting from 1873 to 1876, which established a new field for human study: oceanography. Since then, knowledge of the animals of the oceans, the plants that form the ultimate supply of food, and the dissolved mineral matter all forms of life must have for growth, have received scientific attention. Increasingly the influence of the continents and particularly the great rivers on the nutrition of creatures far out at sea has become known. Now the effects of one kind of land animal—our own—are beginning to outweigh all others. At a pace faster than anyone believed possible, the wastes of mankind are coating the oceans and altering the environment for every marine form. Not only have invisible poisons blown and washed into the sea, endangering most the predators at the peak of the pyramid of food relations, but visible debris coats vast areas of the surface.

The Norwegian explorer Thor Heyerdahl recalls that when he and his crew drifted across the Pacific Ocean on a balsawood raft in 1947 "We on *Kon Tiki* were thrilled by the beauty and purity of the ocean." In 1969, reporting on his experiences while attempting to reach Central America from Africa aboard a papyrus raft, he expressed his shock to find that "Large surface areas in mid-ocean as well as nearer the continental shores on both sides were visibly polluted by human activity." Empty plastic bottles, light bulbs, and other trash floated along, as well as oily particles already coated with tiny barnacles. Hundreds of miles from the nearest land and remote from shipping lanes, the water was sometimes "too dirty to wash our dishes in." Virtually all of this debris, like the persistent pesticides, accumulate because of man's success in manufacturing products for which nature has almost no efficient decomposers.

Policing the vast oceans, whether for the benefit of whales or the survival of lesser animals, still seems too big a task for man. People and their products have become abundant faster than the necessary international cooperation to minimize the damage. The human species now confronts a challenge far greater than the Ice Age: to learn to recycle and reuse the limited resources, to work with and not against all other kinds of life.

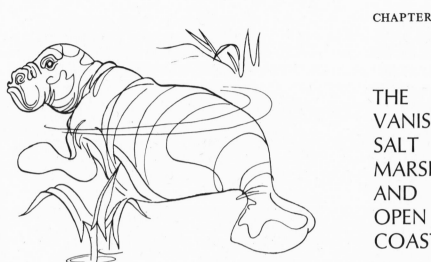

CHAPTER 11

THE
VANISHING
SALT
MARSHES
AND
OPEN
COASTS

NO MAN WHO lives by the ocean's edge can completely overlook the tides. They move its frontier now closer, now farther from the steady landmarks he goes by, on a complex schedule slightly slower than twice each day. In combination with prolonged wind from over the water, they help the sea assault the land. Erosion quickens along open coasts. Into the estuary of every river and up the drainage gutters of the salt marshes, the water floods especially high, only to withdraw without fail before the next incursion. At every mooring the tie line to boats small and large tighten and slacken. Anchors may drag or break loose on the flood, while the ebb lets craft tilt aground. As Robert Burns wrote in 1787, "Nae man can tether time or tide."

Curiously, the tides in the Mediterranean Sea are so slight that the classical thinkers of Greece and Rome paid little heed to these water movements. Nor did people living in other parts of the world find explanations beyond the realm of fantasy for the tides until Isaac Newton recognized the combined role of moon and sun. He forgot to allow for the effects of the earth's rotation, but these were included nearly a century later when, in 1773, the French astronomer and mathematician Pierre Simon de Laplace formulated some equations from which the timing of the tides could be crudely predicted.

The shape of the coast in three dimensions and the water currents still include so many undeciphered features that the best modern computers give no accurate predictions years in advance for the actual level of the tide hour by hour for any point along the sea coast. The tide tables that are published for major harbors and channels as a vital aid to navigation are all based upon past records, not upon any real understanding of the water movements. They are extrapolations, and sometimes err inexplicably.

For most animals, including ourselves, the distinction between the marine environment and that of the land is particularly sharp. We take a special interest in places where tidal changes lower the sea level and then raise it again as much as 43 feet. Two-and-a-half feet is a normal average range around islands remote from shallow water and over the open oceans.

In the tropics, where the conditions seem to have been most nearly constant throughout recorded history, the remains of sea beaches can be seen both well above and considerably below the present level of the shoreline. For each beach, a fairly reliable date can be assigned by studying fossils below where the beach is now. Animals had to move to keep up.

Our human experience, in fact, has been only with unusual sea levels and peculiar climatic conditions. While primitive tribes were spreading from one continent to another, about half of the ice of the Ice Age melted. Sea level rose, but only about halfway to its normal high point. The rest of the water is still frozen on Antarctica, on Greenland, and in smaller glaciers elsewhere. Geologists try to calculate how much more the average temperature of the earth must rise before this ice too will melt, inundating all of the coastal cities and all land less than 330 feet above the sea.

The tidal margins of the sea and waters close offshore have long supplied people with food, a livelihood, or recreation. They caught edible fishes, found tasty mollusks and other shellfish, dug sea worms for bait, and gathered the seaweed as fertilizer or to wash, dry, and eat. Twice yearly along temperate coasts, they could hunt shorebirds pausing on migration. Later they took arctic waterfowl wintering in these places, as a natural source of flesh and feathers. Meat and fur came from seals in spring, when these animals hauled out to pup and nurse. To men along ocean borders, each opportunity seemed God-sent. With no investment other than in boats, tackle, guns, and ammunition, they felt no call to help insure future harvests.

As we think of the time and money that have been invested to increase the economic gains from animals in coastal waters, we realize how biased these men have been toward improving the efficiency of exploitation. Almost nothing has been done to raise the basic productivity of these living resources. The gain that is within reach has already been measured, but planning to develop the potential has not yet been fitted into the pattern of land uses along the marine shorelines. Local pride and historic tradition generally must be overcome to get a worthwhile change begun.

Around North Atlantic shores, history shows many changes during the last few centuries. During the 1600's and 1700's the small fishing enterprises from European shores could not satisfy the market. Enterprising businessmen fitted out larger ships to cross the ocean and harvest the products of New England waters. Enormous quantities of cod, particularly, were dried or salted for markets in Europe. Efforts to keep these operations a monopoly eventually failed because of the determination of independent, private fishermen in America to exploit the coastal resources. Today the descendants of these men see their small-scale efforts being superseded by newer techniques in the hands of foreign fishermen—mostly from the U.S.S.R. in Atlantic waters and from Japan at legal distances beyond the Pacific coast. Generally the American fishermen would prefer to go out of business rather than become a nationalized undertaking to compete with the newcomers. Yet they realize that the large ships with modern equipment paid for by distant governments are harvesting fishes and shellfishes from the surface to the bottom over the continental shelf. Everything big and edible is filleted and frozen, while the remainder is converted into protein-rich fish meal for livestock or for sale; all of these products from the American coasts are being carried away. The supply within the 12-mile limit diminishes because the animals being exploited no longer have a sanctuary anywhere.

Rather than tailor techniques to the actual life histories of the animals sought, the fishermen search for practical ways to benefit from advances in technology as a quick way to restore a semblance of former easy harvests. We saw a similar effort a few years ago in Barbados, West Indies, where housewives and fishermen both fretted because so often the fishing boats returned empty, or with just a few of the flying fish that are favorites in the market. Now that the harvest has deteriorated, the government has attempted to stabilize the supply by building huge freezers to serve as a fish bank. Whenever fishermen catch more than they can sell fresh, the government buys the surplus at a fixed price and freezes it. When demand exceeds the supply, the surplus is offered for sale at cost. Yet no encouragement was given for the fishermen going out at night, with proper lights on the boats, when flying fishes are feeding abundantly at the surface and can easily be brailed into the little boats by the primitive methods now failing day after day.

Our own Bureau of Commercial Fisheries operates a combined research and demonstration ship, the *Delaware II,* out of Gloucester, Massachusetts. Recently we spent a day aboard, while the vessel cruised up and down the New England coast, testing trawls and new sonar equipment that not only measured the distance between keel and bottom but had such high resolu-

This large dogfish, nearly four feet long, was a pregnant female bearing several unborn young (known as pups), each developing with a copious supply of yolk in an attached sac.

tion that individual codfish and dogfish could be detected around dense schools at calculable depths. From their behavior, an expert might even tell which kind of fish the sonar's markings revealed. A fishing vessel similarly equipped could place its trawls in exactly the right place and ignore unprofitable underwater territories—saving time and economic disappointment.

But when we asked about the life histories of the various kinds of saleable fish, where they laid their eggs and when, what the young fry ate and for how long, what decimated their numbers before they reached market size, and whether any migrations could be traced, the enthusiasm and the answers dried up. Equipment and techniques were what interested the fisheries experts. They learn statistics about decline in catch, but little of the web of ecological relationships from which each fisherman seeks to remove what he can sell.

Between the schools of commercial fishes, where the *Delaware II* dragged its experimental trawl that day, it picked up mostly spiny dogfish, cod of small and medium size, herrings less than a foot in length, a few huge anglers (goosefish), a few flounders, a butterfish, and a mackerel. Every female dogfish seemed pregnant, either with transparent young less than 2 inches long or with 6 inch pups that seemed due to be born any day. For American fishermen this means misfortune, for dogfish hunt along the bottom in fast-moving packs, devouring small fish of many kinds that might mature into something saleable. The dogfishes themselves, which are regarded as edible along European coasts, have no market in America, but get caught in fixed nets and tear them while escaping.

We thought of the codfish spawning in great schools, their buoyant eggs rising to the surface, mostly to be eaten by animals among the plankton whose mouths will accommodate a sphere a sixteenth of an inch in diameter. Mackerel eggs, laid by fishes bigger than the solitary individual caught that day, are slightly smaller and drift among the plankton too; about three in a million, on the average, escape to hatch and survive for three months, becoming little fish 2 inches long. How many million became food for something else while the one 10-inch mackerel we saw got that close to becoming mature? We wondered, too, about the flounders, whose eggs are heavy, sticky, and usually laid near shore where the salinity is slightly less than that of the open sea. What proportion hatched, only to be eaten by a dogfish or sucked in by an angler resting lumplike on the bottom? No one had an answer for us.

We yearned for more information about the butterfish, which live in schools on sandy bottoms close to shore. In winter they disappear from northern waters, probably to the place where they reproduce before returning. The herring, we knew, move shoreward in autumn to spawn. The "aristocrat of herrings," the American shad, like its close kin the alewife (or sawbelly), comes into fresh water to lay its eggs in early spring. Once important as commercial fish, the numbers of these two have fallen seriously, due in large part to pollution of the estuaries and rivers. So long as a sewage slime coats the rocks to which a female shad attempts to affix her eggs, they slide off into the muck and suffocate.

Far more than most fishermen and other coast dwellers appreciate, the estuaries and salt marshes hold much of the key to an increase in living resources over the continental shelves. They are the source of nutrients and often the nursery shallows upon which the coastal animals depend. The real hazard for shore-based fisheries and shellfisheries is from inside the one-mile limit, not beyond the 12-mile boundary. It stems from the widespread idea that a salt marsh is "a barren desert of salt hay and mud flats," when actually it is teeming with life at the grass-roots level.

Close to our home is an area of salt marsh amounting to less than five square miles. Its grasses, sedges, and other plants often give a superficial impression of decay. It is easy to overlook the shorebirds and invertebrate animals that find shade and concealment there, the seeds that nourish migratory waterfowl, the organic matter released by decomposition that then feeds bacteria and other plankton in the tidal pools and gutter water. Even in winter, tidal action bares the tide flats and gutter edges of fallen snow and lets algae grow on sun-warmed slopes and films of drainage water. Shellfish filter out the algae. Some of the small fish, particularly herring, depend entirely on this microscopic life. Shorebirds catch the young fish, getting their sunlight from algae indirectly.

Migrant birds are most numerous there during spring and fall migration. But over an 11-year period, a winter census made by the state Fish and Game Department has shown an average of 750 ducks and geese staying in the marsh. Most are black ducks and goldeneyes, a few are fish-eating mergansers, and the rest a smattering of buffleheads and Canada geese. Local ornithologists can always count on seeing many other residents of this habitat in summer, particularly gulls and terns, sandpipers and plovers, rails, gallinules, and coots. Song birds nest on small wooded islands, which are home also to ruffed grouse, muskrats, otter, raccoon, fox, and deer.

The clam flats are not extensive, nor are the sea worms outstandingly abundant. Yet in a typical summer season the value of clams, lobsters, crabs, and worms for bait taken from this small area exceeds $100,000. The people who rent out boats and supplies do several times this much business because visitors come for recreation. Requiring no expenditure for construction or maintenance of man-made attractions, the salt marsh earns an annual return in excess of $250,000. At more than $80 per acre, it produces competitive value and ten times as much animal protein as any equal area of New England farmland or forest.

The plankton and the nutrient materials in solution spread from the coastal shallows into the adjacent sea so silently and inconspicuously that it is hard to measure them and put a value on them. Many species of fish found along the coast use the marsh and its gutters as spawning, nursery, and feeding areas. Others, which stay farther from the shore, eat those that do spawn in the marshes and estuaries. The eels, smelt, flounders, menhaden, and smaller fishes come closest in. Striped bass, cod, pollack, haddock, and others thrive to the extent that their prey comes out to meet them.

The fishermen rarely own much land along the estuary, and seldom a whole salt marsh. Even if they did, they might yield to the urging of local residents to fill the brackish shallows to reduce the number of salt marsh mosquitoes, of biting female horseflies ("greenheads") maturing from larvae that prey on salt marsh creatures of smaller size, and of "biting houseflies" (stableflies), whose maggots scavenge on decaying vegetation in the marshy margins. The owners of salt marshes used to cut an occasional crop of hay, but only as a substitute for hay made from more nutritious grasses growing on dry land; otherwise they get back little income from which to pay the taxes.

The town fathers can easily forget that the nursery shallows are not wasteland—inactive, useless until filled with community garbage or clean

Since late in the Paleozoic era nearly 300 million years ago, horseshoe crabs have been pairing up, the male clipped to the rear corners of his mate's shell until she towed him into shallow water and bulldozed a place for her eggs in the sandy bottom (photographed in New Hampshire).

earth, to become sites for airports, industries, or housing subdivisions. They may approve proposals to convert the area into neat marinas, where the affluent can keep boats. All of these have a tax valuation vastly greater than the natural community that thrives inconspicuously along the coast, as though waiting for man to change it.

We take particular notice of one animal that now meets sea walls of concrete and riprapped stone where its ancestors used to breed. It is the "living fossil" known as a horseshoe crab or king crab. Not a crustacean but a marine relative of scorpions and spiders, it has an extraordinary history dating back almost unchanged for hundreds of millions of years. Its armored body has a low contour, shaped like an inverted washbasin, ending in a long tapered tail spine. Lacking jaws, it chews seaweed, worms, and young shellfish by means of spiny shoulders on its walking legs, which arise from around its mouth in the middle of the lower surface. Occasionally it goes swimming, leaving the bottom in an abrupt 180-degree turn to travel inverted while its legs and gill-cover plates wave in sequence to provide the motive force. At the end of this type of travel, it sinks on its back to the bottom, and uses its tail spine to right itself.

The world has four surviving kinds of horseshoe crabs, three of them Oriental—from Burma around Malaya to the China coast and down through the islands of the East Indies. There people who live along the shore still catch these animals, to eat some of the soft internal parts or to feed them to pigs and chickens. The fourth species frequents American coasts from Maine to Florida, with outliers in Texas and Yucatan. American Indians formerly included horseshoe crabs in their diet, and also used the stiff sharp tail spines to point their spears until European traders introduced metal substitutes in the seventeenth century.

The artist John White, who accompanied the expedition sent from England by Sir Walter Raleigh to Roanoke Island to establish the colony of Virginia, sketched horseshoe crabs and also the special traps the Indians built to catch these creatures. We found white people along New Jersey's shores using almost identical traps in the 1940's, and complaining that the number of horseshoe crabs caught had decreased in just a few decades to a tenth or less. Some of the decline might be due to the fishermen, who were stacking dead crabs to dry until a local fertilizer company could collect them for grinding.

Many shellfishermen approved of the decline in horseshoe crabs, claiming that the ancient animals ate so many young clams in the mudflats that their business was falling off rapidly. Some men helped the gulls attack adult horseshoe crabs by overturning each one they caught along the beach and shoving its tail spine deep into the sand. Actually, these same gulls did far more to reduce the population of horseshoe crabs by catching the young ones, 2 inches or less across and not yet thick-shelled, as they grazed on the mudflats and sandbars in shallow water. These predatory activities of gulls had increased greatly because the gull populations had risen sharply in recent years, supported by food in garbage dumps along the coast.

Today, almost no horseshoe crabs are taken for fertilizer or to feed pigs and chickens in America. The crabs are too few, and people have found more lucrative uses for land near the salt water. We still know some places where horseshoe crabs continue to approach the shore in early summer, each mature female towing one or more males that are ready to fertilize her eggs. Every year, a few of these places become unavailable, unsuited for a female to bulldoze a depression in the beach at the limit of high tide as a simple nest. Progressively the opportunities wane for the eggs to benefit from the sun's warmth and the freshening kiss of rain seeping into the salty sands, to hatch into tailless young an eighth of an inch in diameter. Fewer billions of young means fewer hundreds of middle-sized horseshoe crabs, and fewer dozens reaching maturity.

We are watching the decline of an animal that frequented these shores while the dinosaurs evolved and became extinct. Probably its habits remained essentially unchanged while on land the birds, mammals, flowering plants, and pollinating insects became the obvious kinds of life. In less than 300 years, the activities of enterprising people from the Old World in the New have done more to hurry this particular kind of coastal creature toward its doom than nature's ruthless struggle for survival did in 300 million years. We wonder if the horseshoe crab is merely one we notice, out of hundreds or thousands of species that our own is liquidating at the same pace and in similar ways.

Shellfishermen have tried to provide young oysters with rough areas of discarded oyster shell, to which the juveniles would attach themselves and grow to commercial size. Often by the time the oysters had taken advantage of this improvement in their environment, polluted water from nearby communities forced public health officers to ban oystering in the coastal shallows. The shellfishermen attempted to reduce the depredations by sea stars that force open the shells of oysters and other bivalves, then devour the soft contents. But green crabs, which attack young bivalves, spread northward from more southern Atlantic coasts and reduced the number of shellfish for both fishermen and sea stars. That the green crabs may have sidled through the Cape Cod canal, built at public expense to reduce the hazards and time for coastal ships, is one explanation for the appearance of these crabs in Boston Harbor and to the north. For the commercial shellfishermen the only important fact was that the number of bivalves to exploit was smaller than in previous decades.

Often no easy explanation can be found for the decline of a native animal. We know too little about the essential foods for even the species caught as human food. While too many may be caught to leave a reasonable breeding stock, it is equally possible that too few survive through developmental stages because of nutritional deficiencies, poisons, or new predators.

In recent decades the North Atlantic lobster has declined along New England and Canadian coasts, without much change in the style of traps or the number of them in operation. Along these American shallows, lobstermen seem more conscientious than those in northern Europe about tossing back all females with eggs and all lobsters weighing less than a pound.

Knowledge of life-history details for the American lobster has never been put to use in revising the conservation laws. Not until a crustacean of this kind has lived about 5 years, molted 25 times, and grown to be nearly 11 inches long at a weight of 1¾ pounds does it attain its full reproductive potential. The lower limit in size for marketing should probably be 12 inches long, so that every lobster possible would have a chance to mate and free at least one generation of young. Having mated in May, a female carries as many as 100,000 tiny translucent eggs on the swimmerets below her abdomen, aerating and protecting them until they hatch a year later. Ordinarily she breeds only in alternate years.

Young lobsters are transparent, and so buoyant that they drift upward to join the other small creatures feeding on microscopic green plants at the sea surface. There they are fed on by a hungry multitude of other animals, including young herring (sardines) and mackerel. Those that succeed in running the gauntlet for two months will have molted six times, changing their shape and diet as well as growing. After the sixth shedding and replacement of their body covering, they become heavier than water and sink to the sea floor. There, about their fifty-sixth day and by means of a seventh molt, they attain the shape of their parents and a length of about three-quarters of an inch. Possibly storms and other weather changes in the air above cause a wide variation in yearly survival through these early stages. This would lead later to irregular fluctuations in the luck of lobstermen and cause them to believe that something other than their own activities produces the sad state of their business.

Natural events for which man is not responsible do cause reductions in wild populations of coastal life. One such occurrence was identified after a disastrous die-off of the estuarine flowering plant known as eelgrass, which led in turn in the early 1930's to a sharp decrease in the number of American brant. This small dark goose had previously held first place in popular esteem along the New England coast as the native goose to grace a banquet table. Brant rely upon eelgrass for at least 80 percent of their diet. They found few suitable substitutes after the eelgrass decayed and disappeared.

Wildlife officers found the culprit: a marine slime mold by the name of *Labyrinthula*. It had changed suddenly from being a mild and chronic infection to a virulent, deadly one. Within a year or two, wherever eelgrass was found all around the world's coastal shallows, the same devastation struck. Ecologists noted, however, that some eelgrass survived far up in estuaries, where the salinity of the water was minimal. Botanists saw that only there did the plant reproduce with flowers and fruit, rather than by vegetative extensions of its horizontal stems in the mud. In a few places, where eelgrass had survived the epidemic, seemingly isolated in a brackish lagoon, it went into decline abruptly when a storm breached the barrier from the sea and filled the lagoon with water of full salinity. Experiments confirmed that eelgrass lost its resistance to the disease whenever its environment became too saline. Climatologists provided the remaining clue: on most continents in the early 1930's, drought was followed by a reduced flow in rivers and increased salinity in all of the estuaries where eelgrass grew.

Once the favorite waterfowl of New England diners, the brant geese of the Atlantic coast declined precipitously in numbers when their favorite food, the eelgrass of estuaries, died off.

Some change, perhaps man-made, seems to be preventing a rapid recovery of eelgrass. Through the world-wide weather cycle that brought drought again in the middle 1960's, the coastal plant failed to spread when river flows returned to normal. Consequently the American brant never again had an abundance of their favorite food, upon which to regain their former numbers. Nor did a host of small creatures, which stayed above the bottom in moving water by clinging to eelgrass leaves, have suitable areas upon which to live. With fewer of them dropping into the tide, and few to mature into an animal of different shape (such as a crab or worm), the drifting motes of life upon which oysters and scallops feed were fewer. So now are the coastal shellfishes, the fishes whose young rely upon the same types of nourishment in shallow water, and larger animals we are more likely to notice or miss.

As wildlife shows signs of vanishing near or in salt water, we need to seek an explanation that includes all of the weblike relations of food. Originally, in the temperate zones, these interdependencies of living things were complex and tough. When one strand broke, as so often happened because a newly evolved creature displaced one of lesser fitness, others held the web intact until further change could tighten the mesh. But when too many species disappear, the number of alternatives decreases in the nutrition of the survivors. Wildly fluctuating populations serve as a warning that the web is in danger, having been oversimplified. It needs time to recover, and perhaps a little wise assistance.

The pace of restoration differs for each kind of animal, generally because of unknown natural pressures that resist any increase in each wild population. The contrasts are evident among the shorebirds and other native fowl that nest or migrate along seacoasts. They have now had four decades of legal protection from people who would like to "live off the land" by taking whatever eggs, young, or adult wildlife can be considered edible. During those years most citizens have forgotton how seriously depleted herons and egrets were previously because of market hunting to get feathers of esthetic appeal. Edible species were fast following the passenger pigeons, as living dodging targets for marksmen who enjoyed practicing their deadly art.

The most famous battle in behalf of vanishing birds was undertaken just prior to World War I, while the only remaining passenger pigeon was nearing the end of her life in the Cincinnati Zoo. It struck at the thriving trade in decorative plumes from sixty or more wild species, for use in the millinery business. Statistics for three months during 1913, as compiled by Dr. William Hornaday and published by the New York Zoological Society, border on the unbelievable. In the London market alone, the records for this period include sales of 41,090 hummingbirds, 10,698 birds of paradise, 13,598 egrets and other herons, and 18,936 other birds as essentially whole stuffed bodies. Tail plumes from snowy and American egrets native to southern Florida, Venezuela, and parts of Mexico were sold by the ounce under the trade name aigrettes, each ounce representing six male egrets killed at the beginning of the annual nesting season. This haste precluded the possibility that the nuptial adornment would be harmed by wear and parental duties. The 21,528 ounces of aigrettes sold during the same three months meant the death of 129,168 of these birds and the termination of that many nests at a minimum. Such senseless butchery for so trivial a reason incensed Dr. Hornaday. He found no difficulty sharing his indignation among members of the Royal Society for the Protection of Wild Birds in Britain and the Audubon Society in America.

Since aigrettes and heron plumes were selling for up to $50 per ounce, and the whole birds for even more, business was too good to stop for a few sentimental people. Public relations representatives for the industry spread the word that the plumes came from special bird farms, called *garceros,* in Venezuela, where the egrets bred and multiplied, molting at intervals and shedding their beautiful feathers for the benevolent collectors. Scientific investigators found, instead, that the Venezuelan hunters tied up as decoys any birds that survived being shot and plucked, until these victims died of their injuries, or from attacking ants, or of starvation.

The delicate nuptial plumes of the male snowy egret soon become frayed with wear as he helps his mate with duties on the nest, incubating the eggs and feeding the young that hatch. (ALLEN D. CRUICKSHANK FROM NATIONAL AUDUBON SOCIETY.)

The Audubon Society bought the land where American and snowy egrets nested in southernmost Florida, and hired wardens to expel poachers. One Audubon warden was shot dead for his protests, and the poacher acquitted by the jury in a local court. The incident failed to discourage men from working as wardens, and actually helped get new legislation passed.

At New Iberia, Louisiana, a Mr. E. A. McIlhenny, who had made a fortune with his Tabasco sauce business, established on Avery Island a huge fenced sanctuary in which some 20,000 pairs of assorted birds of the heron family (including the threatened egrets) could have space and safety. But fickle fashion really saved the birds. Feathers went out of style, replaced to some extent by newly invented plastics. The furor died away, leaving moderate laws on the books, and letting the birds recover as best they could.

Perhaps we should be grateful that north of the Mexican boundary most local residents and state governments cooperate with Federal agencies in supervising wildlife over such a big area. Canada meshes its program closely with ours. The ban on possessing or killing songbirds is generally respected. The management of migratory waterfowl, based upon an annual census and a knowledge of migration patterns, has been outstandingly successful. Seasons for hunters can be lengthened, shortened, or closed altogether along the Atlantic Flyway and the Pacific Flyway, and also the Mississippi and the Central flyways, to give the traveling birds a reasonable chance to complete their journeys in sufficient numbers to leave a generous breeding stock of each kind.

Far less can be done to equalize the hazards along the migratory route for birds that continue into the West Indies and Latin America, where the principal limitation is the number of shotgun shells a hunter can afford or can fire while targets are within range. On other continents (except Australia) neither international cooperation nor national averages for education and standard of living allow comparable protection of living resources. Speaking of nature preservation in the Netherlands Antilles, Mr. F. R. Fosberg pinpointed the problem for us: "Hungry people are not easily convinced that anything they can use should be preserved for the enjoyment of posterity."

Florida alone, so far as we can learn, decrees a fine ($500!) for killing a manatee deliberately. Yet all three species of these strange coastal mammals are on the world danger list. Weighing commonly around 700 pounds, an adult manatee surfaces to breathe at 5- to 10- minute intervals. Between times it sculls through marine bays and sluggish rivers, generally in turbid water where its black or dark gray skin makes it exceedingly inconspicuous. Unlike a dugong or sea cow, a manatee has a rounded tail and vestigial nails on its flippers.

Cold weather limits the Florida subspecies of the West Indian manatee to waters around the tip of the peninsula. Daylight generally repels them, and they congregate where they can sink into dark depths between their irregular trips to the surface for air. Only at night are they likely to browse on plants overhanging the margins of canals and channels, rising ponderously to a height of a foot or two out of the water to seize the vegetation in their mouths. More commonly they eat submerged algae, or help clear the waterways of the prolific introduced water hyacinth by pulling it under and devouring it while concealed. Yet too often a manatee rises for air in the path of a motor boat, or shows itself close to someone with a boathook who kills the animal because he "didn't know what it was."

Manatees can still be seen occasionally in the late evening or early morning along the coast of the Gulf of Mexico from Florida to Texas, from Veracruz to Yucatan, along the shores of British Honduras, Guatemala, Honduras, Nicaragua, and Costa Rica to Panama, from Colombia to the Guianas in South America, and in the West Indies at least from the Dominican Republic and Jamaica to Cuba. Seventeen separate governments have been advised how rare the West Indian manatee now is. Brazil alone has the responsibility for protecting the Amazonian manatee. The third of these endangered animals is West African, tempting with its meat and oil the coastal peoples of no less than nineteen countries.

The dugong, which may have inspired sailors to invent tales of mermaids, is still more thinly spread along Africa's east coast from Mozambique and Madagascar to the Red Sea, around the Indian Ocean and the Malayan Archipelago to New Guinea and northern Australia, as well as to the Philippines and the Ryukyu Islands south of Japan. It even reaches Palau in the western Caroline Islands—a United States Trust Territory—making this country and 21 others responsible for its survival. More marine than the manatees, it feeds on algae and such coastal plants as turtlegrass, while dodging tropical people intent on killing it for food or native medicine.

Tropical coasts are dangerous too for the three different kinds of monk seals, which are the only seals of warm waters. The Mediterranean species, which visits the shores of thirteen separate countries because it ranges into the Black Sea and through the Straits of Gibraltar to Madeira and the Canary Islands, seems most numerous, with nearly 5,000 individuals as the best total estimate. But more people hunt it for its meat, oil, and hide than the Hawaiian kind, which dives for shellfishes and fishes among reefs in the western islands of the archipelago, where its population has gradually decreased from larger numbers to between 1,500 and 1,000. The Caribbean monk seal, which formerly lazed along coasts of British Honduras, Mexico, the Northern West Indian islands, and southern Florida, may now be extinct; two of them were seen off Jamaica in 1949 and another in the same waters in 1952, but none since. Probably these are the animals that Columbus' men found sleeping on the sand of Alta Vela Island, south of Haiti, in August, 1494, and described as "sea wolves"— the first native mammals recognized in the New World. Four centuries later, almost none were left in the Caribbean.

Professional seal-taking, called sealing, began in the latter half of the eighteenth century as an offshoot of whaling when whalers began having to go farther from their European home ports. Records for the North Atlantic subdivision of the sealing industry show that 1831 was the peak year, with 687,000 seals taken, mostly harp seals, with smaller proportions of hooded seals and bearded seals. In the North Pacific the years between 1868 and 1897 saw the skinning of more than a million Alaskan fur seals taken at sea by pelagic sealers, and another 2.5 million on land, principally in the Pribilof and the Commander Islands. In the southern oceans, around coasts of South Africa, Patagonia and Tierra del Fuego, Australia, New Zealand's South Island, and more remote bits of land in the midst of cold seas, sealers explored intensively trying to harvest the last of the southern

Breeding on remote islands south of New Zealand, cows of the elephant seal complain loudly when visitors arrive. Cows rarely exceed 10 feet in length, but the bulls grow to be twice as long. (COURTESY CONSULATE GENERAL OF NEW ZEALAND, N.Y.C.)

fur seal, and later of the southern elephant seal. Only in the North Atlantic did the herds stand up under such continuous pressure. Those breeding on the Pribilofs decreased from about 2.5 million to a mere 125,000 while the more than one million on the Commanders shrank similarly. The fur seals of the Southern Hemisphere seemed headed for extinction, a fate from which they were saved mostly by the increasing discrimination of fur buyers, who strongly preferred the pelts from Alaskan fur seals.

In 1911, by international agreement among Russia, Great Britain (for Canada), the United States (which had bought Alaska), and Japan, pelagic sealing was stopped altogether because at least half of the seals taken at sea were pregnant females ready to give birth as soon as they reached the breeding grounds. Thenceforth official crews on shore would do the work each year, culling 80 percent of the unmated bachelors from the inland fringe of the breeding herds. Driving the victims away from the sea to specific killing areas where all but the biggest and those with damaged pelts would be dispatched with a club, the men would skin their catch and have each stamped by the census keeper. The proceeds from the later sales would be divided among the nations according to a formula. An indication of the success brought about by this management program can be seen in the fact that the Pribilof and Commander herds now total about two million, while close to 100,000 skins are taken annually. At present, much of the meat is also salvaged and converted into protein meal. Another proof of value in seal conservation appeared in 1969, when a small herd of Alaskan fur seals was discovered breeding on an island off Santa Barbara, California, thousands of miles farther south than any on record —apparently individuals that had migrated to the vicinity in winter, as this most migratory of seal species has been known to do before, but found no reason to journey to arctic waters to reproduce.

Similarly strict management has partially restored populations of the entertaining marine weasel known as the sea otter. Traditionally, its brown pelt has been the most expensive of all furs, and the prerogative of royalty. To supply the demand, hunting was intense for 170 years until, around 1910, the survivors became too few and scattered to be worth finding. From close to extermination, these few benefited from complete protection and international cooperation. They reestablished breeding colonies among the kelp beds off the Monterey Peninsula of California, in inlets of western Alaska, and around the Kurile and Commander Islands in the Bering Sea. They still occupy only about a fiftieth of their former range, which extended from Alaskan waters to Baja California in the eastern Pacific and to Kamchatka along Asian shores. Nature-minded people enjoy watching them from high lookouts at California's Point Lobos State

Given complete protection, the endangered sea otters have recovered considerably from hunting over about a fifth of their former range in the coastal North Pacific. (KARL W. KENYON, BUREAU OF SPORT FISHERIES AND WILDLIFE.)

Park, for the sea otters among the kelp beds are close enough to be seen well through field glasses. The animals are more active by day than most carnivores, frolicking with one another, coming up from dives with arms loaded with clams or sea urchins, rolling over to float on their backs while cracking their trophies and eating, or just curling an arm around a frond of kelp and letting it moor them while they snooze.

We wish something equally significant could be accomplished for the benefit of sea turtles, of which the world still has five different kinds, all endangered because they come too close to people while concealing their eggs in sandy beaches. The giant is the leatherback, which may weigh 1,200 pounds and measure 7 feet in body length and 9 in span of out-stretched front flippers. Found in all tropical seas and occasionally as far from the tropics as the coast of England, Maine, Vancouver Island, the Argentine, or South Africa, it possesses only irregular plates of bone em-bedded in the smooth thick skin. Despite its size, the leatherback appears streamlined, with seven lengthwise ridges along its back. When her time comes, a mature female hauls herself ashore and digs a hole for her 80 eggs, just like almost any other turtle. But whether she visits more than one beach for this purpose during her life remains to be discovered.

Based at the University of Florida, Dr. Archie Carr is devoting his re-search life to learning more about the four other kinds of sea turtles, which have horny plates concealing bony armor as is customary among turtles, but arms and legs modified for propulsion under water. All are in peril be-cause so few of their eggs are left to hatch. Even along deserted shores of the Galápagos Islands, feral dogs now dig out and devour virtually every egg left by a sea turtle. On many more populated coasts, men in motor vehicles with oversize tires patrol the beach each morning, stopping wher-ever they find the telltale tracks of a sea turtle crossing from the water to the limit of high tide. There they dig up the eggs, then hurry on to the next. Only North Americans and Europeans tend to object to turtle eggs, because the albumen, or "white," does not coagulate when cooked but re-mains clear, jellylike, and sometimes green. In Sarawak, along the north-est coast of Borneo, harvesting the eggs of the green turtle has become a government monopoly. Some effort is made to be sure that many of the eggs are left to hatch. But the number taken varies mostly with the season, least in January and most in August, the annual total amounting to nearly two million from each of the small islands in the Talang Talang group.

The meat of the green turtle is preferred to that of the others, generally with the explanation that this is the most vegetarian of the species and therefore is both more flavorful and less tough. It is named for the color of its fat. Between the middle row of closely fitted plates in its shell and

The sea turtles of the world are most vulnerable when they come ashore and lay their eggs in sandy beaches. Wild animals and people dig out the nests, seriously reducing the number of young that hatch and go to sea.

the marginal row, the green turtle has four large plates, whereas the very similar loggerhead turtle has an extra (fifth) plate as well as a larger head. The loggerhead is primarily carnivorous, feeding largely on crabs. It is also the most likely to breed and lay its eggs well north and south of the tropics. The hawksbill turtle, with a more hooked beak and generally overlapping plates atop its shell, is omnivorous, taking even Portuguese man-of-wars but closing its eyes before actually biting close to the stinging tentacles. Regarded as good eating in the Caribbean, the hawksbill is best known as the principal source of tortoise shell for ornamental use. This commodity retains its appeal in parts of coastal South America, Africa, and Australia, but elsewhere has lost much of its former appeal because ornaments made of synthetic plastics are cheaper and often more ingenious than those carved from real tortoise shell. The final sea turtle, the ridley, is a mystery animal. Found from the East Indies west to Ceylon and east to the Pacific coast of the Americas where the water is warm, it mates and lays its eggs in the same vulnerable way as the other three. But small ones, rarely 2 feet long and often only 8 inches, are famous for their pugnacity from the Texas coast to the Florida Keys and northward to St. Augustine. Missing from the West Indies and the Bahamas, they get carried by the Gulf Stream and turn up occasionally on the coasts of Britain and the

Azores. No one knows where the Atlantic ridleys come from, for no really small ones have been seen nor any female with eggs developing inside her.

It would be a pity if these sea turtles vanished, ending forever the chance to solve the mystery of the Atlantic ridley's life and answer all the other fascinating questions raised by turtle survival. Since Cretaceous times these ancient reptiles have been coming to sandy open coasts of the temperate and tropical world. They are linked to the land unbreakably, although otherwise they desert it. Their developing embryos must occasionally be wetted by the salt-free water of rain or dew—escaping briefly from the sea's salinity. On land the sea turtles' space requirements seem minimal, their competition with terrestrial life negligible, their use of the beach sand so temporary that some way should surely be found to accord them this limited hospitality. If we deny them this modicum of privacy, we and the world will be the poorer, with never a second chance to rescue our peace of mind.

CHAPTER 12

DANGERS
IN
THE
EXPANDING
DESERTS

NOW THAT WE have explored parts of the world's great deserts, in the American Southwest, North Africa, the Arabian Peninsula, and Australia, we marvel more than ever at the many people who regard these arid lands as desolate wastes to be crossed as quickly as possible. "There's nothing to see, so drive through nonstop at night when the heat will be more bearable. Be sure the automobile air conditioner is working well." "Take gallon jugs of water with you. Have an extra spare wheel with inflated tire, and replacement fan belts, in case you're stranded." We remember one couple in a convertible with the top down, who decided to tackle the Arizona desert by day. They hunted out the only place on the desert fringe where ice could be bought by the block, and had the man set a 50 pound piece on the leather upholstery between them!

Each word of advice has some basis, but together they are overdrawn. At night the desert is often chilly in midsummer, because the day's heat from the sun soon radiates away to outer space through the clear, dry air. Where the temperature was 110 degrees in the shade at 2 P.M., it may be 55 or 60 at 2 A.M. Quite often the air that seemed so desiccated by day becomes saturated with water vapor before dawn, and dew condenses on everything shiny in the desert. These are the hours when most of the desert animals are active. Soon after sunup they disappear below ground, benefiting from the earth's thermal insulation and having no need to draw upon their previous store of moisture to cool themselves by evaporation. They are invisible to travelers through the desert by day, and also to those

195

at night who drive on without stopping to walk with a flashlight away from the road.

At least indirectly, all of the desert animals depend upon moisture and nourishment from the vegetation—plants that are highly specialized to tolerate the daily heat and the chronic drought. In America we think of them as the cacti, the century plants, and the creosote bush. In North Africa and Arabia, the camelthorn acacia, the salt-secreting tamarisks, and tufts of esparto grass survive under similar conditions. Deserts of South Africa and South West Africa have their aloes and leathery plants with no familiar names. Australia has its mulga shrub (another acacia) and mulga grass.

Some areas of desert lack conspicuous plants. The wind tends to roll pebbles for mile after mile (as on the hard-baked flat surface of Australia's gibber deserts), or to move huge sand dunes like wave crests (as in parts of the Sahara, and near Yuma, Arizona). Even in these inhospitable places, a few plants get a roothold. In the early slanting rays of the morning sun we have found the tracks of mice and other animals that scampered in darkness from one clump of vegetation to the next. Occasionally we discovered a darkling beetle still plodding along, seemingly safe for the moment in its armored body, or an alert lizard, peering about for one more ant before digging in for the day.

Most desert plants have an extremely thick cuticle, and almost no pores through which they might lose water by evaporation. Those that retain their foliage generally are densely hairy below each leaf, and curl the leaf when dry, tangling these hairs together and reducing still more the possibility that moisture will escape. They tolerate greater reduction in their water resources than most plants can without fatal wilting. Creosote bush leaves, which possess a thick coating of secreted wax outside the cuticle, can recover after desiccation to a water content equal to 50 percent of their dry weight.

Many of the plants in arid areas have small leaves for only a few weeks after a rainstorm, or shed them permanently as a normal step in early growth. Their succulent stems carry on photosynthesis as well as water storage, and often are protected from animals by sharp spines, a poisonous milky juice, or other means. In this respect, as well as in general appearance, some of the African spurges and strange stapelias simulate American cacti, and African aloes resemble the century plants and yuccas of the New World. Africa and Australia both have gigantic trees called baobabs, that remain leafless most of the year, with enormously bulky trunks conserving water for life until the next rainstorm.

Digging down into the sun-baked soil of almost any desert, we encounter roots close to the surface, connected to trees and shrubs that are far apart, often separated by bare ground. Whenever moisture from a rain seeps into the soil, these roots produce absorptive root hairs and obtain as much water for the plant as possible. Then the root hairs die and shrivel, while the plant lives on its hoard of moisture and waits for the next storm. With no scarcity of light, its growth is limited by the quantity of water available for photosynthesis.

The desert animals are at least as highly adapted as the plants, and show many features of behavior that help them take full advantage of each specialization in structure and function. Rodents that burrow, such as the kangaroo rat of the American Southwest and the gerbils of North Africa and Arabian deserts, carry home the seeds they find and store these for a week or more underground. At first the seeds contain no moisture, for they have been sun-dried. They can absorb no water from the rodent's saliva, because the animal carries its trophies in dry, hair-lined cheek pouches. But in the underground storage chambers the air has moisture to share. Gradually the water content of the seeds increases until, by the time they are eaten, it may be 50 percent or more. This moisture is pure gain for the rodent, a bonus in addition to the metabolic water it can get by digesting the carbohydrates in the seeds. Combined, they may suffice for the animal's limited needs, letting it live its whole life without a drink.

In its selection of seeds and fruits on the desert floor, a kangaroo rat shows a pronounced preference for those high in carbohydrates and low in protein. If none of this type is available, it will accept other kinds with higher protein to save itself from starving. But how it chooses without a chemical analysis for guidance remains a mystery. The inherited wisdom of its action is understandable for, on a diet containing more than the minimal requirements of protein, the animal has some amino acids in excess and must dispose of them through its urine. Even though the kangaroo rat's kidneys are extraordinarily efficient, producing a urine several times more concentrated than usual among mammals and thereby conserving water, extra urine requires extra water to flush out the waste. On a high protein diet the little rodent becomes dangerously desiccated and will then take any opportunity to sip dew—a liquid it ordinarily ignores.

On the arid fringes of the Sahara and other deserts in North Africa and the Arabian Peninsula, the one-humped camel relies upon comparable adaptations. Unable to hide underground by day or to store its food where humid air will add moisture, it takes advantage of the thermal inertia of its own body by letting its blood temperature sag at night as low as 93 degrees Fahrenheit. Not until after noon does the summer sun ordinarily heat the 1,000 pounds in a camel's body to 105, which is the temperature above which the animal starts sweating. Merely by having its body fat mostly in its hump, a camel is able to slow its daily heating by dissipating its body heat to the surrounding air. So little fat underlies its skin that its blood vessels are close to the surface. From them the heat generated by muscular work and glandular activity escapes readily so long as the surface of the skin is 2 degrees cooler. By comparison, the fatty tissue in the skin of the thinnest person retards the outward flow of heat from the blood enough to block it altogether unless the body surface temperature is at least 3 degrees cooler than the blood. The fatter the person, the cooler the skin must be to permit outflow, and the greater is the need to chill the surface by evaporation. Most of us begin to sweat when the air next to the skin gets above 80 degrees. The camel need waste no water until its skin is at 103.

During the winter, camels need no drinking water at all if they are free to eat the ordinary desert vegetation. As summer approaches, they develop a mild thirst, but can slake it with bitter and brackish water that would upset a human's digestive tract. Not only can a camel tolerate magnesium sulfate (epsom salts) in its drinking water, but it can load its tissue spaces with moisture from alkaline or saline waters and keep it available to sweat with, without affecting its blood. During a long trip over the hot desert sands, the camel uses its spare water and soon appears emaciated, while its blood continues with the same consistency as ever, bringing heat from inner organs to the skin to be dissipated. If a person is similarly prevented from drinking in hot desert air, sweat loss soon robs so much water from the blood that it becomes viscous, straining the heart, and eventually moving too slowly to transfer the heat. Internal body temperature rises quickly and fatally. Nor can a person nearing this calamitous condition remedy it by drinking copiously, whereas a camel at the end of its journey can restore itself completely in five minutes with a few gallons of water and a meal of its favorite foods.

Probably a number of the larger mammals that enter the fringe of the desert are as well adapted as the one-humped camel, although none of them has been tested so thoroughly. The medium-sized antelopes known as addaxes possess hoofs that are harder, less padlike than those of the camel, but equally able to splay widely for better traction on loose sand. Both sexes of this white animal are heavily built and develop long horns with consecutive rings and a spiral twist. Originally widespread in the deserts from Senegal to the Sudan, they became familiar sights to many soldiers in North Africa during the early part of World War II. But addaxes became rare, unable to get out of range of modern weapons or to outrun hunters on camels, on horseback, or in military jeeps. With the ability of these animals to live most of their lives without drinking, to travel as necessary to find the scanty desert vegetation, they always appeared in good condition. This often exasperated nomads in the desert, who could not find enough food for their flocks.

Scarcer still today are three of the four kinds of oryx, whose long straight horns, excellent meat, and tough skins were their undoing. The pale sand-colored Arabian oryx has been virtually eliminated from its original territory in Iraq and the great Arabian desert by soldiers with machine guns in jeeps; a sanctuary for this spectacular animal has been established near Phoenix, Arizona, with the hope that it will breed in moderate confinement and be available some day to restock its original desert homes.

The scimitar-horned oryx of the Sahara and Libyan deserts is threatened, and now survives only in remote local herds of small size. The beisa oryx ranges from Eritrea through Ethiopia and Somalia south to the Tana River of central Kenya. Its numbers are much reduced, although herds of from 5 to 50 individuals can still be seen in some of Kenya's national parks. The related gemsbok of the Kalahari Desert in South Africa and Botswana is in least danger, partly because the South Africans are determined that it will never follow into extinction a somewhat similar animal with curved tapered horns, the bluebuck, which vanished about 1800 from its last territory in South West Africa.

The only wild sheep native to Africa, the aoudads or Barbary sheep, no longer find safety in the barren, rocky, waterless deserts between Morocco and the Red Sea. Unlike most sheep, these animals have a wonderful mane of soft long hairs hanging down over the throat, chest, and upper parts of the forelegs. Otherwise their spreading heavy horns remind us a little of rams of the Rocky Mountain sheep, except that similar armament is carried by both sexes in the aoudad whereas ewes of mountain sheep have slender horns with no real curl. But the African sheep have ceased to be an important source of meat, hide, hair, and fibers now that desert people have better weapons and faster transport with which to clear out every possible refuge.

In North America, the Southwest has afforded a desert sanctuary to the strange pronghorn, misnamed pronghorn antelope, which is the only animal in the world that sheds an antlerlike covering from over its branching bony horns. Until a century ago, while bison were still numerous on the grasslands from Alberta to Mexico and from the foothills of the Rockies to the western slopes of the Appalachians, pronghorns to a total of perhaps 40 million accompanied the great herds and evaded the same wolves. By 1910 the bison were gone as wild animals, and the pronghorns were down to a comparatively small number of fugitives, which took refuge from the colonists and the Indians in areas that seemed too arid for any native animal weighing up to 130 pounds. Nothing in the New World can outrun a

Displaced by man over most of their former range on the Great Plains, the pronghorns have moved to the desert fringes. Both sexes wear horns, from which the outer covering is shed each year. (E. P. HADDON, BUREAU OF SPORT FISHERIES AND WILDLIFE.)

pronghorn, coursing along at 40 miles per hour on hard ground, making occasional leaps of almost 20 feet. Even at top speed, the sexes can be distinguished, for the buck has the longer horns (longer than his ears), holds his nose lower (not so horizontal), and is marked conspicuously under the throat with a black patch which the doe almost lacks.

A combination of natural curiosity and sharp vision has brought many a pronghorn within range of a hunter's gun. A person whose scent the animals cannot catch because of the wind has only to tie a white handkerchief to a stick and wave it to attract a herd's combined attention. Pronghorns communicate among themselves in a similar way, by raising the hairs of a white rump patch when they sense danger. It is a signal that a man can see on a sunny day for a distance of more than two miles. Apparently it is meaningful to a pronghorn only when the animal can recognize the body outline of its neighbor. Otherwise a buck or a whole herd moves slowly over to investigate.

Well-planned conservation measures followed the drastic decrease in pronghorn numbers early in the present century, with the result that they can be seen again along the desert fringes and into sagebrush country from Canada to Mexico. Unlike sheep and cattle, they browse on such a variety of vegetation and keep moving so much of the time that they rarely damage the range. To us they are a sign of the Old Frontier that can spread much more widely and be enjoyed by many people who otherwise might notice no moving mammal native to this once-wild western land.

Australia's deserts have a counterpart to the pronghorn and the addax in the red kangaroo, of which the male is red and the female so bluish she is called a blue flier. Fast-moving and outstandingly versatile in finding vegetable food where only the most highly adapted plants can grow, they cause sheep herders to conjecture how many sheep could live well on what a red kangaroo does. The answer, emphasizing the words "live well," is "none," for sheep lack the appropriate adaptations and tastes in vegetation. Yet, today, mobile refrigerated vans are being driven over the Australian Outback to hold the meat from kangaroos that are shot and slaughtered, partly for the benefit of the sheepmen and partly to supply flesh for pet food. Already many Australians are concerned over the rapid decrease in the number of red kangaroos and wonder at what stage in the decline they should begin a program to ensure that these distinctive animals do not become extinct. That stage may be already at hand, for our own explorations along the eastern fringes of Australia's desert heartland did not result in our seeing in the wild a single member of this highly adapted species.

The proportionately large ears of the kit fox serve a dual role in the deserts of the American West: they provide surface for radiational cooling of the body and gather sounds where prey animals tend to be few and far apart. (BOB LEATHERMAN FROM NATIONAL AUDUBON SOCIETY.)

Marsupials in Australia never evolved into foxlike predators with over-sized ears, to correspond to the kit foxes of deserts and arid lands in North America, the fennec fox of North African and Arabian deserts, and the bat-eared fox of eastern and southern Africa. These foxes are all largely or completely nocturnal, hiding for the day in burrows and needing little water so long as they can find a reasonable number of the small rodents and reptiles they hunt. Seldom failing to eat any insect they find, they also take advantage of fresh grass and moist fruits. But all of these agile foxes seem unable to learn to avoid poisoned bait set out for rodents, and too often come within range of a gun in the hands of someone using a "game call" to summon a target. The American kit foxes, in particular, are now en-dangered animals despite their almost perfect adaptations to life in arid lands.

Probably a kit fox is too swift to be caught by the bobcats that have be-come desert dwellers for lack of safer places to live. Once bobcats ranged from southern Canada to northern Mexico and over all of the United States except the midwestern corn belt. Now they are almost extinct ex-cept in the American Southwest, but there they seem to eat well on rabbits, rodents, birds, and lizards of the desert. So far the bobcat is not on the danger list of animals dwindling to the vanishing point. By watching carefully toward sundown, we can still see one stretch itself after its daylong nap under a mesquite tree, then step jauntily over the gravelly ground as though to work up an appetite before really hunting for its breakfast.

The American Southwest does have a good many sanctuaries for all kinds of life, including bobcats and kit foxes. More national parks, national monuments, and similar sanctuary lands have been set aside in the arid Southwest than in any other corner of the country. Yet this conservation effort, intended primarily to preserve Indian artifacts and spectacular geological formations, has not been enough to safeguard some of the rare and peculiar desert animals or to keep near normal the number of native predators.

The Vegas Valley leopard frog has not been seen since 1942, and probably is extinct. The springs and seepage areas near Las Vegas where it formerly was found were used first as a potential recreation center by introducing bullfrogs (which eat smaller frogs) and trout (which eat tadpoles). Then the need for more fresh water for human settlers led to capping the springs, largely eliminating any place where the leopard frogs could live. Similar hazards beset the small black Deep Springs toad in the dry desert valley between California's White and Inyo mountains, and several kinds of minnowlike pupfishes. One pupfish, once abundant in sloughs within the northern part of Owens Valley, seemed lost about 1940 due to drainage operations, but it was rediscovered in 1964. Another has not been seen since sixteen specimens were collected near Fort Stockton, Texas, in 1851. A third species seems to have lived in the bottom of Death Valley, along the Nevada-California border, since the Ice Age; the sole surviving population, numbering between 50 and 300 individuals, inhabits a spring known as Devil's Hole, measuring approximately 40 feet in one direction and 15 in the other. No other vertebrate animal in the world seems to have so restricted a natural distribution.

The state of Arizona acted in 1952 to give legal protection to one of its peculiar desert animals: the Gila monster. Surely this is the smallest monster, rarely more than 2 feet long, but it is a reptile not to be trifled with. Ordinarily slow-moving, it can turn quickly and close its blunt black mouth on a finger or toe, then hold on and let its poisonous saliva work into the wound. This habit lets the Gila monster subdue small rodents in the desert and increase its dietary range beyond insects, birds' eggs, and other lizards. Like its only near kin and the world's sole other poisonous lizard, the Mexican beaded lizard, the Gila monster has a coarsely pebbled surface. Usually it is salmon pink, mottled with black spots, and not par-

One of the only two kinds of poisonous lizards in the world, the Gila monster of Arizona deserts is more threatened than a threat. It is now a protected species.

ticularly conspicuous as it crawls about. Those we have found always seemed ready to defend themselves as best they could. This earns our respect, rather than enmity, just as it has among the considerate legislators who would like to see this animal survive.

One feature in favor of Gila monsters is that they are unlikely to kill sheep. Other predators and scavengers that might feed on a sheep of any age, alive or dead, have largely been eliminated by sheepmen with traps, guns, and poison. On all sides of national park and monument land in the American Southwest, this program has been carried on so consistently that few beasts or birds of prey are left. Sheep may have prospered. Certainly the rodents have multiplied. In consequence, many of the highly adapted desert plants have a poor chance to reseed themselves. The giant saguaro cacti in particular get fewer every year as old ones die and new ones fail to start. Ecologists discovered this recently in Saguaro National Monument, near Tucson, Arizona, and countered it to some extent by providing special rodent-proof germinating plots in which these tree-sized cacti might get a start. Later, when the little saguaros are able to contend with their altered environment, they will be transplanted to places where old cacti of this kind have fallen. Every extra Gila monster, bobcat, and kit fox improves the chances for saguaro cacti and for many other desert plants as well.

A chapter in our book *Because of a Tree* tells how many kinds of animals can live in the deserts of the Southwest because the saguaro cacti grow tall there. Any decrease in the number of saguaros diminishes the opportunities for the Gila woodpecker, which normally chooses one of these big cacti as the place to excavate a nest. Using its powerful beak to cut through the tough skin over the pulpy center, and somehow avoiding the rosettes of stiff spines that stud the accordionlike ribbing of the upright stem, the bird prepares an entranceway and then a space in which to tend its eggs and young. The saguaro might drown a smaller attacker in viscous sap. Against so large an unnatural cavity, the plant produces a hard callus tissue which prevents entry of insects and bacteria. So thoroughly does the cactus harden this insulation that, long after the plant itself has died and disintegrated, the wall remains. Prospectors in the desert found these strange remains, each with its central cavity, and named them "desert shoes" before the origin was discovered.

After a Gila woodpecker tires of its nest or vacates it for the season, the smallest of American owls—the elf owl—generally moves in. Often we have spotted an elf perched facing out of the doorway from the cavity where it had roosted silently all day, waiting impatiently for the sun to set and the sky to grow dark enough for it to emerge and forage. No other bird seems so expert at finding scorpions in the dim light under the starry sky, at nipping off the stinger on the scorpion's tail and then eating the disarmed creature. More bobcats, fewer rodents, more saguaro seedlings, more Gila woodpeckers and elf owls, fewer wood-boring insects and scorpions, all are part of the food web of the desert. In our scale of values, all of these changes that match an increase in the number of bobcats are improvements.

From our travels and reading, of course, we realize how often the welfare of sheep raisers runs counter to the welfare of other inhabitants of most nations. The countries around the Mediterranean in general, and Spain in particular, have deserts created and maintained by sheep and goats. The Scottish Highlands and many of the British moors turn more and more into heatherlands because flocks of sheep avoid heather and eat the competing kinds of plants to death. A desert is often a place with insufficient rain and mist for heather, and no other vegetation shunned by sheep and goats that can form an impenetrable cover. Only in New Zealand have we seen sheep raisers working to improve the growth of the grass and clover preferred by their animals—adding fertilizer by airplane to the rounded tops of the volcanic hills. There, wet, low clouds and hungry sheep combined to keep the soil supporting a lawnlike growth more continuous and lush than any Mediterranean herder ever saw.

Elsewhere domestic animals are expected to find nourishment in weeds and native plants that grow without attention, often among outcroppings of rock that would damage the machinery used for cultivating crops. Where rainfall is slight and seldom, as in arid western Texas, the distinction between ranch land and sheep country varies somewhat from year to year and according to the season. But the critical point is an economic one: if a square mile (a section, or 640 acres) will support one or more beef animals, it is a cattle ranch. Anything poorer is sheep country.

The point we can hardly overlook is that after land deteriorates through poor management or other cause until it is unsuited to grains or vegetables, cane or cotton, it is let grow up in weeds and called pasture. If drought or soil erosion make the pasture too unproductive, it is turned over to sheep and goats. These animals can survive where a cow will starve. They tolerate more kinds of food among the plants of the world, and have the right shape of mouth to be able to bite closer to the roots or woody stems. Often they prune each plant so severely that, to save its life, it must draw upon its reserves and quickly put out new growth. If this is eaten too, the plant may die. Wherever sheep or goats are overstocked on arid land, they destroy the vegetation. Their small, sharp hoofs accelerate the devastation by digging into the soil, severing roots and increasing the surface from which soil moisture can evaporate. The broken soil, dry as dust, blows away when the wind is strong.

On our first visit to the deserts of North Africa, from Morocco all across to Egypt and the Sudan, we found ourselves far more willing to believe that a change in climate since Caesar's day had brought increasing aridity than that nomadic people with their flocks were responsible for the desolate landscape. It seemed too uniform, too barren, for a scattered population to maintain. But with more intimate exploration, with side trips to oases, we met some of the Arabs whose ancestors have followed the nomadic life for centuries. To them the barest desert held stark beauty as luring as a lonely lake in a northern forest is to us. They assured us that, while "following the green" with their flocks, they and their animals crisscrossed every inch of ground in their area, and that all other areas were equally patrolled. After the sheep and goats had eaten everything green, the stems and roots were pulled up, dried in the sun for a few hours, and used as fuel for simple cooking. Nothing edible or combustible remained when the nomads moved on.

In the Sudan, just beyond the city limits of Khartoum, a small but dedicated group of government workers led by Mr. M. Shawki has demonstrated how quickly the desert can be reclaimed—mostly by fencing out people and their domestic animals, and patrolling the fence. Mr. Shawki began by enclosing a small area irrigated by the effluent of the Khartoum sewage disposal plant, and setting out a miniature plantation of drought-resistant trees. His "forest" grew at an amazing pace, shading the ground and reducing the loss of water by simple evaporation. He expanded the area by moving the fence and added more seedling trees. Within a few years his forest was no longer miniature but productive. From it he pruned low branches and sold them in the city as fuel, earning in this way nearly all of the income needed to pay his workmen. Almost daily, nomads and their flocks arrived at the fence, eager to get at the firewood and foliage. As regularly they were briefed on the experiment and sent away—advised to start their own forage-growing and turn the desert green again.

In earlier days, the Roman Empire imported great quantities of wheat from areas of modern desert in Morocco, Algeria, Tunisia, and Libya. Now we are convinced that much of this unproductive territory could be reclaimed if given suitable care. An incredible number of seeds and spores arrive by air, some brought by birds but mostly windblown. Many are of plants that possess extraordinary tolerance for chronic drought. But to let them grow and support a native fauna that is equally well adapted to desert life will require a wrenching change in values and habits among local people, particularly among the nomads who most vigorously resist change in anything except an address.

We wonder what changes would follow the erection of a people-proof fence in the most forbidding of Africa's deserts, the Namib, along the "Skeleton Coast" of South West Africa. There, small family groups of Bushmen are the principal nomads, possessionless people whose numbers match closely the amount of drinkable water, plant, and animal life they can find. Meaningful answers are likely to come from this area because, since 1963, the South African Council for Scientific and Industrial Research has been maintaining a field laboratory at Gobabeb in the Namib. Already the presence of rollers and other insectivorous birds in this desolate wasteland has been accounted for. Several hundred different kinds of beetles have been found crawling about, apparently surviving on plant material passively carried into the desert by the wind.

Since the fringes, at least, of both the Sahara and the Namib are parts of what our friend Marston Bates calls the "man-altered landscape," we may need to rethink what we mean by the word "desert." No longer do we feel comfortable with Webster's distinction that a desert is uninhabitable through barrenness, whereas a wilderness is habitable but pathless. Nor does the common limitation of annual rainfall at 10 inches or less seem suitable, since so many plants and animals can be active despite such relative drought. It can scarcely be "deserted" if so many nomads and their flocks make their home in it, and if a different program of use could make it support wheat and trees again.

Today we can recognize a new style of deserts produced by people, as well as the old style. The old are inhabited either by primitive tribesmen (such as the Bushmen and the Australian aborigines) who rely almost entirely on their own senses and skills, or by nomads with sheep and goats. New-style deserts are marks of industralized society. We must include the new style, which are expanding fastest today, if our measure of a desert is simply that its green plants are few and highly specialized and its animals, if big enough to be seen, in constant danger of sudden death at human hands. New-style then includes the world's paved streets, highways, airport runways, and parking lots. For native vegetation and wildlife it means urban and suburban land and fields of plant crops, where a dandelion or a ragweed is a blemish on perfection.

Recently we walked among the native desert plants in the vicinity of Palm Springs, California. Many of them were in bloom, giving the arid land a special glory. Beyond, on the mountain peaks, white snow glistened while the hot sun glowed in a cloudless sky. Hummingbirds and insects probed the flowers and helped share the pollen where it would instigate the growth of seeds and fruits to carry on the many patterns of adaptation. Jackrabbits with enormous ears, the better to get rid of body heat by day, had browsed everywhere beneath the shrubs and herbs during the night. Brown egg-shaped pellets they left were bleaching in the light. But in many places, we saw also the first signs of change to come: surveyor's stakes, each with a distinctive number and an eye-catching swatch of orange cloth. Soon the local denizens would be displaced by private homes and motels for people who could pay for water from great depths or far off, for air conditioning, and for largely unproductive living remote from rain clouds, ragweed pollen, and the contaminated air of industrial cities.

Progressively less of the earth's surface remains for native vegetation and wildlife, because progressively more of it is claimed by people. Yet so often, and perhaps in the American Southwest too, the destruction of habitat may be to satisfy a temporary need or a use that cannot be continued. We think of the artesian wells that must be drilled ever deeper to reach water, because the rate of withdrawal is so much greater than the rate of natural recharge. Most of this deep water has been there since the glaciers melted at the end of the last glacial period. It may not be renewed until after another Ice Age. The surface water that is diverted from the Colorado River, following a legal apportionment that assigns every gallon of normal flow to human uses, brings with it dissolved salts in small amounts. But as year after year in this naturally arid land the diverted water evaporates, the salts remain behind. With too slight a rainfall to carry them deep into the earth, they accumulate at the surface. Each light rain, in fact, redissolves the salt in the top inch or so of soil and helps it rise by capillarity into the sunlight. Dry air carries off the moisture and leaves a white crust in which almost no seed can sprout.

While engineering feats permit a temporary, expedient use of natural desert land, the native plants and animals grow cramped for space. Deprived of the habitat for which they are so outstandingly adapted, they have nowhere else to go. Under increased competition, a good many may become extinct, with no descendants to recolonize the land when, for some newly expedient reason, it is abandoned.

The conversion of wild desert, rich in variety, into tame desert, poor in this measure, concerns us most where it consists of developing truck gardens on irrigated land. We know that these are to replace formerly productive areas in regions with generous rainfall where the rain, which is so nearly distilled water, still falls. It falls, however, on pavements and roofs, where it serves no useful role, and now is hurried off as quickly as possible through storm sewers. This waste of fresh water and degradation of farmland, matched by gradual salination of naturally arid tracts, may be expedient and good economics. Yet it seems equally arrogant and immoral in an age when we are aware, as never before, of the number of starving people and vanishing species.

When, we wonder, will mankind—the self-styled "wise" *Homo sapiens* —realize how unreliable both expediency and economics are as guides? Future generations of our species seem sure to look back on the twentieth century as a time of willful desecration, through short-sighted spectacular engineering, of living resources that could have renewed themselves and served indefinitely.

CHAPTER 13

COUNTRY
ANIMALS
IN
THE
SPREADING
CITIES

ONE MAPLE TREE grew from a seed that the wind set down. The other one we planted, unaware of the first. Both grew sturdily and at just the right distance apart to swing a hammock between them. We lay in the hammock and looked at the foliage overhead, the creatures of all sizes moving about, listened to the tree frogs, the tree crickets, the tree swallows that found the place congenial. We marked down a few thoughts:

By staying home this summer, we had a chance to see what animals from the country used our lawn, each bush and tree. Just a few seemed over-eager to move right in with us: some ants and earwigs, a pregnant whitefoot mouse. Catbirds, robins, waxwings, could hardly wait to eat each red, white, or orange fruit as though it were a treat. The bluejays took every seed the sunflower heads produced. The starlings came for suet and then messed up their roost. Purple finch and goldfinch ate bird-seed by the pound. House wrens raised three families, and filled our world with sound.

A snapping turtle ambled in with thirty eggs to lay. She dug a nest in our gravel drive, continued on her way. Chipping sparrows, chickadees, and squirrels (gray or red) flew and jumped from every branch before they went to bed. Nurseries of paper wasps appeared below our eaves. White-faced hornets built their nests in two of our cherry trees.

Although we walked and mowed and gardened, wondering when we'd be stung or bitten, only mosquitoes and flies proved ardent. Until fed full or finally smitten, they kept on whining, buzzing, diving—at us, at squirrel, at turtle, at bird. On native creatures the pests were thriving. That we were special was clearly absurd.

211

We remember the challenge an old friend accepted: to list just the insects on his lot in the city. It led to a book, *A Lot of Insects,* an inspiration to those who knew Dr. Frank E. Lutz of the American Museum of Natural History. Now we wonder about the future for these country animals that continue to live in the spreading cities. If they become attracted to vegetation the city dwellers have set out to beautify the urban environment and begin to eat it, they earn a reputation as pests and may be eliminated. If they rely upon plants in which man is not interested, they suffer from any program of weed control. Almost the only food a wild animal in the city can take with man's blessing is insects that are eating foliage or bothering people. In this respect, swallows and flycatchers win special approval.

The smallest wild things from the country that reproduce in cities are probably the most cosmopolitan and least in danger of extermination. They live in our eaves troughs and every little puddle—thriving in the birdbath if we just refill it without scrubbing it out. Mostly they are so minute that a microscope is needed to recognize the different kinds: blue-green algae, green algae, golden diatoms, countless euglenas, colorless animalcules that resemble euglenas closely, other protozoans, wheel animalcules (rotifers), bear animalcules (tardigrades), and at a size larger —insects such as water boatmen bugs.

When we recall how many of these miniature denizens inhabit wet places so close to our homes, we think of the Dutch microscopist Anton van Leeuwenhoek discovering them with the aid of his homemade instruments, writing about them to the Royal Society in London, where his descriptions were translated, appreciated, and published. We recall our own delight with Rudyard Kipling's story, *The Eye of Allah,* about a medieval monk who secretly used a strong lens imported from the East to see these amazing animalcules and to use their shapes to whet his own imagination in portraying devils as he illuminated a Biblical manuscript with creations no one else had discovered. All of these creatures possess the special ability to withstand being desiccated to dust and blown by the wind. Many of them eventually get wetted again and resume their rapid cycles of growth and reproduction.

Above its gutters, our peaked roof affords almost no sanctuary and a minimum of food to any creature. The fire-resistant asphalt shingles even have an under layer of cementing material to hold them tightly together where they overlap, preventing the wind from riffling them and perhaps leaving a space where a fly might hide. Roofs of slate and tile have far more crannies. The thatched cottages we slept in while traveling by automobile through Britain, Scandinavia, and Africa south of the great deserts were far more hospitable to living things. Sparrows and weaver birds, rodents and lizards of many kinds, sometimes a snake or two, always an assortment of insects and spiders, went in and out rustling and squeaking as though the spaces were not quite big enough. So well did the carpenters and painters fill any chinks around our roof with plastic wood and putty that not even a bat finds a cranny to squeeze through to hide among the glass wool thermal insulation during the daylight hours. How many native animals that would take advantage of a thatched roof, if we had one, are dwindling in numbers for lack of privacy? For almost none of them is a census kept, from which we might extract an answer.

One of our neighbors has a flat roof coated in tar and pebbles, rimmed by a low parapet. An attic window overlooks this portion of his house and has let us see on several occasions that a nighthawk accepts this city surface as a haven safe from cats. Close to the parapet, where for most of the day the bird has shade from the sun, it crouches shortlegged on the pebbles as though it were the decaying remains of a thick branch that had fallen from a tree. Occasionally it opens its eyes to a narrow horizontal slit, then continues its sleep. Toward evening and on dull days it rouses itself and, stretching its long angled wings, flips into the air and away to pursue flying insects. When it twists and dodges after them in its erratic flight, we can understand the name "bullbat" given to this bird. But much of the time it seems to trawl the air, mouth open wide, swallowing whatever tiny fliers chance inside. Any nighthawk that chooses to sleep on our lot must find a place on a horizontal limb, despite the traffic of the squirrels. We see no way to learn whether the urban air has food for more nighthawks, if house roofs afforded them more roosting sites. We approve of their diet, for a majority of the moths they catch have caterpillars that eat holes in leaves on plants we cherish.

Only in Europe have we seen hospitality extended to favored birds on housetops, and there too the traditional welcome seems on the wane. Changes in architecture eliminate the flat capstone on chimneys, reduce the number of flues now that a separate fireplace is not needed in each room, and diminish the opportunities for white storks to build their bulky nests and rear their young with great ceremony close to man. The old belief that a family of storks on the roof is a good omen for the people who live below has been replaced by a feeling of unease at the contamination from droppings. The ancient tale that storks bring babies is no longer popular where people favor birth control. And worst of all, storks have a way of colliding with television antennas and electric power or telephone wires, bending the antenna array, breaking some wires and short-circuiting others, increasing the costs of maintenance and—incidentally—maiming or killing the birds. Add to this the fact that the storks find fewer frogs and fishes near urban areas because low wet places have been filled in and built on, and closed storm sewers have replaced marshy gutters for carrying off the rain. Paved streets and parking lots offer few grasshoppers. The Old World is changing fast, and the number of storks shrinking toward the danger point.

In the New World, we sense a similar catastrophe in store for smaller birds: the darting, wheeling, insect-eating chimney swifts that seek nest sites all over North America after spending each winter in one mountain valley of Peru. Until hollow trees grew scarce and unused chimneys common, these chittering birds brought twigs and used their own saliva as a glue to fashion a basketlike nest against the inner wall of the dark vertical cavity. Resourcefully, they transferred their nest building to chimneys that were seldom used. Now economy, efficiency, and centralization are shutting them out. Some of our neighbors and many new large buildings have no chimney because none is needed for electric heat or constant indoor temperatures maintained through concealed pipes from a central climate-control plant. Our chimney has two flues, but both are used too often for chimney swifts to move in with us. Older houses, built around World War I, have unused chimneys still; they were built for kitchen ranges that burned wood or coal, and for fireplaces in individual rooms which now have metal radiators. But these structures, like public buildings erected longer ago and equally attractive to chimney swifts, are being torn down to make space for new-style replacements. No hollow trees, no unused chimneys, no chimney swifts? We used to think these birds were vulnerable because they clustered in the one remote wintering area of South America and perished in thousands during the summer whenever a combination of storms kept insects from flying for several days in a row. Our new apprehension is that they will have nowhere in North America to nest.

Much as we would like to encourage chimney swifts, we see no way to provide them with imitation hollow trees, no likelihood that enough people will go to the expense of building suitable cavities that have no other function. Even the multiple apartment house that would appeal to purple martins takes more space around it and more costly construction than city dwellers will normally spare. Our smaller efforts with individual bird boxes fit better the time and sites on the corner "mini-acre" that we call home. But so far as we know, no woodpecker or owl has so much as inspected the boxes with a 3- to 4-inch circular doorway. Neither house sparrows nor starlings take chances nesting where the entryway is so big. House sparrows cannot enter other boxes we have built because the door is less than 1¼ inches in each direction; for these the chickadees, house wrens, and tree swallows vie, with no two within less than 50 feet of each other and no two of the same kind on our lot nesting simultaneously. Tree frogs and flying squirrels accept the leftovers.

We used to believe that when horses were replaced by internal combustion engines for motive power, in cities and suburbs and the farms around, the belligerent house sparrows introduced nearly a century ago from Europe would have no manure in which to find undigested seeds and soon would disappear. The gentle bluebirds, which the sparrows (and starlings) displaced from nest sites with entrance holes in the 1½-inch range, might then return—at least to nest boxes put up in good locations. (One of our childhood memories is of being held high by a fond parent so that we could reach a still-small hand gently into a nest hole of bluebirds in a wooden fence post and feel the warmth and softness of the unfledged young; today the eastern bluebirds are so uncommon that any bird-watcher would be unkind to risk disturbing a nest in any way.) Somehow the house sparrows have survived the conversion, and still roost noisily by the dozens among the long-stalked leaves of Boston ivy on brick buildings. Now we despair for bluebirds and for hearing each summer their sweet warbling as they perch, alert for a worm or an insect or a small soft fruit in the short grass.

Our grass is kept short with a push-type lawnmower, but the weeds in it thrive and so do the ants. At first we accepted what some neighbors advised: that grasses chosen to match climate and soil would form a turf of such vigor no weed could invade. But after months of coddling with sprinkler and fertilizer, our dream sward still needed constant defense. We put away the spudder and the weed-killer and accepted the better-adapted plants. Watching carefully for any toad in its hole, detouring around the johnny jumpups, the bluets, and the daisies, we mow over the dandelions, plantains, and hawkweeds, and hardly touch the crabgrass that spreads flat against the ground. When crabgrass seeds are dry, the chipmunks come like vacuum cleaners and haul away this booty to underground chambers—enough to last all winter. Chipping sparrows and goldfinches find trophies in our mowed weeds that no respectable lawn would have. Flickers come at intervals and regale themselves on ants. Even the neighborhood skunks find a detour worthwhile in our direction and occasionally have a need to remind a cat that wild animals have rights to defend.

Everyone seems to enjoy the goldfinch's roller-coaster flight, its call of per-CHICK-o-ree or po-TAT-o-chip, its semblance of being a "wild canary." These delightful birds instinctively wait until late July or even August before beginning to nest. By then they can gather thistledown to line their cup-shaped nurseries, built low in the fork of a bush or tree. Our neighbors' lawns produce no thistles. Neither does ours. If we can help it, for we draw the line at prickly weeds and poison ivy. When the last vacant lots are built on, where will a goldfinch get its thistledown? Can we offer a substitute that would not disturb our neighbors, just as we supply string for nesting birds? In our community, not even a Scotsman should let a thistle go to seed.

Thistles, burdock, and the small-flowered everlastings known as cudweeds are among the plants our neighbors eradicate. They are also the foods of the caterpillars from which come the handsome butterflies called painted beauties and painted ladies. To eliminate the plants is to neglect these delightful insects. To rid the streamside and wet places of nettles is to do away with red admiral butterflies. Clearing out the milkweed gets rid of milkweed butterflies (monarchs). And now that the American elms are going down, killed by an introduced fungus, the Io and Polyphemus moths will be fewer, and so will the mourning cloak butterflies that still can surprise us on a warm winter day by coming out of hibernation to flit in the welcome sunshine. Tended lawns and introduced shrubs are like many of the horticultural varieties of trees now replacing our native kinds: they let our beautiful moths and butterflies starve and disappear.

In Britain and on the European continent, the question is being asked: "Where have our butterflies gone?" Generally the answer is sought in some application of toxic chemicals, which struck cherished insects as well as pests. But these are no longer the only poisons added to controlled land. Herbicides, sprayed repeatedly on roadsides and rights-of-way by communities, railroads, and electric power companies, selectively destroy herbs as well as shrubs upon which butterfly caterpillars used to feed; they leave ferns and grasses, for which few of these attractive insects have evolved a taste or tolerance.

Our own state of New Hampshire leads the country, and perhaps the world, in applying de-icing chemicals to its highways to keep them free of snow in winter. It is a doubtful honor, and questionable economy since despite undercoating, automobiles exposed to the salty slush rust to pieces before wearing out. The latest figures (1966–1967) show almost 30 tons of salt added per two-lane mile. Already the roadside trees are dying from the chemicals around their roots. Sugar maples, which have so long graced the highway margins, yielding sweet sap in spring, welcome shade in summer, and glorious color in October, are succumbing quickly. So are white pine, red pine, and hemlock, whose contrasting evergreen added so much to the autumn display. The juniper called red cedar, which made good fence posts and lead pencils before people turned to substitutes, the oaks (both red and white), and the black cherry seem more tolerant of salt. Intermediate are red maple, Norway maple, and American elm.

Our own sympathies go to the sugar maple and the elm, trees of special magnificence. For the sake of helping people travel faster to work and home again in winter, must we destroy the beauty they wish to inhabit? The elms in particular have no need to be hurried to their doom, for a fungus is doing quite well enough—almost as well as another fungus did to the American chestnuts half a century ago. Already we recognize the fountainlike branching of dead elms close to the road and far from it, and marvel that the Northeast had so many of them in its cities, villages, and open country. But what of the Baltimore orioles, which regularly hunt out the elms while their new foliage is beginning to expand? Scarcely ever have we seen one of the socklike nests of these beautiful, melodious birds swinging from the delicate branch tips of any other kind of tree. Must they find tall American elms alive, or nest vulnerably, and then go? We have no idea what native tree would be second choice, or if a foreign import would be an acceptable substitute. What other animals may be homeless if this elm goes the way of the chestnut? So far, we have found no account of the change that took place as chestnuts died in town and beyond. Surely the nation was poorer for the loss in more ways than one.

Our attitude toward animals from this or any other country changes sharply when we come indoors. Only a pet that is behaving itself according to our rules is welcome in most of the house. No animals of any kind are to go into closets, the stove, or the refrigerator. A select few kinds are killed on sight, and a few more (such as scorpions and black widows) would be if we lived in a part of the country where they were a problem. Other animals get boosted or transported through the nearest door or window—except in the basement storage area. For some reason, we tolerate a few house spiders and camel crickets, suspecting that anything they eat we would not want there anyway.

Indoors too the city world offers less than it used to for animals from the country. No longer is there a wooden box in the basement where potatoes bought by the big burlap bag waited in darkness for their day of use, where centipedes and sow bugs found shelter. How we hated, as youngsters, being delegated the chore of breaking off the sprouts from those potatoes in the cellar! Now we can buy a few potatoes at a time, each treated with hormones to retard sprouting, and keep them in the sealed refrigerator.

In the city, cold storage of meat came first. Animal-proof jars and cans have long appealed. Now frozen vegetables and desserts, to be stored in a freezer until actually needed, have deprived the house mouse and rats of much of their former livelihood. And the whitefoot mice from the forest edge that occasionally get into our house seem never to open the sealed packages of cereal products we keep in the kitchen cabinets. Instead, they raid our store of sunflower seeds and manage to leave the empty shells in the strangest places: behind books in bookcases, inside the open back of the hi-fi set (as though attracted by its warmth), or atop the baseboard behind heavy furniture. Often the mouse has come and gone again before we find these remnants of its trophies. This suits us well, for we hold these attractive wild animals no grudge and enjoy neither killing them with a snap trap nor freeing them from a live trap in midwinter in territory far from home.

As we think of the wild animals of every size all over the world, we realize how few large species can find space in cities unless they give up their country ways and almost become pets in parks. The mute swan, which is native from Poland to Turkestan, and the black swan of Australia take readily to cruising on small lakes and ponds, even nesting on islets or secluded peninsulas along the margin. Both have been introduced into New Zealand, southern Scandinavia, the eastern United States, and the mute swan into Britain and South Africa. In all of these places the big birds are much admired. But their numbers do not threaten native animals because so many swans, both young and old, are killed each year by colliding with overhead wires while flying. In the United States they have the additional hazards of snapping turtles, which often eat young birds, and of a malaria-like disease spread by biting black flies.

The squirrels, which visitors from Australia and New Zealand find so entrancing because their homelands have none, find safety among the city trees in most countries. Individual squirrels sometimes playfully risk their lives by taunting cats and dogs, relying upon greater agility and ability to climb, for escape at the last possible moment. They rarely get caught by a pet that they see. Occasionally a patient cat pounces successfully from concealment. But if city people have reduced the number of predators a squirrel need fear to well-fed cats and dogs, by virtually eliminating hawks, owls, weasels, martens, and wildcats, a compensatory hazard has been added. An onrushing automobile seems to call forth only confusion in a squirrel that is hopping across the street during a lull in traffic. Although the animal usually has plenty of time to get away, it squanders the opportunity in fruitlessly changing direction, giving the best-intentioned driver in his less maneuverable vehicle no clue to which way to swerve.

Newspapers make much of the occasional animal that finds seclusion and enough to eat in the midst of a busy city: the fox at Yankee Stadium in New York, that grew bold enough to be seen catching rats that ate the peanuts, popcorn, and sandwiches the sports fans dropped; the family of raccoons that raids the garbage cans; the opossum with similarly scaveng-

The prolific muskrat manages to find food and a place to live even along the edge of city reservoirs and marsh-bordered ponds. (V. B. SCHEFFER, BUREAU OF SPORT FISHERIES AND WILDLIFE.)

ing habits; the marmots and the scent-bearers—skunks in the New World and polecats in the Old. Almost anywhere in North America north of the southern states a family of muskrats will move into a city pond with a marshy margin and make themselves at home.

Unusual as these animals seem so close to human dwellings, we prefer to regard them not as vanishing relics from a richer past but as pioneers probing the city environment for a chance to occupy new territories. We, not they, are aware that formerly these same areas were occupied by their ancestors. The city resembles in this respect the desert, which undergoes a natural restoration when fenced off to exclude the influence of mankind for a few years. A vacant lot, proof of a change in human plans, grows up in weeds as the first step in this age-old succession. It becomes an oasis for wildlife in inverse proportion to the number of people and pets who visit.

On our most recent trip to Texas we paid a memorable visit to an un-used parking lot. It helped maintain our confidence in the readiness of animals to recover their land. The lot had been graded, divided into lanes, and gravel-topped for the automobiles of workmen who never were hired. It was part of an engineering dream, from which the management of a big industrial complex awoke, at the edge of the community of Freeport. A hurricane was the alarm clock, for it caused disastrous floods in the low-lying town beside the Gulf of Mexico. Old inhabitants, who decline to move

A chick of the American skimmer, tolerating the scanty shade and intense heat on a disused parking lot in Freeport, Texas, feigns death to escape being detected until it can grow up and fly expertly over the open waters—anywhere from Argentina to New Jersey.

away, are still haunted by the memory. New families look and learn and leave. This gives weeds and animals a chance to colonize.

Only the hardiest weeds can colonize the gravel of the unused parking lot, for under the summer sun the temperature rises above the tolerance range for most seeds and seedlings. But among this scanty cover, hundreds of seabird eggs and young stood silently. Had not the parents been flying shuttle service with food for their young and crying noisily while locating their own, we could not have guessed that the immature stages were those of skimmers. Previously we had seen these strange birds only at a distance, and marveled at their peculiar adaptation—an extended lower beak—and their technique of using it. Cruising expertly on slow-flapping wings just above the waves, the skimmer lowers its jaw tip into the water. At unpredictable intervals, the momentary furrow leads to a small fish or crustacean at the surface. Reacting immediately to touch, the bird bends its head and closes its mouth over the struggling prey. Predigested food caught in this way from the Gulf waters was regurgitated for the young skimmers, which had no other source for nourishment or moisture.

The parking lot was to us a piece of unused desert, to which virtually no person had a reason to come. For the wild things it offered an opportunity, a place for each to reproduce its kind and stave off the perpetual night of extinction. They benefit in many ways from the discontinuities in human plans, recouping their losses in one region through gains in another, using adaptations and versatility in far more directions than we generally expect. The apparent sterility of the city center, from which human inhabitants have moved to "bedroom suburbs" leaving only a few watchmen to patrol the silent streets, may be just the chance for which some wild pioneers are ready. By living on the night shift and lying low by day, they may adjust their country heritage to fit our urban sprawl.

CHAPTER 14

WHAT ANIMALS CAN LIVE WITH TEN BILLION PEOPLE?

SINCE 1962 THE Statistical Office of the United Nations has been releasing each June its careful estimate of the number of people in the world on the preceding July first. With the total now close to four billion, it seems incredible that as recently as 1840 A.D., there were only one billion (a thousand million). The two-billion mark was passed before 1930, the three-billion in 1961. A fifth, sixth, and seventh billion are expected before the year 2000. Although the mind boggles at a growth rate that could bring the human population to 30 billion a century from today, it is challenging enough to consider what animals could live with ten billion people just forty-odd years from now, around the year 2015.

We can predict confidently that mankind in these larger numbers will compete more strenuously than ever for space on land. Some people may have moved underground, particularly in the deserts, or be living below the sea on the shallower parts of the continental shelves. A lessening of the land area available, due to a rise in the sea level following the disappearance of ice on Greenland and Antarctica, seems more probable than any significant increase. Continental engineering projects, such as the proposed North American Water and Power Alliance, might inundate areas in one region to let people live in others that now are too arid or remote from electricity.

If ten billion people could be redistributed evenly over the land that is now available, each one would have about two acres in which to live and make a living. (For comparison, the world average in 1967 was 9¾

223

acres.) But the twentieth century has shown a progressive decrease in the area occupied, fewer people choosing to work on ranches and farms, and more moving to the cities. The number of ranches and farms in North America having less than 100 acres is diminishing rapidly because of inefficiency, while those of 1,000 acres or more continue to increase. Only a minority of the ten billion people will stay in open country to manage the ever-larger and more mechanized operations yielding meat, plant foods, and fibers from living domesticated animals and plants. Humanity seems destined to cluster on about ten million square miles, in metropolitan areas separated by dense suburbs.

For ten billion people and whatever animals can associate with them, the ten million square miles offer an average plot per person measuring 160 feet square. This includes not only space for a house or apartment, but also for a share of whatever parks, streets, shopping centers, offices, factories, storage warehouses, hospitals, churches, cemeteries, waste-disposal and water treatment plants, schools, theaters, bowling alleys, and airports are maintained to furnish important services. By the time the population has reached 30 billion, the area democratically available to each person for all these uses will have shrunk to less than 95 feet square.

Although the predicted "standing room only" state for the city dweller is still another century or two into the future, assuming that no significant reduction in population growth rate has been achieved, we see no reason to expect a matching disappearance of nondomesticated animals. In the most densely populated parts of modern cities, and in facilities such as food factories and hospitals that have been built for a year or more, wildlife of certain sorts is well adjusted to the daily routine. It finds space to colonize, to crouch in, and to utilize for nesting. While people are asleep or away at work, or machines are providing the labor smoothly and unsupervised, the animals are free to circulate, to feed, and breed.

If we think about our own home and all the unmonitored spaces in which animals could live, the opportunities seem impressive. All interior walls are sandwiches of plasterboard on both sides of air chambers almost 4 inches thick, 17 inches wide, and nearly 9 feet high between the vertical two-by-fours used for studding. Except for electrical wiring strung in these spaces before the plasterboard went on, they are vacant territory awaiting colonists. Outside walls have the same construction and plasterboard in inner surfaces, but the spaces are loosely filled with rock wool insulation which a pregnant rat or mouse or squirrel could easily fashion into a snug nest. The floors and ceilings are separated by even bigger cavities between two-by-eight joists set at 18-inch intervals, each almost uninterrupted for nearly 12 feet. No one looks in any of these places. So long as we notice no hole through which an animal could slip, we assume they are empty.

Behind books in bookcases are shadowy spaces. Still darker, except when the solid doors are opened momentarily, are those behind dishes stacked in kitchen cupboards or pots and pans in under-counter cabinets. With luck, these places are housecleaned twice a year. Occasionally we find evidence of animal traffic but, so far, no inhabitants.

These spaces—opportunities for animals—would remain unaltered whether the house sheltered one human occupant per two rooms or six per room. If our private home were replaced by a multistory apartment house built of reenforced cement and brick, the sandwich construction of inner walls might still be repeated. The cupboards and cabinets would offer seclusion for animals whose dimensions are less than ours, and space requirements in proportion. Unprotected food to lure the colonists would substantially increase if, on the same area of land, more people were bringing home groceries, storing edible materials, dropping crumbs, and postponing disposal of their garbage.

Mice and rats travel without help to buildings that have had none. The rats, at least, often demonstrate their ability to actually gnaw through concrete walls and foundations to get inside. An occasional mouse and many a cockroach (or a whole packet of cockroach eggs that soon will hatch) ride as stowaways from the grocery store straight through an opened door to the kitchen, generally in a clean-appearing carton that stood empty overnight in the store. Once in a while we detect one of these colonists ready to move in with us, as it scuttles out of groceries we are unpacking. Every open package offers free, fast transportation.

In this or any other country, when we learn of people matching low incomes by limited space, by crowding together several to a room, we sympathize first for their lack of privacy in that one room, without thinking of other consequences. If more people must share the same kitchen facilities, they are less likely to organize a schedule than to keep whatever snacks they can among their few belongings—where rodents and insects can enter and leave most easily. Programming people in and out of a shared bathroom is close to impossible, which explains to us why any dark corner in a hall or elevator gets abused repeatedly, each time in a moment of emergency. Odors and residues of food are the very cues to which rats, mice, and cockroaches respond.

These animals have been taking a share of man's possessions for centuries, perhaps thousands of years, and are in no present danger of being exterminated. The black rat remained a denizen of Asia Minor and lands to the east until the time of the Crusades, when it managed to accompany returning crusaders to Europe and to make itself at home in roofs, most of which then were thatched. It rode to the New World on the ships of early explorers, and later used its ability to climb in escaping on West

Indian islands from the Asiatic mongooses that were introduced to extermi-nate it. The rat and the mongoose now coexist, the rat nesting in the coco-nut palms and the mongoose on the ground. When not feasting in the plantations of sugar cane, they harry native animals and have already caused many species to vanish forever.

The Norway rat probably originated along the shores of the Yangtse River in China and has nothing to do with Norway. It reached Europe by ship about 1553, perhaps from Shanghai. Only over food does it conflict much with the black rat, for it is a natural burrower, well fitted to live in city sewers and garbage dumps. In concert, these two kinds of rats damage food in shipment and storage, buildings by gnawing through concrete, lead pipe, and electrical insulation, and other human possessions to an an-nual cost of many billions of dollars, despite efforts to control them. Fully half of the grain shipped to India to help starving people during the past decades has nourished rats there instead.

Only the albino strain of the Norway rat has been put to work for human benefit in medical, psychological, and genetic research. Some of this value comes from the fact that both kinds of rats are susceptible to rabies and to salmonella food poisoning, and can harbor disease to which people are prone. At various times in the Christian Era, rat fleas transmitted bubonic plague from sick rats to well people, and from person to person, so effec-tively that a quarter or more of Europe's human population died of the disease, which was called the "Black Death." At other times, and particu-larly during military campaigns when head lice and body lice had ample opportunity to multiply and consort with rats, the lice carried typhus fever from rats to people, and then from people to people, causing disastrous epidemics. The late Hans Zinsser, professor of bacteriology at the Harvard Medical School, gathered together some of the explicit historic records of typhus into a discursive and informative biography of the disease, entitled *Rats, Lice and History*. At one point he claimed:

> Typhus, with its brothers and sisters—plague, cholera, typhoid, dysen-tery—has decided more campaigns than Caesar, Hannibal, Napoleon, and all the inspector generals of history. The epidemics got the blame for defeat, the generals the credit for victory. It ought to be the other way round . . .

He also mentioned the estimate made by a Dr. Lantz, who had gathered in-formation on damage by rats in the United States and the United Kingdom around 1910, "that in most of our cities there are as many rats as people." The proportion of rats to human inhabitants may have decreased in the intervening decades, but the cost of their destructive activities has correspondingly risen.

The house mouse, which rarely weighs more than an ounce as compared to the pound of a big rat, began running in and out of human habitations in Asia Minor during prehistoric times. It went along with people on shipboard, and is now cosmopolitan. Like the rats, it destroys more than it eats, and it carries infections that can be transferred to mankind. Yet it retains somewhat more independence than the rat, and commonly moves into the fields during the summer to feed on vegetation and insects, finding its way indoors in autumn before the weather gets too cold. Its smaller size gives it much more freedom, for we have seen house mice squeeze silently through the crack below a door, where a rat would have to gnaw its way noisily, leaving clear evidence of its passing.

Indoors, the house mouse shows by its high-pitched squeaking that it is active around the clock within the hollow walls or other places in which it nests. Ordinarily it adjusts its hours for foraging to times of quiet, but it is seldom alert enough to avoid a patient house cat. Outdoors, it is almost strictly nocturnal, and thereby escapes the attention of hawks, crows, and gulls, but provides attractive prey for owls, prowling cats, foxes, coyotes, and other beasts of prey. The degree to which these predators depend on catching mice becomes evident after an intensive campaign has decreased the house mouse population. The animals turn in their hunger to wild birds, domestic fowl, and even house cats.

Probably most house mice are caught and killed in less than six months, but in captivity (where their inheritance has been studied more thoroughly than that of any other mammal) they often live for six years, breeding until near the end. Each house mouse usually is born as a member of a litter of four to seven, becomes fully furred and has its eyes open within two weeks, is weaned a week later and goes off on its own, begins breeding at seven weeks of age, and gives birth after a gestation period of three weeks. A female mouse born January 1 could have 14 litters by the end of the year, with 100 young of her own, and be a great-great-great-great-grandmother.

Since a house mouse can survive on any food that people eat, and also on soap, glue, and many household articles stiffened or sized with starch, it may live well in a deserted house and make the closed building reek from the ammonia in its urine. In the open, a combination of factors occasionally allows an explosive increase in the population of house mice. Irruptions of this kind in the Central Valley of California during 1926–1927 and 1941–1942 brought numbers estimated at more than 82,000 mice per acre—about two to the square yard. They dug for food so thoroughly in the semiarid soil that it appeared cultivated. The people frantically borrowed cats from hundreds of miles around to reduce the number of mice invading houses. Mousetrap makers could not supply their products fast enough. Gulls swarmed into the area, feasted, and then stood around waiting for digestion to make space for more mice in their crops. By then, the mice were already dwindling, perhaps from starvation, and soon vanished. No actions of mankind seemed to have caused either their sudden rise or equal fall.

One kind of animal that moved in with man long ago, possibly even before the house mouse, is facing extinction locally after a long, unenviable record of destroying human treasures. Probably the ancestral moths lived in the fur of wild mammals, as some of their relatives still do. We can easily imagine that the first fur garment made from a pelt a caveman gave to his chilly spouse became bald in patches due to this insect—the clothes moth—rather than from any wear. Today's clothes moths are just as active as any wild ones could have been, but beyond human habitations they are now unknown. Nor can they survive the sterilization of garments by dry cleaning, or their caterpillars digest the synthetic fibers that threaten to replace wool. Seemingly this explains why the last time we saw clothes moths flying in a home was while on a trip in Europe. In North America so many buyers have turned away from wool to escape problems with clothes moths and with shrinkage that the wool processors are meeting the challenge. Recently we found some wool yarn with a label reading "Chemically treated. Guaranteed mothproof." We bought some and made it into a colorful seat for a favorite chair, wondering whether the chance we took was likely in a few years to make us vulnerable to an insect we would just as soon see extinct.

A competing insect, the carpet beetle, is still in evidence. Some day we hope to see the last of them as well, by eliminating from our possessions everything for which their larvae have the digestive enzymes. This presents a larger order, for this scavenger will eat holes in any fabric of animal origin. A stain from any food we eat may induce it to chew through fibers of inert material. It thrives on accidents, including dust-sized particles of spilled food. For the present, its future seems very well assured.

Cockroaches are a much more ancient type of insect, represented by fossils among the coal seams of Carboniferous times, more than three hundred million years ago. Even then their bodies were flat, suitable for slithering through crevices, perhaps to hide in these shadowy places during the day. Out of more than 1,600 modern kinds, most of which are tropical insects, three different cockroaches have moved in with man and are now cosmopolitan in buildings that are heated during cold weather. The half-inch European ("German") cockroach and the 1½-inch American cockroach both fly well as adults. Oriental cockroach females have vestigial wings, and the males only very short ones. Like rats and mice, they are omnivorous and destructive. Attracted by human food—even food stains on clothing, through which they chew holes in getting the nourishment, they attack sized paper for the starch coating, eat the glue of book bindings (causing the books to fall apart), devour leather belts and shoes, scrape at bones and many other kinds of organic matter. Their droppings foul much that they have not yet eaten.

In New York City the German roach is often called a "Croton bug" or a "water bug" because it invaded the city first around 1842, when piped water from the new reservoir at Croton, New York, reached private homes. Like other cockroaches, it needs moisture and commonly comes to kitchen sinks and bathroom basins to quench its thirst. We recall one photographic darkroom in a Philadelphia hospital that was so popular with American cockroaches that they came to it from all over the building. Dark and warm, due to poor ventilation, it had sinks that usually contained water. Often cockroaches that had not yet departed toward areas of the building where they could find food could be recognized because they crouched in the black crevice around the supposedly light-tight door, waving their 2-inch feelers into the lighted room beyond. Before entering that darkroom, it was good practice to run a finger quickly along the line of quivering feelers, frightening all the roaches into dropping to the floor and scuttling off. All of the water pipes in that room were coated with a strange rough material that we finally identified as a crust of cockroach droppings at least a sixteenth of an inch thick.

The only building in which we have seen all three common cockroaches in abundance was in a huge cannery in southern Ontario, Canada, where the machines seemed spotless, the floors and walls immaculate. But for so many insects of all sizes to be living exclusively on the glue used to attach labels to the cans and to keep the corrugated cardboard cartons from collapsing seemed too simple an explanation. Somewhere, perhaps in the drains, scraps of vegetables, fruits, and meats must have been within easy running distance for a cockroach. The temporary storage room in which we found them was merely shelter for the day, and an embarkation point for those headed for grocery stores and supermarkets all over the country.

If we lived somewhat closer to the Equator, we would share with neighbors a dread for termites, commonly called "white ants." Pale bodied and soft, for the most part, the insects of this order that can thrive with ten billion people are the ones with microscopic partners in their digestive tracts, enabling them to get nourishment from cellulose. The termite chews up the wood of dead and dying trees as its natural food, swallows the macerated fibers, and lets its protozoan partners take over. Its own digestive action keeps the numbers of its intestinal protozoans within bounds and converts both some of them and their products into absorbable nourishment. The unnatural foods that termites accept so readily are objects made from wood and wood fibers: houses, furniture, books, and other treasures of civilization.

Dry air, carnivorous ants, and insectivorous animals of larger size tend to reduce the damage termites cause. From dry air the termites shield themselves by tunneling in the soil to the wood they seek, or by constructing covered tunnels built grain by grain of mineral and fecal particles. Working night and day in complete darkness, the termites extend their passageways, plugging any small hole or crevice where daylight enters as a place where precious humidity could be lost and ants could enter. All of this labor is shared by juvenile and adult members of the termite society, which also share by regurgitation their partly digested food and the protozoans that are essential for their survival. This habit, which seems fundamental in termites, assures the food supply for adults, called soldiers, which have matured with enormously enlarged jaws and heads, and with reactions that cause them to seize and hold any ant or other foreign insect they encounter. In many termite species, an additional caste of adults that have difficulty feeding for themselves are equipped with special glands and nozzles for chemical warfare against ants and other intruders; known as nasutes, they spray jets of formic acid and other repellants when defense of the colony is needed. When these measures fail, as they do with ant-eaters of various kinds, the termite colony relies on the rapid reproduction of its king and queen to compensate for losses.

Termites extend their covered runways right up the face of concrete foundations and steel supports for buildings. In the same way they pass creosoted timbers and reach untreated wood products they can use as food. Often their presence goes undetected until a piece of furniture or a whole house collapses, or a book is opened, exposing their galleries to light. Or the colony reaches a state where winged reproductive individuals are sent forth, to begin new infestations.

We have no fear that termites, cockroaches, house mice, black or Norway rats will falter merely because the world contains ten billion people. In tropical rain forests, where native people eat almost every edible animal and plant, termites (especially the heavy-bodied queens) are sometimes relished. Cockroaches seem to have little appeal. No heaped platters of them are offered for sale in the markets of Latin America alongside the trays of cooked caterpillars and fried grasshoppers. People there are well acquainted with *las cucarachas,* but not as an item of diet. Mice seem similarly taboo on any bill of fare. Only in some parts of Ghana have we learned so far that freshly killed rats are being sold at inflated prices to meat-hungry people, now that their country has been cleared of virtually every other nondomesticated mammal. Until rat-, mouse-, cockroach-, and termite-eating become acceptable, these animals are likely to thrive wherever many people live—particularly where the weather is warm in winter.

Human dietary preferences still have much to do with the degrees of success for a herbivorous land snail named *Achatina fulica,* which is already a serious pest in parts of the world it reached, only with human help. Originally discovered on the island of Mauritius in the Indian Ocean, it is perhaps native also to Madagascar, the Indian Ocean coast of Africa from Somalia to Natal, and along the continent's Atlantic side from Angola to Ghana. Over much of this territory native people gather the snails as food and to obtain their shells as raw materials from which to fashion spoons, other utensils, and objects for the tourist trade. Young snails of this kind, which have developed neither a heavy shell nor the ability to pour out a copious mucus in self-defense, are preyed on by a civet cat, a land crab, at least two kinds of carnivorous snails, and a few kinds of beetles. These wild predators and man keep *Achatina fulica* in check so well that no one cares what plants the snail itself eats to grow to full size, at which it weighs about a pound.

The earliest recorded move for the big snail came in 1847, when Sir David Barclay, a shell fancier on Mauritius, gave a few large live ones to a Mr. W. H. Benson, a British conchologist who was visiting the island. But upon reaching Calcutta, Mr. Benson had second thoughts about these souvenirs from Mauritius, and decided not to carry them in his luggage all over India. Gently he released them in the Chouringhie Gardens just outside the city, perhaps with an intention of contributing a new source of edible meat in a region where starvation is common, partly because there are 5,000 or more people trying to farm each square mile. Unfortunately, custom kept the Indians from killing the newcomers for food or any other reason. The snails joined the sacred cattle, the sacred monkeys, and other animals in devouring vegetation that otherwise might have alleviated human hunger.

No records show whether *Achatina fulica* spread on its own or received further human help in reaching Ceylon about 1900, and the tip of Malaya around 1911. They quickly became agricultural pests in these areas. In 1928 they received free transport to Borneo. An attempt was made to exterminate the invaders, and a bounty was offered in 1931 for snails of this kind and their eggs. Within a two-week period some 500,000 snails and

20 million eggs were destroyed without visibly affecting the *Achatina* population. Two years later they appeared on the islands of Sumatra and Java and began attacking young trees in the vital rubber plantations. Almost simultaneously, some of the Malayan stock of *Achatina fulica* was carried by way of Amoy, on the Chinese mainland, to Japanese-controlled Formosa.

Japanese people on Formosa welcomed the new snails as a delicious food and atrributed to them special medicinal virtues. Exuberantly, they sent living specimens to the home islands, although laws forbidding import of these pests had already been enacted because of the agricultural damage done by *Achatina* in Ceylon and Malaya. But the laws proved unnecessary, for the winters on even Japan's southernmost island are too severe for the snail, despite its habit of burrowing into the soil during cold weather.

From Formosa, a Japanese resident of Honolulu brought home some *Achatina* to Hawaii in 1936. Soon the snails were out of control on Oahu and the island of Maui too. Reluctantly, the Hawaiian Sugar Planters' Association summarized the crash program of measures aimed at the prolific mollusk: "Eradication is impossible without the expenditure of vastly more money than the Territory can afford."

During 1938 and 1939 the Japanese introduced their new food animal on tropical islands mandated to them after World War I. From Palau in the Caroline group, the snails were taken to Ponape and Yap, to Tinian and Rota in the Marianas, and to Saipan in Micronesia.

Following World War II, the United States Navy was dispatched to restore order in the islands of the Pacific Trust Territory. By then billions of snails had spread through the East Indies, parts of the Philippines, as well as New Britain, New Ireland, and New Guinea. As war equipment was salvaged and shipped to Pacific ports of the United States, millions of snails were scalded out with live steam from jeeps, ambulances, bulldozers, and other machines.

California, with its truck gardens and citrus groves, is one of the few states with a strong program of law enforcement aimed at keeping out potential pests. Already growers there are having enough trouble with a European land snail (*Helix aspersa*), which reached the West Coast many years ago. Yet no one can be sure that *Achatina* will not infiltrate the defense perimeter and conquer America. Already it seems the real winner of World War II in the South Pacific, for the damage it continues to do to vegetation far outweighs that from all the explosives used by military actions. It may limit the size of the human population, rather than be seriously hampered by the presence of more people.

We cannot help but wonder about changes in *Achatina*'s homelands along Africa's coasts, on Madagascar and Mauritius. All over that conti-

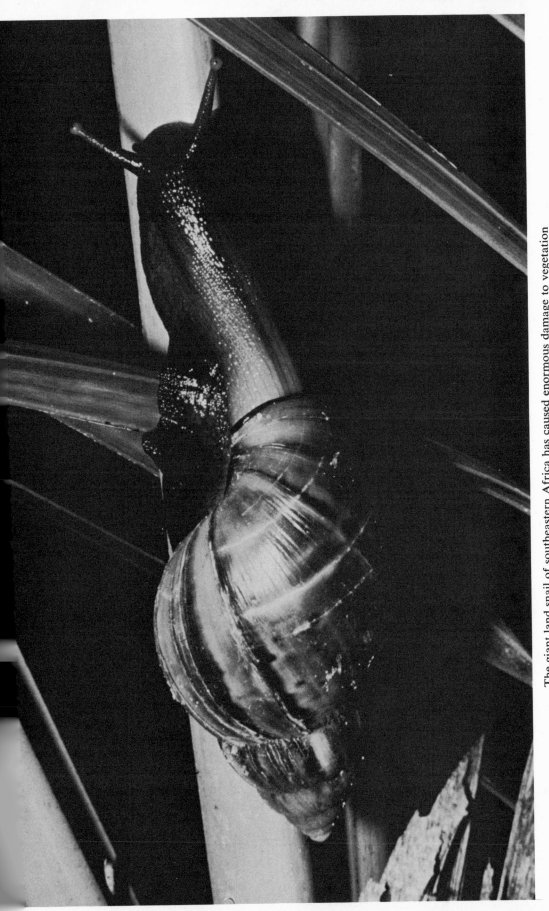

The giant land snail of southeastern Africa has caused enormous damage to vegetation where it was introduced in Southeast Asia, the South Pacific, and Hawaii. A new colony in southern Florida was quickly exterminated in 1969.

nent we have seen native people gaining independence and an expensive urge to adopt white man's ways—having exotic food and utensils as well as clothing, radios, and automobiles. If Africans cease to eat great quantities of this snail, and to use its shell in the old ways, will the snail turn on their vegetable gardens too and become a pest no one can control? The critical point may not be how many people live in the same area, but what they do to the animal in their midst.

The first snails of this disastrous species that we met alive were rasping away at some decorative lily plants on Coconut Island, off the northeast coast of Oahu, where the University of Hawaii has a fine marine science laboratory. We were still examining them and getting pictures for future reference when the wife of one of the scientists came striding up the path, towed by two huge dogs. Among the topics that entered our conversation was the high cost of dog food—pet food in general—as part of the price of enjoying Hawaii's charm and climate. Now that we think about it, why are *Achatina* and other pest animals not the ideal solution to the problem of high-protein food for pets. Rather than continue to hunt the vanishing whales, red kangaroos, and mustangs to supply meat to pet owners and fur-farm operators, a really worthwhile effort might be made to use and hence reduce the populations of giant snails, rats, perhaps mice and cockroaches. The product would still be "all meat." Cheaper cuts of domestic animals could reappear on the market for people with lower incomes.

Nowhere in the world, it seems, is control exercised over what supposedly harmless animals are kept as pets, so long as they do not annoy the neighbors. Pet keepers often lavish on these live possessions more care, particularly in diet, than they do on themselves. Consequently, all over the globe (and not just in the affluent nations) important amounts of grain and meat are diverted from supply channels that could lead to hungry people, to feed these animals with primarily a sentimental value. So long as this trend continues, no danger threatens the existence of dogs, cats, cage birds, tropical fish, and other indoor pets, or the pigeons, sparrows, starlings, squirrels, and similar beneficiaries of regular feeding schedules outdoors.

All parts of the Western world have experienced this changed status of pets, matching improvements in technology as well as increased numbers of pet owners. Newspapers and magazines from the European continent and Britain, from Australia to South Africa, point to the effect of modern cooking methods and refrigeration on the availability of scraps and leftovers, "unconsidered trifles" to feed a pet. Portions tend to come out even, or the surplus is kept chilled for people to eat at a later meal. Pet food comes from the grocery store in cans and cartons, dried or frozen. Its total weight or price is almost impossible to learn for any country or given year. But manufacturers of metal cans know that, although perhaps half of the pet food is marketed in bags and boxes, the fraction canned requires more cans than are bought by any other industry except motor oil and beverages (soft drinks and beer). In the United States alone more than half a/ billion dollars is spent annually to feed dogs and cats. This exceeds the sales of human baby food, and about equals those for instant coffees.

The five boroughs of New York City house about 8,000,000 people, 350,000 dogs, and at least 575,000 cats. Unlicensed dogs are not included. Nor is the estimate for cats reliable, for no registry of these animals is kept. Many are fickle in their attachment to a family. Nevertheless, about one family in three has one or both kinds of pets at some time each year. In the suburbs, the proportion is higher and still growing.

Of the money spent on special food for these two major kinds of pets in North America, about one seventh is for cats. Cat food is somewhat less expensive since the trash fish used is a commoner ingredient than meat from mammals. An adult cat generally weighs around 5 pounds, perhaps about a third as much as an average city dog since few are as big as a muscular wild wolf (30 pounds) or as small as a chihuahua (one pound or a little more). If we multiply 15 pounds for an average dog by 350,000 licensed dogs in New York City, and divide by 150 as a reasonably average weight for a person, we calculate that the dog population in this one metropolitan area is about equivalent to 35,000 people in weight, in food requirements, and in quantity of wastes to be disposed of each day. It equals approximately the human population of Culver City, California, or Middletown, Connecticut, or Orange, New Jersey, or Auburn, New York. No community of this size in the country would permit its citizens to discharge their wastes on the city streets, as is the custom in New York City where signs implore people "Curb your dog."

A few years ago, before our neighbors assembled at the annual Town Meeting, we made a suggestion in regard to money needed to install a number of new fire hydrants: instead of raising the property tax to pay for the improvement, why not increase the charge for dog licenses, since the hydrants in town served dogs so much oftener than people. We drew a laugh, and then the information that the price of a dog license is fixed by the state and relates to the reparation fund from which sheep herders can be compensated when free-running dogs attack their domestic animals. How long ago, we wonder, was the last sheep killed by a dog in our community, let alone in the boroughs of New York City. The only live sheep in the metropolis are likely to be caged at the zoo.

Increasingly, zoos are places where animals can live with millions or billions of people. They used to be parks where children could be shown the monkeys, the lions, and the elephants. Today an equal attraction is found among domestic animals and their young, particularly if they can be touched and fondled. To hear a lamb bleat and see it nuzzle for nourishment, to examine a live cow or horse, adds a new dimension to the experience of a city child. Zoo animals, like our household pets, now live longer than formerly because of improved food and veterinary care. At present attempts are being made to attend to the mental welfare of animals in confinement, relieving their boredom and letting them get exercise more varied than pacing back and forth.

At least as important are the new efforts being made within the safety of the zoos and with the expertise of zoo keepers, to save from extinction those creatures for whose survival in the wild the outlook is particularly bleak. The bison, the wisent, the Hawaiian goose, and the whooping crane are just the first to be aided in this way. The white-tailed gnu (black wildebeest) and the bontebok of South Africa, and the Arabian oryx, are antelopes now testing their inherited reactions in large enclosures established for the purpose, as their last chance to live with people.

Quite often a sanctuary that is set aside for one endangered kind of animal proves inadvertently to have helped another. The Wood Buffalo Park set aside by the Canadian government for their remaining bison was later learned to include the nesting territory of the last surviving whooping cranes. Similarly, when the Red Rock Lakes region in Montana became an official National Wildlife Refuge for the benefit of trumpeter swans, it saved from extinction a kind of native fish—the Montana grayling. Both the swan and the grayling came from ancestors in the Old World, which crossed the land bridge at the present site of Bering Strait and adjusted their distribution in America during the Ice Age. As such, they are regarded as glacial relics.

The trumpeter swans, which are the counterpart of the whooper swans in the arctic and near-arctic parts of the Old World, once nested from Indiana to western Alaska, migrating for the winter in two large contingents. One group traveled regularly to open water and suitable food from British Columbia to the Sacramento Valley of California, the other to Chesapeake Bay, the Mississippi River, and along the coast of the Gulf of Mexico. But as colonists spread westward from the Atlantic Coast, these largest of America's waterfowl decreased in numbers. A hunter could hardly miss a white bird weighing up to 30 pounds, with a wingspan of 10 feet—particularly one with edible flesh and saleable feathers. Most of the 17,671 swan skins which the Hudson Bay Company bought and sold between 1853

Benefitting from strict protection, the handsome trumpeter swans of western North America have recovered in numbers from close to extinction and now are regarded as no longer endangered. (WINSTON E. BANKO, BUREAU OF SPORT FISHERIES AND WILDLIFE.)

Grayling attain a foot in length in waters of Red Rock Lakes Wildlife Refuge, Montana, benefitting from a sanctuary established to save the continent's trumpeter swans. (WINSTON E. BANKO, BUREAU OF SPORT FISHERIES AND WILDLIFE.)

and 1877 were trumpeters; only a minority were whistling swans, a smaller and warier bird that nests farther north and east.

By 1932 the eastern trumpeters had been exterminated, and the western flock gravely depleted. In the United States, only 69 trumpeters could be found. All of them remained inconspicuous because they had lost their migratory behavior. They huddled instead where thermal springs kept the water open all year in the Red Rock Lakes, in Yellowstone National Park (Wyoming), and along the Snake River Valley into eastern Idaho. The survivors prospered when given complete protection. The 1968 census showed at least 2,842 trumpeter swans taking part in the annual migration between Alaska and the British Columbia coast, while the nonmigratory birds numbered 365 in Montana, 126 in Wyoming, 94 in Idaho, and additional offspring transplanted from Red Rock Lakes into suitable places in Washington, Oregon, Nevada, South Dakota, and Minnesota. In addition to trumpeters nesting in western Canada, about 5,000 of these birds seemed to be under United States' care. Accordingly, in 1969 this species was removed from the list of the world's rare and endangered wildlife.

The grayling, which shared some of this success, is a troutlike fish with a sail-sized dorsal fin. It thrives in cold streams, but seems unable to tolerate either a rise in temperature or the introduction of competing brown trout from Europe or rainbow trout from rivers flowing into the Pacific Ocean.

The species of grayling in northern Michigan disappeared during the 1930's, when logging operations let the sun warm the woodland waters and charge them with silt. The Red Rock Lakes population, which inhabits cool parts of the sanctuary, is all that survives from a second species that formerly was common throughout the tributaries of the Missouri River in Montana. The only other fish of this type in America is a strictly arctic species in northern Canada and Alaska, where it seems safe for the present.

The number of people to whom the existence of trumpeter swans and graylings is important continues to rise, despite the inexorable drift of farm families to the cities and city families to the suburbs. Those who live in proximity to neighbors tolerate their constricted freedom best when they can count on escape at intervals into open country. The esthetic role of wilderness gains in appeal and seems likely to continue to do so as the world population approaches the ten-billion mark. Many people long for some time in unpolluted air, with native plants and animals on all sides. Others, who are fewer but easily counted because they buy hunting and fishing licenses and special equipment for their recreation, expect to see a return from their license payments in live deer, ducks, or fishes.

A visitor from another continent is often puzzled by the welter of regulations in the United States and Canada as these apply to hunting and fishing on public and private lands. To some extent, this is because the two large nations cooperate so magnificently in regard to endangered species, to migratory waterfowl, and to songbirds. Nowhere else is so large a continent coordinated by migratory flyways, with hunting seasons and bag limits adjusted according to the latest shared information from regular censuses of wildlife. Yet an animal that is protected inside a National Park and rare enough to be listed among endangered species may have a bounty on its head if it steps beyond the park boundaries onto land administered by the state. This confusion is more understandable between adjacent small countries in Europe than within the subdivisions of the supposedly *United* States.

Nor are citizens in this or other countries generally aware how subversive were the hunting and fishing rules deliberately established by the Europeans who colonized the Atlantic coast of North America, and how tenaciously these have been clung to in most states. Elsewhere in the world, the mammals and birds and fishes regarded as "game" animals are part of the property on which they grow, to be harvested only upon written invitation of the owner and then in ways rich in style and long tradition. Any taking by others of this living property is poaching, and a serious offense. These rules enforced on large estates have persisted along with class distinctions, and contributed importantly to the survival of pheasants and grouse, deer of various kinds, and even the predators such as the European wildcat and lynx. Only a wealthy European seems willing to share his world with large predators.

The American colonists decided that all animals other than domestic ones belonged to the state, and not the landowner. In this they agreed perfectly with the Indians. But the white men refused to go the extra step toward the philosophy of the indigenous people, to agree that once a hunter or fisherman had a license to take a specified game creature the manner of accomplishing this end was no one's concern. Instead, the hunter or fisherman must follow rules much like those of gentlemen in a private estate. The important change was that public and private lands alike were available. Only a small tract could be set aside and closed to all citizens of any age. This difference colored the task of those who wished to safeguard vanishing species, since efforts to improve an area for the benefit of the rarity were liable to frustration by license holders who could legally enter the sanctuary. Today it leads to the anomalous situation where a motorist who collides with a deer that dashes without warning across a highway in front of his car at night may not sue the state for damage to his automobile or self; but the state will prosecute him for destroying its property out of season and without a license if he ties the dead deer atop

Basking in the sun, an American alligator remains alert and ready to slide into deep water, escaping from danger that might come through the swampy margins. (REX GARY SCHMIDT, BUREAU OF SPORT FISHERIES AND WILDLIFE.)

his car and drives off with it. The penalty is still more if he shoves the carcass inside his car for lack of a rope, unless he drives with it immediately to the nearest game warden and relinquishes the remains.

These rules do not endear the hunter and fisherman to the landowner except in those states where hunting and fishing are by permit with payment. We fear that this relationship carries over into the national parks and monuments as an arrogance on the part of many who regard themselves as sportsmen. What they see and want, these men tend to take. Those who have taken alligators from the Everglades National Park in Florida for the sake of hides to sell have reduced the numbers of these reptiles from 1,000,000 to less than 20,000 in just a few years.

The Everglades is the country's only subtropical national park, and a refuge for no less than 22 different endangered species. In addition to the American alligator, they include the Everglades kite, the roseate spoonbill, the great white heron, the snowy egret, the osprey, the bald eagle, the manatee, and the Florida race of the cougar. Established in 1947 to encompass 2,188 square miles of coastal mangroves and islands, sawgrass savannas with low eminences clad in cabbage palm or slash pine or tropical hardwoods, it is visited annually by more than a million people. They come to see the wild alligators and the flocks of unfamiliar birds, and to fish where nourishment generated in the park supports a wealth of marine life just beyond the boundaries.

The life of this unique park depends upon a continuation of flowing fresh water from areas to the north and northeast, like a strange river about 50 miles wide and a foot deep, bringing some 153.5 billion gallons each year. Change in the quality, quantity, or seasonal rhythm of the water supply brings death and decay where visitors expect to find the full richness of subtropical wildlife. Yet two years after the Everglades National Park was created, another branch of the Federal government through its Army Corps of Engineers began endangering the whole area. More than 1,400 miles of canals were built to regulate the water level in agricultural land near Lake Okeechobee, generally by hurrying into the Atlantic Ocean many billions of gallons that otherwise would have flowed southward and nourished the resources of the park.

During 1968, the Dade County Port Authority, which operates the congested Miami International Airport, began quietly to buy up private land north of the park as the first step toward a gigantic new airport and a projected community of a million people. The Federal Department of Transportation made a substantial grant toward development of the first runway and the planning of high-speed ground movement of people and luggage between debarkation points and the city. Whether the jetport is put into operation as originally projected by 1980, to accommodate the largest aircraft in service, or some alternative use is found for the land and its water, the problem of maintaining the National Park seems likely to increase with rising population. Similar conflicts can be expected over every other sanctuary set aside for wildlife and native vegetation.

Most of the national wildlife refuges in the United States are designed more specifically to improve the hunting of waterfowl. They offer breeding and feeding areas along the principal migration routes of ducks and geese. Rarer species benefit if their needs are served by the manipulations of water level and vegetation aimed at providing more waterfowl for the annual harvest. Never are the local managers able to forget that their policies must be biased in this direction, since the tax money that supports their activities comes from levies on guns and ammunition. Generally, however, the refuge boundaries do not enclose the source of the fresh water that makes the operation successful. It too can be rendered useless if development of adjacent land and rivers becomes worthwhile to meet the needs of more people.

Perhaps the last to be affected as the human population rises will be the small popular efforts to save a species, or the really remote wildernesses which offer attractions only to those rugged people who enjoy pitting themselves against whatever the natural world can produce. We think of Isle Royale National Park in northern Lake Superior along the boundary between Michigan and the Canadian province of Ontario. Its main islands are mostly forested, and have campgrounds but no roads. Possibly the moose arrived there during the first decade of this century, reached a stage of overpopulation by the mid-1920's, died off to a low point in the early 1930's, increased again after the disastrous fire of 1936, and now seem to be in balance with their habitat because some eastern timber wolves arrived and stayed. Whether the wolves walked to the island across the ice from the mainland during the extremely cold winter of 1948 is not known. Today, preying on moose and smaller fare, there are at least 26 wolves on Isle Royale, as compared with about the same number in the wildest parts of Michigan and between 300 and 400 in northern Minnesota. Minnesota has canceled its bounty on wolves. So has Michigan, which has now included the wolf among protected animals. Wisconsin protects wolves too— without having any yet to protect. These and the related population of wolves in Canada are all that are left of these powerful animals, which once ranged from eastern Canada south to Ohio over most of the northeastern United States.

In other parts of the world, international cooperation is even more essential toward the success of programs for saving vanishing species, since most countries are smaller and sanctuaries harder to patrol. We think of famous Kruger National Park, 200 miles long and 40 miles wide, with an extensive boundary along the border with Mozambique. A poacher who enters to a depth of 20 miles can go out equally well in either direction—into a different country, if this serves his purposes.

To help with international cooperation, two closely linked agencies maintain central offices at Morges, near Lausanne in Switzerland, where they work in conjunction with the United Nations. One, the International Union for the Conservation of Nature and Natural Resources (abbreviated to IUCN) acts as a clearing house for information, for stimulating research programs, for convening scientists from all countries, and for advising governments throughout the world of needs and possible solutions in conserving both threatened species and environments. The other, called the World Wildlife Fund, attends to public relations, collection of charitable contributions, and some of the major expenditures in establishing research programs or sanctuaries.

The IUCN has been able to coordinate its efforts with those of the World Health Organization (WHO) and the United Nations Educational, Scientific and Cultural Organization (UNESCO) to the advantage of all. Generally the successful introduction of conservation measures depends on overcoming apathy through education, which takes time, on changing age-old customs that no longer suit a world with so many people, and on showing that an economic gain will be assured—preferably in less than five years. Diplomacy of the highest order is necessary to institute a program in a developing nation, where only an elite few have the education, where national pride is easily bruised although foreign exchange is desperately needed, and where local people—generally the least educated ones—must be shown another way to satisfy their hunger for meat than by continuing to hunt native animals. To rename their hunting "poaching" makes no sense unless these people gain quite specifically (and without harm to their self-respect) from the large sums of money spent by tourists who find recreation in viewing wildlife that otherwise seems useless.

Our own discussions at all levels of society in Africa, Latin America, Southeast Asia, and Australia have convinced us of the difficulty in protecting native wildlife from more people—people who live on the land and compete directly, people who live in the cities and know little of the outlying countryside, people who travel and route themselves where they are most likely to find remnants of vanishing ways of life.

From among aboriginal people on wild land, it is possible to educate a few as game guards and guides, to teach them to converse in the languages of international travelers, and to have them paid for showing wildlife to visitors. This does not mean, however, leading tourists on foot to stalk large animals, or sharing with them the types of food and lodging that indigenous people for generations have relied upon as matching the resources of the land. It means meeting the visitors at the airport, driving them in a comfortable vehicle to a good hotel, getting them to the kinds of beds and meals and drinks familiar to them on the schedule to which they are used, while fitting in the game-viewing and native-visiting between times.

As an intelligent man (we have never seen a woman as a guide or game guard), the educated aboriginal may do a superb job. Gradually, however, his values change along with his increasing affluence. He longs for city shoes, new clothes, house, furnishings, and automobile, for an administrative position that matches his knowledge and income. Never having traveled, he has no realization that the city ways and buildings that impress him lack novelty for visitors. In his limited experience they are the only signs of progress. His kin who live in grass-thatched shacks and cultivate the land with primitive equipment are part of a past he has outgrown. He feels secure in their company, but superior; not quite ready to sever his ties to them, but often ashamed to have visitors see and photograph their way of life. In this attitude, he is generally supported by officials in city offices, who prefer their nation to be represented as up to date. They cannot comprehend why a modern city, except at meal times, the cocktail hour, and the night, has no attractions for world travelers, in comparison with vanishing wildlife and unchanged people.

Within the shaky cultural framework holding the old to the new ways is room for new relationships between people and the rare animals so needing in protection. One novel procedure was begun in the 1950's by the approximately 262 British inhabitants of the remote volcanic islands of the Tristan da Cunha group, midway between South America and the Cape of Good Hope in the South Atlantic Ocean. The resources on these rocky bits of land are extremely limited and in constant peril of another major volcanic eruption such as occurred on August 6, 1961. The people who live there (and almost all of them returned in 1963 after being evacuated for their own safety during the eruption) adjust their fondness for the eggs, meat, and fat of native birds and use principally the two commonest species. About 50 other kinds are to be disturbed only by permit and payment of a fee ranging from a shilling to two pounds according to rarity for each egg or bird. Nests are carefully protected so as to "farm" the different species, so that good specimens can be taken to a self-taught taxidermist and prepared in a scientific manner for sale to museums all over the world. A regular census of each species is kept so that control under the Wild Animal Protection Ordinance can be effective. Seemingly in consequence, the three species of birds on the world list of rare "and endangered" kinds are scarcely threatened there.

This adjustment to endangered wildlife made by people who have grown used to remote existence shows determination of a character quite different from that creating a conflict we encountered near Speyside in Scotland. Learning that the Scottish Trust for Ornithology was according special surveillance over the only occupied osprey nest known in the British Isles, we found our way to the place and paid the viewing fee that permitted us to walk through a leafy tunnel to a camouflaged observation post and there look through high-power binoculars at the nestlings on their treetop a great distance away. Through daylight hours a constant watch was kept by volunteers to prevent any interference with the nest. At night fresh guards took up positions at the foot of the nest tree to block any vandals in darkness. That vigilance of this type was needed is one measure of people; that so many took their time in such grim insistence on the safety of the ospreys is another. Between the two we look for the answer to a question that recurs as we think about the kinds of animals that can coexist with a progressively increasing human population: What kinds of people can live with ten billion people? Among ten billion the world seems sure to have all kinds.

BACKGROUND
FOR
THE
FUTURE

MOON WALKERS AND space probes continue to redirect our attention to the planet Earth as the only place within reach where there is any life. Awareness of the richness this heritage affords us deepens every year. Among the many communications of new discoveries and fresh interpretations, some, more than others, shape our thoughts and earn a place of reference. From among those we recently have found most stimulating, we list a few for readers to enjoy:

Introduction: The Vanishing Act

Allen, Durward L., *Our Wildlife Legacy* (rev. ed.). New York: Funk & Wagnalls, 422 pp., 1962.

Crowe, Philip K., "Must they die like the dodo?" in *New Hampshire Audubon Quarterly,* vol. 15, no. 4, 109–113 (Oct., 1962).

Dasmann, Raymond F., *The Last Horizon.* New York: Macmillan, 279 pp., 1963.

Dasmann, Raymond F., *A Different Kind of Country.* New York: Macmillan, 276 pp., 1968.

Matthiessen, Peter, *Wildlife in America.* New York: Viking, 304 pp., 1959.

Paddock, William, and Paul Paddock, *Famine, 1975.* Boston: Little, Brown, 276 pp., 1967.

Udall, Stewart L., *The Quiet Crisis.* New York: Holt, Rinehart and Winston, 209 pp., 1963.

1. Animals in Succession through the Garden of Eden

Beerbower, James R., *Search for the Past* (2nd ed.). Englewood Cliffs, N.J.: Prentice-Hall, 512 pp., 1968.

Bramlette, M. N., "Massive extinctions in biota at the end of Mesozoic time," in *Science,* vol. 148, 1696–1699 (June 25, 1965).

Brancazio, P. J., and A. G. W. Cameron, *The Origin and Evolution of Atmospheres and Oceans.* New York: John Wiley, 314 pp., 1964.

Durham, J. Wyatt, "The incompleteness of our knowledge of the fossil record," in *Journal of Paleontology,* vol. 41, no. 3, 559–567 (May, 1967).

Grant, Verne, *The Origin of Adaptations.* New York: Columbia University Press, 606 pp., 1963.

2. The Rise of Culture and the Fall of Wildlife

Darling, F. Fraser, and John P. Milton, eds., *Future Environments of North America: Transformation of a Continent.* Garden City, N.Y.: Natural History Press, 767 pp., 1966.

Line, Les, "The bird worth a forest fire," in *Audubon Magazine,* vol. 66, 371–375 (Nov./Dec. 1964).

Shepard, Paul, and Daniel McKinley, eds., *The Subversive Science: Essays Toward an Ecology of Man.* Boston: Houghton Mifflin, 453 pp., 1969.

3. Nonhuman Partners of Man's Choosing

Dembeck, Hermann, *Animals and Men: An Informal History of the Animal as Prey, as Servant, as Companion.* Garden City, N.Y.: Natural History Press, 390 pp., 1965.

Thomas, W. L. Jr., ed., *Man's Role in Changing the Face of the Earth.* Chicago: University of Chicago Press, 1193 pp., 1956.

4. Outdoor Harvests and an Ethic for the Land

Hickey, Joseph J., and Daniel W. Anderson, "Chlorinated hydrocarbons and egg-shell changes in raptorial and fish-eating birds," in *Science,* vol. 162, 271–273 (Oct. 11, 1968).

Milne, Lorus J., and Margery Milne, *The Balance of Nature.* New York: Knopf 329 pp., 1960.

White, Lynn Jr., "The historical roots of our ecologic crisis," in *Science,* vol. 155, 1203–1207 (March, 1967).

Wurster, Charles F. Jr., and David B. Wingate, "DDT residues and declining reproduction in the Bermuda petrel," in *Science,* vol. 159, 979–981 (March 1, 1968).

5. Perils in Open Country—On Grasslands and Savannas

Allen, Durward L., *The Life of Prairies and Plains.* New York: McGraw-Hill, 232 pp., 1967.

Madson, John, "Dark days in dogtown," in *Audubon Magazine,* vol. 70, 32–43 (Jan./Feb., 1968).

6. Dwellers in Forests, Swamps, and Streams

McCormick, Jack, *The Life of the Forest.* New York: McGraw-Hill, 232 pp., 1966.

Rounsefell, George A., "Factors causing decline in sockeye salmon of Karluk River, Alaska," in U.S. Fish and Wildlife Service *Fisheries Bulletin,* vol. 58, no. 130, 83–169 (1958).

Carlozzi, Carl A., and Alice A. Carlozzi, *Conservation and Caribbean Regional Progress.* Yellow Springs, Ohio: Antioch University Press, 151 pp., 1968.

7. Animals on Remote Islands

Carlquist, Sherwin, *Island Life*. Garden City, N.Y.: Natural History Press, 451 pp., 1965.

Dawbin, W. H., "The tuatara in its natural habitat," in *Endeavour,* vol. 21, no. 81, 16–24 (Jan., 1962).

Mayr, Ernst, "The challenge of island faunas," in *Australian Natural History,* vol. 15, no. 12 (Dec. 15, 1967).

Walsh, John, "Aldabra: Reprieve for an Island," in *Science,* vol. 158, no. 3805, 1164 (Dec. 1, 1967).

Wolfle, Dael, "The tortoise and the jet," in *Science,* vol. 157, no. 3786, 8 (July 21, 1967).

8. Animals of the High Peaks

Hey, Douglas, *Wildlife Heritage of South Africa*. Cape Town, Johannesburg, London: Oxford University Press, 246 pp., 1966.

Milne, Lorus J., and Margery Milne, *The Balance of Nature*. New York: A. A. Knopf, 329 pp., 1960.

Milne, Lorus J., Margery Milne, and the Editors of LIFE, *The Mountains*. New York: Time, Inc., 192 pp., 1962.

9. In Lands of the Slanting Sun

Hillaby, John, "The wind, the white man and the caribou," in *New Scientist,* vol. 38, no. 595, 222–224 (May 2, 1968).

Kraft, Virginia, "A search for some bear facts," in *Sports Illustrated,* vol. 29, 56–64 (Aug., 1968).

Matthiessen, Peter, *Oomingmak: The Expedition to the Musk Ox Island in the Bering Sea*. New York: Hastings House, 85 pp., 1967.

Perry, Richard, *The World of the Walrus*. New York: Taplinger, 162 pp., 1967.

Pruitt, William O., Jr., "Caribou year," in *Harpers Magazine,* vol. 220, no. 1319, 66–70 (April, 1960).

10. Hazards for Animals of the Endless Seas

Heyerdahl, Thor, quoted in *Time,* August 15, 1969, p. 40.

McVay, Scott, "The last of the great whales," in *Scientific American,* vol. 215, no. 2, 13–21 (Aug., 1966).

11. The Vanishing Salt Marshes and Open Coasts

Amos, William H., *The Life of the Seashore*. New York: McGraw-Hill, 231 pp., 1966.

Baker, Ralph C., *Fur seals of the Pribilof Islands*. Booklet. "Conservation in Action," no. 12, Washington: U.S. Fish and Wildlife Service, 24 pp., 1957.

Brown, Leslie, and Dean Amadon, *Eagles, Hawks and Falcons of the World*. New York: McGraw-Hill, 2 vols., 945 pp., 1969.

Fogg, Forrest F., *Salt Marshes of New Hampshire*. Concord, N.H.: Fish and Game Department Report, 24 pp., 1964.

Gilmore, Raymond M., "Is the West Indian seal extinct?" in *Sea Frontiers,* vol. 5, no. 4, 225–236 (Nov., 1959).

Hillaby, John, "Seals, scientists and stalemate," in *New Scientist,* vol. 37, no. 580, 140–143 (Jan. 18, 1968).

Hillaby, John, "Seals, scientists and sentiment," in *New Scientist,* vol. 38, no. 592, 75–77 (April 11, 1968).

Pimlott, Douglas H., "The whitecoat in peril," in *Audubon Magazine,* vol. 69, no. 5, 77–81 (Sept./Oct., 1967).

Stout, Gardner D., ed., *The Shorebirds of North America.* New York: Viking, 270 pp., 1967.

Teal, John, and Mildred Teal, *Life and Death of the Salt Marsh.* Boston: Atlantic Monthly Press; Little, Brown, 278 pp., 1969.

12. Dangers in the Expanding Deserts

Niering, W. A., R. H. Whittaker, and C. H. Lowe, "The saguaro: A population in relation to environment," in *Science,* vol. 142, no. 3588, 15–23 (Oct. 4, 1963).

13. Country Animals in the Spreading Cities

Kieran, John, *A Natural History of New York City.* Boston: Houghton-Mifflin, 428 pp., 1959.

14. What Animals Can Live with Ten Billion People?

Allen, Robert P., *The Whooping Crane* (Research Report No. 3). New York: National Audubon Society, 246 pp., 1952.

Baker, John H., "Saving man's wildlife heritage," in *National Geographic Magazine,* vol. 106, no. 5, 581–620 (Nov., 1954).

Banko, Winston E., *The Trumpeter Swan: Its History, Habits, and Population in the United States* (North American Fauna, No. 63). Washington: Bureau of Sport Fisheries and Wildlife, 214 pp., 1960.

Hillaby, John, "Saga of the saiga," in *New Scientist,* vol. 37, no. 585, 408–409 (Feb. 22, 1968).

Lint, Kenton C., "Hope for the whoopers," in *ZooNooz* (San Diego), vol. 42, no. 4, 5–8 (April, 1969).

McNulty, Faith, *The Whooping Crane.* New York: Dutton, 190 pp., 1967.

Schaller, George B., *The Year of the Gorilla.* Chicago: University of Chicago Press, 260 pp., 1964.

Schaller, George B., "The vanishing wildlife of India," in *Audubon Magazine,* vol. 70, no. 3, 80–91 (May/June, 1968).

Also past and current issues of *Bulletins* and *Red Books* published by the International Union for the Conservation of Nature and Natural Resources (Morges, Switzerland): especially *Bulletin,* new series, vol. 2, no. 3 [334 species and subspecies of rare and endangered birds; June, 1967], no. 6 [258 species and subspecies of rare and endangered mammals; Jan., 1968], no. 8 [162 species and subspecies of birds extinct since 1600 A.D.; July, 1968], and looseleaf *Red Data Books,* vol. 1 [210 species and subspecies of mammals], vol. 2 [259 species and subspecies of birds], and supplements annually to at least 1970.

Also past and current issues of *Wildlife Abstracts,* published by the U.S. Bureau of Sports Fisheries and Wildlife.

INDEX

258